Profitability and Mobility in Rural America

Profitability and Mobility in Rural America

Successful Approaches to Tackling
Rural Transportation Problems

Edited by William R. Gillis

The Pennsylvania State University Press
University Park and London

Library of Congress Cataloging-in-Publication Data

Profitability and mobility in rural America.

    1. Rural roads—United States. 2. Rural transit—
United States. I. Gillis, William R.
HE355.3.R85P76 1989   388.1'0973   87–43187
ISBN 0-271-00632-3

Contents

Part I

Overview

1

Introduction: The Relevance of Rural Transportation

William R. Gillis

Educational outreach programs, including those sponsored by Cooperative Extension Services, provide assistance to citizens, businesspeople, planners, and public officials in solving rural transportation problems. Educational programs resulting in improved rural transportation facilities and services can play a critical role in supporting both commerce and quality of life in rural America. The cost and availability of freight transportation services affects the profitability of farms and businesses that depend on those services to bring production inputs and consumer products into rural areas and to carry local products to markets. Similarly, passenger transportation services are important to the mobility of rural residents in order for them to gain access to the opportunities and culture of the nation. Thus, the concern for maintaining and enhancing transportation systems in rural areas is rooted largely in a broader concern for supporting the future social and economic vitality of rural America.

The perspective of educational and technical assistance providers for rural areas forms the orientation of this book. Critical transportation problems faced by rural regions and successful approaches that have been used to help state and local governments as well as rural enterprises deal with those problems are documented. The text is based primarily on the experiences of the Cooperative Extension Services and transportation institutes affiliated with land-grant universities. This chapter provides a brief overview of emerging rural transportation issues and the educational challenges associated with those issues. The remainder of the book examines these issues in greater detail.

Changing Transportation Environment

The transportation environment of the 1980s is much different from that of previous decades. Shifts in the rural economic base, policy changes, and technological and organizational innovations each have influenced transportation needs in rural areas.

Most of today's local roads and bridges were built in the late 1800s and early 1900s when overland transportation for passengers and freight was limited to horse and wagon, canals, and recently built railroad lines. In 1910, 35 percent of the U.S. population lived on farms. Farms were small, and local roads provided farmers needed access to homes, fields, schools, churches, and markets.

Transportation networks designed to support the needs of a rural economy based on small-scale agriculture, mining, and forestry are not adequate to meet the transportation needs of today's rural economy. Today less than 10 percent of the people living in nonmetropolitan areas are employed in farming, forestry, fisheries, or mining industries. Present-day farms tend to be larger and more capital intensive than those of previous decades. Large tractor-trailer trucks are rapidly replacing smaller vehicles in the delivery of production inputs to farms and products to markets.

Nonagricultural demands for rural transportation have increased dramatically in recent decades. Between 1960 and 1980, manufacturing employment in nonmetropolitan regions grew at a rate three times that of metropolitan regions of the nation. Approximately 20 percent of nonmetropolitan residents are presently employed by manufacturing firms. A growing number of tourists travel to rural areas for pleasure trips. A recent national travel survey found that small towns in rural areas were second only to ocean beaches as the most frequent destination for American tourists. A growing number of commuters travel rural roadways on their way to work in larger population centers. The most recent census of population indicates that nearly 18 percent of the nation's nonmetropolitan residents travel outside their county of residence for work.

As a result of these changes, the quantity and type of traffic using rural roads have changed dramatically. The larger, heavy vehicles on these roads require major investments in bridges and in surfaces of paved roads. A recent U.S. Department of Transportation survey suggests that more than 50 percent of the local road mileage in America is structurally inadequate. This problem is the result of surface type and condition and even safety deficiencies, such as, inadequate lane widths or lack of shoulders. In addition to highway shortcomings, one-half of the nation's rural bridges are rated either structurally deficient or functionally obsolete.

The ability of state and local governments to upgrade deficient rural transportation facilities has been complicated by recent federal policies shifting financial responsibility for constructing and maintaining transportation routes to state and local authorities. This policy is represented by a combination of cutoffs in federal funds for secondary road and railline preservation, curtailments in rural public and program transit assistance, and shifts in responsibility for roadway maintenance decisions and financing to nonfederal levels of government or to the private sector. These policies will place new, more intense responsibilities for decision making and transportation financing on state and local governments.

Increased financial responsibility of local governments for construction and maintenance of rural road systems suggests a special concern for those rural regions suffering economic stress due to recent declines in farming and manufacturing employment. Rural road systems are financed through a combination of local revenues, which are property taxes in many states, and state-shared motor-fuel taxes. The dependence on shared state-highway user taxes and fees varies from state to state, but the financing of rural roads is a state/local partnership in all states with a local system. A faltering local economy can severely limit local government's ability to raise revenue for road system improvements. The likely result is a cycle of decline. Without additional revenues, local road systems will continue to deteriorate, reducing the future attractiveness of the area for business and industry and further eroding the area's tax base. Innovative public-finance solutions are needed to help local governments avoid this potential cycle of decline.

Transportation deregulation is a second major federal policy change likely to influence the cost and availability of transportation services and facilities in rural areas over the next decade. Until recently, transportation has been regulated as a public utility. Carriers were partially protected from competition in return for fulfilling public service (common carrier) obligations. Under this arrangement, common carriers were not free to choose customers, nor were they free to delete parts of their services without the consent of the public. They also had to provide safe delivery of goods and persons in care of the common carriers. This obligation placed liabilities for loss and damage with transport companies. Third, common carriers had to serve all customers without discrimination. Finally, common carriers had to have their rate proposals reviewed by regulatory bodies to determine whether rate changes were reasonable.

In return for fulfilling these public obligations, common carriers were protected from new competition. When a company proposed to expand service, an existing transportation company could argue that it currently served the traffic adequately and could oppose entry of a new carrier. Often, opposition of existing carriers prevented entry of new carriers.

In the early 1980s Congress passed major legislation changing the government's role in transportation. Recent policy changes have essentially replaced the common carrier system with a market-transaction system similar to any other private business. The new market approach allows shippers and receivers to actively negotiate for transport services rather than accept one of a few alternatives offered by carrier consortiums. Deregulation should increase economic efficiency in the provision of transportation services due to new flexibility on the part of carriers in adjusting to demand. Opponents of transportation regulation reform fear that a transportation system operating in the market place will leave people residing in sparsely populated areas without transportation services.

Technological and organizational innovations have accompanied the new deregulated transportation environment. Railroad mergers, for example, have resulted in reduced rail rates and single-line service on many routes, potentially affecting relative competitiveness of regions as a location for business and industry. Developments of unit-train facilities and railroad contracts encourage consolidation and growth of agricultural service and processing firms. Carriers are developing flexible movement equipment that will enhance the feasibility and the competitive necessity of backhauls.

The changes in the transportation environment that have occurred in recent years will significantly affect the quality, cost, and availability of transportation services in rural areas over the next decade. The ability of citizens, businesspeople, planners, and public officials to adjust to the changing transportation environment will in turn play a critical role in determining the future social and economic vitality of rural America.

Transportation's Contribution to Rural Economic Development

Transportation plays an important role in determining the profitability of operating both farm and nonfarm businesses in rural areas. Farms, business, and industry in rural areas rely on available transportation services to obtain necessary production inputs and to deliver commodities and products to markets. Where transportation expense represents a significant portion of total input or product value, small changes in transport rates can influence net farm or business income substantially.

Transportation improvements that result in lower operating costs for area enterprises aid rural communities in efforts to attract new business and industry and encourage the expansion of existing firms. Business surveys consistently find that firms rank transportation access, cost, and quality as high-priority considerations in choosing a business location. The availability of highway transportation is particularly important to a wide variety of rural businesses and industries. The reliance on the highway network will probably increase, since many rail lines that previously served rural areas are now being abandoned.

Industries that have bulky inputs or outputs tend to be influenced most by the availability of rail service and port facilities. Air service is particularly important to firms with multiple locations. Airlines provide corporate executives with access to branch plants.

Passenger transportation can also play a key role in rural economic development. Highways, railways, and airways are the arteries that enable shoppers and tourists to travel within the area to purchase locally produced goods and services, as well as enjoy available recreational opportunities. Many rural industries draw their workers from surrounding communities up to fifty miles away. For these industries, the highway system is a critical link providing them access to the labor force. Commuting also occurs in the opposite direction. A significant number of rural residents find it necessary to commute to surrounding population centers for employment. Paychecks brought home by these outcommuters create local economic vitality when spent for goods and services sold by local businesses.

Policies and investments that reduce the cost of transporting freight and passengers within rural regions are a potential catalyst for rural economic development. However, transportation improvements should not be viewed as a panacea for local economic ailments. Other factors such as the lack of skilled labor, distance to key markets, or lack of capital may override any benefits that could be obtained through transportation improvements. The implications of transportation policies and investments for rural economic development must be assessed within the broader context of a wide range of factors affecting local business profitability.

Transportation's Contribution to Rural Quality of Life

Quality of life is integrally related with economic development. Quality of life is one of the key factors considered by firms in choosing locations to start or expand operations.

Communities offering a high quality of life have a comparative advantage in retaining area residents and in attracting new residents. Maintaining the local population base in rural communities is critical to the future economic vitality of rural America. A major loss of rural residents means fewer customers to support rural businesses and a lower tax base to support the provision of necessary local services.

Transportation facilities and services contribute to the quality of life in rural communities. Mobility is particularly important for rural residents due to the geographic dispersion of homes, churches, markets, and places of employment. Opportunity for safe travel at a reasonable cost is a necessity of life for most rural residents.

Mobility is a particular problem for the rural poor and elderly. Households owning no automobile represent 57 percent of the rural poor and 45 percent of the rural elderly. Public transportation is usually not an alternative as less than 2 percent of the nation's communities with populations of 50,000 or less are served by local public transportation systems.

An emerging new transportation issue affecting the quality of life in rural areas involves the movement of hazardous materials. The volume of hazardous materials transported on the nation's highways and railroads has increased substantially in recent years. More than 700 billion ton-miles of hazardous materials are shipped annually. Public attention has focused on the need to transport hazardous materials versus the potential for accidents involving these materials. We use many products—clothing, paint, cleaners, car parts, pesticides, cosmetics, building supplies, gasoline—that are hazardous in nature or are by-products of hazardous materials. As we consume more, we demand that more be available and we have more to dispose of.

When hazardous materials are transported, emergencies can occur unexpectedly anywhere. The probability is high that such an emergency will not occur in the presence of persons with expertise in the materials involved. It is more likely to occur in a small community whose police and fire departments are unprepared for such emergencies. Communities need to be able to estimate risks. They need to know the types and amounts of materials they are exposed to, and they need to know potential dangers. They need to have knowledge of the proper source of expert information for any category of hazardous material. They need training programs to acquaint personnel with necessary information. Lastly, particularly in smaller communities and rural areas, they need to know how to develop an organizational structure for an emergency response program.

A final transportation concern affecting the quality of life for rural residents is access of school buses and emergency vehicles to homes, farms, and businesses. Highway obstructions such as weight-limited or narrow bridges are a particular concern. Obstructions that hinder the safe movement of fire trucks, ambulances, and other emergency vehicles is of vital importance to saving both lives and property in cases of emergency.

Educational and Technical Assistance Challenge

The preceding sections provided an overview of rural transportation concerns and the rationale for undertaking systematic efforts to improve transportation facilities and services in rural areas. Educational and technical assistance programs can play a critical role in helping rural residents, shippers, planners, and public officials recognize and develop solutions to the transportation problems they face. Because of the broad range of transportation issues, it is not possible to characterize a single educational approach that will deal with these issues. Instead, a series of four focus areas is suggested, which can be used to tailor educational programs in addressing specific problems. These four areas are understanding the issues, management and analytical decision tools, obtaining transportation services, and technology transfer.*

Understanding the Issues

Ensuring that audience groups adequately understand the issues is basic to developing effective educational and technical assistance programs. An important role for education is to provide perspective on the broader context of policies and economic changes that affect the provision of transportation facilities and services. For example, audience groups need to understand how the changing economic base and use of larger transport equipment will affect future rural transportation facility and service needs. Agricultural interest groups and rural businesspeople should grasp the basic intent of transportation deregulation in the context of the market-oriented policy and economic trade-offs concerning public service versus market allocation of transportation. State and local officials need to understand the implications of federal budget cuts and transfers of responsibility for the maintenance and construction of rural roads, particularly in economically distressed areas. Citizens should recognize the extent to which growing consumer demands for products containing hazardous materials increases the risk of an emergency happening in their community and their need to be prepared.

A second important aspect of helping rural residents, businesspeople, planners, and public officials better understand transportation concerns and potential solutions is to ensure that they ask "the right questions." For example, agriculture and rural-business interest groups facing a potential rail branch line abandonment often ask the question, "What can we do to keep the rail branch line in operation?" The proper question for the groups may be, "Will abandonment of the rail branch line significantly affect the profitability of farms, business, and industry in the area?" or "Are there alternative modes of freight transportation available to shippers at a similar or perhaps reduced cost compared

*Many of the ideas for this section were provided by James C. Cornelius.

with rail transportation?" Someone outside the process can often help frame the question that local groups ask and improve the value of the answer in the decision process. The earlier in the analytic process that the right question is asked, the more effective the analysis will be in affecting the outcome.

Understanding the issues is a prerequisite to discussing specific actions to remedy transportation problems. Once groups are familiar with the basic issues, the educational opportunities become more specific in terms of responding to individual situations.

Management and Analytical Decision Tools

Management and analytical tools to help firms and transportation planners identify and analyze transportation alternatives can provide valuable assistance in making transportation improvement decisions. For example, at the firm level, many of the tools and techniques for enhancing business management skills can be adopted for use by shippers and carriers.

Management decisions at the firm level center on particulars of the transportation service, from the perspective of either the shipper or the carrier. Key criterion in either case is efficiency of operation. Educational programs can be developed to improve efficiency of operation in areas such as least-cost route design or improved capacity utilization. In such applications, technical assistance can provide the analytical tools, such as linear programming, to aid in the designation of the transportation service routes to provide least-cost service by the shipper.

Initially designed by the U.S. military during World War II to route naval vessels, linear programming has evolved to the state of firm-level applications and represents the sophistication and precision of decision-making tools that can be provided by the Extension Service. Specialized expertise in operations research or computer programming may be necessary to tailor such analytical tools for individual firm use, but linear programming has been successfully used in a variety of agricultural production applications, including least-cost feed rations and efficient allocation of farm equipment. In agricultural transportation, linear programming might be used in such applications as developing transportation routes to minimize the cost of distributing farm inputs or in routing commodity flows through a variety of alternative storing and processing facilities.

Similar applications of existing analytical techniques may be useful in transportation decisions involving more efficient utilization of capacity through scheduling backhauls or in traditional capital budgeting decisions such as lease-versus-purchase of transportation equipment. Econometric forecasting models might be developed to project transportation equipment availability or service demand. Again, the focus on educational programs designed to enhance efficiency of operation capitalizes on proved business and economic decision making procedures applicable to a variety of market-oriented industries.

At the broader level, management and analytical decision tools can help in making maintenance and investment decisions for rural roads and railways. Computer simulation models can aid in comparing the costs and benefits of public transportation improvements. This information is particularly useful in setting priorities among competing transportation improvement projects.

Obtaining Transportation Service

A third educational opportunity is to help clientele groups obtain necessary transportation service. One of the recurring problems faced by small shippers is generating sufficient freight tonnage to attract motor carriers. The organization of formal or informal shipper cooperatives offers one solution to this problem. Similarly, providing smaller shippers with the techniques and information necessary to negotiate contract rates with carriers could become part of the solution to the apparent disadvantage small shippers have in obtaining lower rates.

At the other extreme, specialized technical assistance may be provided to clientele groups facing abandonment of rail service or increased rates. The role of the educational program in this case is to provide expertise on alternatives. Similarly, small or remote shippers may need advice on procedures for protesting rate increases. The role of the educator is, not so much to forestall abandonment or ensure low rates, as to develop and discuss alternatives in the light of such actions.

Educators may also play a role in helping communities organize public passenger transportation. Specifically, the educational programs can provide valuable information about small-scale rural transportation alternatives and assistance in organizing the implementation of chosen alternatives.

Technology Transfer

Keeping up with the latest highway maintenance and design technologies is a difficult task for most rural road maintenance personnel and elected officials. The majority of the persons responsible for making maintenance and improvement decisions for low-volume roads in rural areas have only limited training and experience. Many are volunteer community leaders or part-time employees with a broad range of responsibilities. Inappropriate decisions can be very costly for both taxpayers and operators of vehicles and, in some cases, may even endanger lives.

Forty-two university-based technology transfer centers supported by the Federal Highway Administration have pioneered efforts in providing up-to-date technical information to rural leaders on highway maintenance and improvements issues. Technology transfer centers located at universities throughout the nation provide individual assistance and workshops to rural leaders on a diverse range of topics, including design of drainage systems, surface preparation and maintenance techniques, bridge repair and maintenance, pavement technologies, highway salt management, engineering innovations, and planning. Programs are developed specifically for road maintenance personnel and public officials in rural areas. In many cases programs are carried out in cooperation with Extension Service personnel.

Purpose and Organization of Text

Transportation will play a critical role in determining the future social and economic vitality of rural America. Education and technical assistance programs will be needed to resolve the emerging rural transportation needs of the next several decades. Cooperative Extension Service and other University personnel are likely to have major responsibility for developing and delivering needed rural transportation and technical assistance programs. This text provides perspective on the issues as well as practical ideas to help providers of educational programs and technical assistance to rural areas to meet this important challenge for almost seventy-five years.

Profitability and Mobility in Rural America contains fourteen chapters. After this first chapter, which discusses the relevance of rural transportation, a second chapter reviews the historical role of Cooperative Extension Services in helping rural communities meet the transportation challenge.

The next three chapters provide perspective on the changing transportation environment. Chapter 3 identifies emerging local rural road and bridge problems and various solutions available to local governments dealing with these problems. Chapter 4 analyzes the impacts and implications of the economic and public finance policy changes over the past decade for the financing of rural low-volume roads and bridges. Problems and issues associated with deregulated agricultural transportation are discussed in Chapter 5.

Chapters 6 and 7 focus on transportation's contribution to rural economic development. The importance of transportation for business profitability is discussed from the perspective of industrial development groups as well from the perspective of an individual firm.

Chapters 8 and 9 provide perspective on emerging rural passenger transportation issues and the movement of hazardous waste. These two transportation topics were chosen because of their importance for quality of life in rural areas.

The final five chapters are case studies of successful approaches to tackling rural transportation problems developed by University and Extension Service personnel. The case studies are intended to stimulate ideas on how educational programs and technical assistance can facilitate solutions to critical rural transportation problems

2

Extension Involvement in Rural Transportation

Donald L. Nelson

This chapter discusses the evolution of Extension's involvement with rural transportation. Efforts to improve rural transportation began even before the creation of Cooperative Extension at the turn of the century. In 1893 the Office of Roads Inquiry was organized within the U.S. Department of Agriculture. The work of this office focused on demonstration and education. In 1905 an Office of Public Roads was organized to replace the Office of Roads Inquiry. Its function was to construct demonstration roads and to test road-building materials. By 1912 Office of Public Roads received appropriations to supervise building of rural post roads (Rasmussen 1985). These developments led to improved rural mail delivery and began to make rural America accessible to the economic benefits of highway transportation.

The Extension system has been called "the lengthened shadow of a man and an idea" (Evans 1938, 5). The man was "an uncommonly successful agricultural teacher with the unlikely name of Seaman A. Knapp, who obviously preferred the soil to the sea" (Extension Service 1976). Knapp, who spent "seventy years of preparation for seven years of service" (Evans 1938, 5) is generally credited with developing and disseminating the idea of "community demonstration farms" which, in turn, was used by Extension. Knapp's demonstration work began in Louisiana and Texas in 1903 when he was seventy years old. For the next (and last) seven years of his life, he cultivated and put into practice the demonstration idea.

After receiving a charge from the Secretary of Agriculture to find ways to bowl over the pesky boll weevil, Dr. Knapp decided to "call a conference on 27 January [1903], of the agricultural and industrial agents of the various railway systems in Texas" (Evans 1938, 9). It was decided at this conference that a small force of field men would be necessary. This small force would travel on the railroads, spreading Knapp's knowledge. One of the agents, author J. A. Evans, said, "The state [Texas] was divided into districts embracing all or part of ten to twenty-five counties, with an agent[1] assigned to each district. We were furnished with railway passes. My territory extended to the Louisiana line on the H.E. & W.T. Railway (locally known as Hell Either Way You Take It)[2] and for a distance of 100 or more miles along two other railway lines." Knapp's agents' work was very much dependent on the transportation technology of the time, as even today a 100-mile-long territory is a formidable strip of ground for an agent to cover.

At the same time in Iowa, "from 1904 to 1911, railroad demonstration trains carried speakers discussing selection of seed corn and other subjects to several stops each day. One leader was Professor P. G. Holden, Iowa State College. In 1911, 62 trains carried 72 lecturers more than 35,000 miles and reached almost a million people" (Extension Service 1976).

Remarkably, the demonstration train as a means of transporting educational technology persevered for another forty years. "When the last [Indiana] Extension train ran in 1947, it consisted of eight exhibit coaches, two sleeping cars and a dining car for staff, electric generating car, and a car for the railroad crew. The New York Central remodelled coaches especially for the exhibit, and the train was accompanied by the NYC agricultural agent" (Reeder 1979, 29).

Extension was officially formed by the Smith-Lever Act of 1914 and the eager new agents began to seek ways to demonstrate effective, efficient farm and home practices throughout rural America, Knapp's famous homily ringing in their ears: "What a man hears, he may doubt; what he sees, he may possibly doubt; but what he does, he cannot doubt."[3]

Extension's mission, as outlined in its charter, is "to aid in the diffusing among the people of the United States useful and practical information . . . and to encourage the application of same." The only effective way to diffuse that practical information in the early days was to transport it out of the classrooms and laboratories and off the demonstration plots to farmers and their families. Extension agents carried this information by rail or over dirty, muddy, flooded, or ice-covered roads. Transportation was not actually taught, but there were lessons to be learned regarding how to get information delivered and applied to nearly isolated and nearly inaccessible rural areas. As Reeder put it: "If the chief concern of these Extension pioneers was finding the needs of their people, then they had first to find ways of getting to those people. They went by horse, on foot, in a train, motorcycle, or automobile—often a Model T—recalled with affection by many of the pioneers. While they loved their Model T, their hate seems to have been devoted to the bad roads enroute" (Reeder 1979, 18).

One pioneer, Tommy Bryant of Kentucky, said: "Oh, my, bridges across streams were a great help to Extension" (Reeder 1979, 27). So as the governments built bridges, Extension crossed them, building bridges of another kind (bridges to understanding) as they traveled.

Reeder relates another anecdote which illustrates how prominently transportation figured in winning the acceptance of the Extension agent by the skeptical country folk: (Pennsylvania agent) Dutch Bucher said, "There were 12,000 farmers in my county—that's a lot of people to get acquainted with. I tried suburban trolley cars, saddle horses at 50 cents a day, a bicycle—all for a year and all too slow. Then I borrowed a motorcycle."

"People in the county were not satisfied with his work," the Reeder passage continues, "and the newspaper condemned the spending of money on a young fellow with no experience who was trying to tell old-time farmers how to farm. A country doctor in that county owned two of the biggest orchards, and Dutch went out to help him prune the trees. When the doctor asked him how things were going, Dutch told the doctor about being young and inexperienced and trying to build a reputation. 'I had the same problem when I started,' the doctor told him, 'so I got me a team of horses and a buggy and drove fast down the dusty county roads. After a while people began to think somebody must be calling for me and I started to get business.' With that advice, Dutch began to do the same thing on his motorcycle, although often, he recalls, he had no place to go" (Reeder 1979).

But Extension, it turns out, did have places to go and started getting there. The early Extension agents' experiences did not alone put rural America on wheels, but they almost certainly contributed greatly to the spread of improved roads and bridges and the cars and trucks plying them. Evans, under the heading "Impact of Technology," muses about the impact of the automobile on Extension's farm family clients: "In 1911, the year of Dr. Knapp's death, there were only 210,000 passenger automobiles made and sold in the United States and Canada. In a few years the number had increased to one million, then two million, then three million, made and sold annually. The census of 1930 showed 1,182,819 passenger cars *on farms* in the 12 Southeastern States alone. At retail prices this represents a farm investment of nearly a billion dollars. As the life expectancy of the average car is four or five years, it is safe to say that approximately two to three billion dollars have been spent by farmers in the South alone for family cars in the last 25 years. I mention particularly the automobile because it is at once the most alluring and the most costly of all the many products of technology during this time."[4]

Advancing transportation technology was certainly a major contributor to the productive development of rural America, along with hybrid corn, crop rotations, and all the other innovations that Extension championed. A USDA publication of the late 1930s reveals some of the transportation statistics that helped foretell the trend to bigger, more productive (and fewer) farms, a trend that continues today:

A recent State study has provided some figures on the changed relation between time and distance in rural communities. Families that had lived on farms for the 25 years from 1905 to 1930 were asked about the cost to them, in minutes of time, of going to school, grange, church, bank, lodge, hardware, drug and grocery stores, and the like. The replies showed that while it took 1,000 minutes in 1905 to reach these institutions, in 1930 it took only 276 minutes. When measured in miles instead of minutes, the bank, church, and the grange had changed very little in their distance from the homes of the families who went to them; the time required to go, however, had been cut about 70 percent. While the average distance to the school had increased 70 percent during the period studied, the time required to go and come had lessened about half. Likewise, distance to shipping points and livestock markets as measured in miles had increased about a half while the time was lessened about 65 percent. (U.S. Department of Agriculture, 1940)

After World War II, Extension expanded its diffusion of inform
to include marketing farm products. "Marketing work with assem
processors, distributors and consumers grew widely; by 1961 there were
about 350 [Extension] marketing specialists" (Noordhoff, 10). In earlier
times, farmers themselves did the marketing or the marketing process
was not specialized or costly enough to merit separate studies and learning. Extension transportation education was mainly the job of the marketing specialist. Specialization, urbanization, technology, burgeoning
farm trade, and competition were among the factors making marketing
and its imbedded transportation component increasingly important to
the agricultural industry and rural America. For this reason an Iowa Extension news release of 1964 poses the question, "Bulk Milk Handling—
Is It For You?" Marketing specialists helped farmers find ways to
"shrink" the loss of weight of livestock in transit to market. And so on.

Transportation as an independent Extension subject matter program
began in the early 1970s with the energy crisis, since energy and transportation were bound tightly together. But energy for transportation
was not the only problem. Agriculture and farm communities were
troubled by rail abandonment and restructuring, rail car shortages, and
decaying infrastructure just when increased foreign demand for American food and other natural resources like coal was booming. Also,
transportation regulation suddenly seemed to be onerous rather than
protective. The Extension marketing specialists were joined by community development specialists, agricultural engineers, policy experts, and
even a few transportation specialists to address the worsening transportation situation.

By 1974, Extension Service-USDA had at least two of its program
leaders deeply immersed in transportation issues. In his inaugural
"Transportation Notes" of June 1974, one of them, Marvin Konyha
said: "There are three basic dimensions to the issue of rural transportation facilities and services. There are (1) the transporting of goods,
either agricultural products, agricultural and industrial inputs, or manufactured goods, (2) the transporting of people, and (3) related to both
of these, the community development impacts of the availability of
adequate transportation facilities and services, or the lack thereof."

This and succeeding "Notes" of the 1970s spoke of "the crisis now
facing shippers and rural communities in the Northeast and North Central Regions . . . (which) has been a long time coming. The financial
plight of the Penn Central and other railroads and the continuing dete-

rioration of rail facilities and rail service throughout the regions made it just a matter of time until the crisis came." Also, "three recent events of gigantic proportions served to focus national attention on transportation issues—the Arab oil embargo and its related energy crisis in 1973–74; the collapse of the railroad industry in the Northeast and North Central States and the passage of the Regional Rail Reorganization Act of 1973 to deal with that crisis; and the shortage in transportation facilities capacity to handle the huge increase in shipments of grain for export in 1972–74.

"Each of the issues and their proposed solution contain major significance for transportation needs and services in nonmetropolitan areas. Each will also have serious implications regarding the future of rural development efforts in this country.

"The transit needs of the transportation-disadvantaged citizens of rural areas will also continue to receive increased attention at the National level."

In the late 1970s, Extension was involved in the Rural Transportation Advisory Task Force (a requirement of Public Law 95-580) and the Carter Administration's Small Community and Rural Development Policy, which included "Transportation and Communication" in its "action agenda."

Extensions organization and policy body established the first national rural transportation task force in 1975 and more recently declared rural transportation "a critical national issue" needing more Extension attention.

Extension today is taking a new look at how to approach rural transportation education, because the issues are in flux again. A drop in foreign trade, the abatement of the energy crisis, a restructured rail system, deregulation, and other factors have combined to change the educational agenda. But farmers, ranchers, families, and rural communities must address the isolation, the inaccessibility, the weak infrastructure, the ever-advancing technology, and the suspicion that energy shortages could return. Extension's teaching today includes such broad topics as roads and bridges, rail (including rail abandonment), personal transit, and other modal concerns, plus planning, routing, public policy, de- and re-regulation, economic development, costs and competition, in addition to others.

The third national Extension transportation task force is addressing these issues and its findings should complement this book (Extension Committee on Organization and Policy 1987).

Extension involvement in rural transportation can be said to be so old that it was the first issue Extension addressed ("If the chief concern of these Extension pioneers was finding the needs of their people, they had first to find ways of getting to these people") or so new that it has not yet had time to coalesce into a defined program area.

The first view could be supported by those who would say that the Extension idea was to diffuse practical information among the people of the United States and that the only way to diffuse that information was to transfer it out of the classrooms, laboratories, and demonstration plots on horseback, on foot, in a train, motorcycle, or automobile.

The second view could be supported by those who would point out that Extension has considered rural transportation in a formal and organized way for only about the past twelve or fifteen years.

It may never be possible or even desirable for Extension to allocate scarce resources to a full-bodied rural transportation program, as such, since transportation is a means to an end rather than an end in itself. Transportation education concerns developing the means to move goods and people, rather than about developing product, place, and human potential. But, while not an end, transportation will certainly continue to be an important means for which rural America will demand Extension education.

Notes

1. Thus, notes the Extension Service Review, Extension had "area agents" before it had "county agents" and the area agent concept popular in the 1960s was not really new.

2. Evans does not say what the "H.E. & W.T." properly stood for.

3. The Knapp quotation is all masculine, but he was a women's rights advocate of the first order: "Dr. Knapp's last visit to the [General Education] Board was to arrange for the expansion of the Girls' Club work. He was already stricken with illness, but he was not too feeble to foretell what might be accomplished through this work for Southern womanhood. This was indeed his last legacy" (Evans 1938, 18).

4. Now, nearly fifty years after Evans penned this comment, the allure and the cost of the family car still rings true for rural Americans and, in fact, for all Americans.

References

Evans, J. A. 1938. *Recollections of Extension History*. North Carolina Agricultural Extension Service. Extension Circular No. 224.

Extension Committee on Organization and Policy. 1987 (scheduled availability). *Extension Transportation Programming Guide and Directory of Assistance* (working title). Being prepared by the "New" Rural Transportation Task Force. Steve Murray and David Chicoine, Chairs.

Extension Committee on Organization and Policy. 1985. *Rural Transportation Education: Challenges for Cooperative Extension*. A report prepared by the Transportation Task Force of the Subcommittee on Community Resource Development and Public Affairs. Marc Johnson, Chair.

Extension Service. 1976. *Extension Service Review* 46, No. 3 (May–June). U.S. Department of Agriculture.

National Extension Transportation Task Force. 1980. *Transportation Policy Primer*. Publication No. 4. Gary M. Mennem, Project Leader.

Noordhoff, Lyman, and E. B. Winner. *50 Years of Cooperative Extension Work, 1914–1964*. Federal Extension Service, U.S. Department of Agriculture.

Rasmussen, Wayne D. 1985. "90 Years of Rural Development Programs." *Rural Development Perspectives* 2, Issue 1 (October). U.S. Department of Agriculture, Economic Research Service.

Reeder, R. L. 1979. *The People and the Profession, Selected Memories of Veteran Extension Workers*. National Board of Epsilon Sigma Phi.

U.S. Department of Agriculture. 1954. *The Yearbook of Agriculture, Marketing*.

U.S. Department of Agriculture. 1940. *Rural Communities: What Do They Need Most?* Bureau of Agricultural Economics with the Extension Service.

Part II

Changing Transportation Environment

3

Alternatives for Solving the Local Rural Road and Bridge Problem

C. Phillip Baumel
Eldo Schornhorst
Wesley D. Smith

In this chapter local rural roads and bridges refer to those rural roads and bridges that are under the jurisdiction of county and township governments. A major characteristic of the local rural road system in the United States is the large number of roads. About 2.3 million miles are in the local rural road system. This figure represents 71 percent of the 3.2 million miles of rural road in the United States. A primary characteristic of the local rural road system in the Midwest and West is the rectangular road grid. The grid usually conforms to a one-mile spacing. The density and regularity of the county road system dates back to the Ordinance of 1785. This act, which was intended by Congress to open the land for settlement, established townships and the one-mile survey grids.

Many of today's local rural roads and bridges were built in the late 1800s and early 1900s when overland transportation for both passengers and freight was limited to horse and wagon or the recently built railroad lines. Farms were small, and farmers needed road access to homes, schools, churches, and markets. Technological change soon took its toll on the rural roads and bridges. First came the steam engine and the four to five ton threshing machine. Some of the bridges collapsed under the weight of these machines. The discovery of large petroleum reserves in Texas and Oklahoma spurred the development of the automobile and small truck industries during the 1920s and 1930s and created a need to get rural America "out of the mud." Roads were surfaced, and some bridges were replaced to accommodate the trucks with gross weights of six to seven tons. About 70 percent of today's rural bridges were built before 1935. Most of the bridges constructed in the 1940s were designed for 15-ton loads. By 1950 about 50 percent of the local rural roads were improved with all-weather surfaces. Thus, the widths, grades, bases, surface designs, and capacities of many local rural roads and bridges are based on the traffic needs of the 1940s and 1950s.

Agricultural technology has also changed the type of local rural roads and bridges needed in rural America today. Agricultural output has increased sharply and large amounts of grain move over the local road system. There are no weight limits on "implements of husbandry"—farm equipment—in many states. Today, it is common for farmers to use a tractor and two wagons to haul 200 to 900 bushels of grain with a gross weight of 28 to 36 tons to the local elevator. Many bridges are 55 feet long or longer, so that the entire load is on the bridge simultaneously. Some single-axle wagons hold over 800 bushels of grain. Deducting about 6,000 pounds of hitch weight, the loaded weight ranges up to 50,000 pounds per axle.

Farm equipment manufacturers have been forced by farm consolidation and farmer demand to create larger, more efficient machinery. Present day disks and row-crop cultivators are up to 54 feet wide. These types of equipment can be folded to 18 to 20 feet wide. But even the folded equipment will not pass through the 16- to 18-foot widths of many local rural bridges. One country engineer in Iowa reported that the entire railing and posts from two wooden bridges located about one thousand feet apart were missing. There was no doubt in the engineer's mind that some frustrated farmer used a chain saw to "widen" the bridge to accommodate his wide farm equipment. Moreover, wide farm equipment uses almost the entire width of the road, creating hazardous conditions for approaching traffic, particularly in hilly country with limited sight distance.

Advanced agricultural technology creates pressures for larger farms. In most instances the only way a farmer can obtain more land is to buy or lease from neighboring farms, thereby reducing the total number of farms. The large reduction in the number of farms means that some rural roads may no longer be needed for access to homes, schools, and markets. Many observers believe that the number of miles of rural roads might be reduced and still provide needed access to the remaining farms.

As the farm size has increased, feed, fertilizer, and petroleum delivery trucks and bulk-milk trucks have become larger. Tandem-axle trucks with gross weights of 27 tons are common on rural roads and bridges. In 1975 Congress permitted states to set higher weight limits for trucks on the Interstate system, and most states have raised the weight limits to the federal standard of 20,000 pounds per axle, 34,000 thousand pounds per two-axle tandem, and 80,000 pound maximum overall weight. The introduction of low-cost, unit-grain trains in the Corn and Wheat Belt states has encouraged the use of larger farm vehicles to haul grain longer distances. Some farmers are buying used semi-trailer trucks to move grain out of the field quickly, to increase their marketing options, to reduce hauling costs, and to eliminate the safety hazards of farm tractor-wagon combinations.

The declining rural population has resulted in a reduction in the number of rural schools. To help minimize the cost of transporting school children longer distances to fewer schools, school boards are purchasing 72 to 89 passenger school buses. Loaded buses of these sizes weigh between nine to ten tons. These buses can not cross bridges posted at less than ten tons.

Condition of the County Road and Bridge System

Precise data on the current condition of off-system rural roads are not available, since no ongoing coordinated data-collection system exists for local roads. A report on a 1984 survey of local government officials in Illinois, Ohio, Minnesota, and Wisconsin indicated that 50 percent of the miles of local rural roads needed more than regular maintenance and 20 percent of the total miles needed major repairs (Chicoine and Walzer 1984, 55). Common complaints about the local rural roads include: overweight vehicles breaking up road surfaces, lack of hard surfaces creating dust and rideability problems, road widths and other design characteristics being inadequate for today's large farm equipment and heavy trucks, and narrow lanes creating safety problems.

There is ample evidence to suggest that the system is deteriorating rapidly. While the local road deficiencies are significant, the condition of local bridges is of even greater concern. Deficient bridges on local rural roads are creating serious safety and traffic constraints. Table 3.1

Table 3.1 Count of deficient bridges by state off-federal-aid system as of 1 January 1986

	Bridges in inventory	Structurally deficient bridges	Functionally obsolete bridges	Total deficient bridges	Percent deficient bridges
Alabama	7,753	2,995	1,508	4,503	58
Alaska	253	60	15	75	30
Arizona	803	90	59	149	19
Arkansas	7,244	1,196	3,078	4,274	59
California	7,487	1,089	2,511	3,600	48
Colorado	3,734	1,880	303	2,183	58
Connecticut	1,146	340	357	697	61
Delaware	262	47	32	79	30
District of Columbia	13	0	0	0	0
Florida	4,197	603	871	1,474	35
Georgia	6,295	2,939	439	3,378	54
Hawaii	369	38	102	140	38
Idaho	2,053	464	382	846	41
Illinois	14,662	3,987	1,853	5,840	40
Indiana	10,438	3,400	2,721	6,121	59
Iowa	18,975	5,310	5,209	10,519	55
Kansas	15,046	4,884	5,175	10,059	67
Kentucky	7,587	1,353	3,361	4,714	62
Louisiana	8,401	3,168	1,659	4,827	57
Maine	1,351	283	278	561	42
Maryland	1,891	248	480	728	38
Massachusetts	1,207	625	33	658	55
Michigan	4,735	1,849	394	2,243	47
Minnesota	7,876	1,420	1,621	3,041	39
Mississippi	9,270	5,025	843	5,868	63
Missouri	15,095	4,919	6,835	11,754	78
Montana	2,334	526	1,052	1,578	68
Nebraska	11,001	6,407	1,703	8,110	74
Nevada	225	29	45	74	29
New Hampshire	1,335	390	445	835	63
New Jersey	1,775	482	293	775	44
New Mexico	571	118	87	205	36
New York	8,491	5,441	893	6,334	75
North Carolina	10,429	4,212	3,236	7,448	71
North Dakota	3,371	1,913	511	2,424	65
Ohio	16,825	2,680	1,441	4,121	24
Oklahoma	14,877	7,078	2,410	9,488	64
Oregon	2,816	327	400	727	26
Pennsylvania	11,179	3,159	1,454	4,613	41
Rhode Island	133	32	17	49	37
South Carolina	4,670	727	333	1,060	23
South Dakota	4,292	1,514	1,420	2,934	68
Tennessee	11,103	4,617	1,421	6,038	54
Texas	18,546	6,636	5,098	11,734	63

Table 3.1 *continued*

	Bridges in inventory	Structurally deficient bridges	Functionally obsolete bridges	Total deficient bridges	Percent deficient bridges
Utah	964	212	83	295	31
Vermont	1,364	277	466	734	54
Virginia	5,676	563	2,122	2,685	47
Washington	2,833	290	445	735	26
West Virginia	3,261	1,655	601	2,256	69
Wisconsin	6,608	2,468	1,137	3,605	55
Wyoming	942	269	252	521	55
Puerto Rico	794	69	198	267	34
Totals	304,948	100,303	67,682	167,985	55

Source: U.S. Department of Transportation, "Seventh Annual Report to Congress, Highway Bridge Replacement and Rehabilitation Program," Federal Highway Administration, Washington, D.C., 1986.

shows the number of bridges inventoried in each state as of 1 January 1986, the number of structurally deficient and functionally obsolete bridges, and the percentage of deficient bridges (U.S. Department of Transportation 1986, 58). A structurally deficient bridge will not carry a legal load. A functionally obsolete bridge will carry a legal limit but is too narrow or has other characteristics that do not meet minimum standards. Nationally, 167,985 bridges or 55 percent of all the off-federal-aid bridges that had been inventoried are deficient or obsolete. Moreover, Table 3.2 indicates that 40 percent of the inventoried bridges were posted or should have been posted at less than legal load limits or were closed (U.S. Department of Transportation 1986, 60). Even this more current number understates the magnitude of the problem. Bridges under twenty feet long were not included in the inventory. There are thousands of structures under twenty feet in length that need replacement or rehabilitation.

The distribution of deficient bridges among states indicates that the off-system bridge problem is national in scope. States with more than 70 percent deficient bridges are North Carolina, Missouri, Nebraska, and New York. States with 50 to 70 percent deficient and obsolete off-federal-aid bridges are Alabama, Arkansas, Colorado, Connecticut, Georgia, Indiana, Iowa, Kansas, Kentucky, Louisiana, Massachusetts, Missouri, Montana, New Hampshire, Oklahoma, South Dakota, Tennessee, Texas, Vermont, West Virginia, Wisconsin, and Wyoming.

Table 3.2 Count of open, closed, and posted bridges off-federal-aid system as of 1 January 1986

	Bridges in inventory	Closed bridges	Posted bridges	Open-should be posted but are not posted bridges	Percent closed, posted, or should-be-posted bridges
Alabama	7,753	67	862	5,584	84
Alaska	253	20	64	39	49
Arizona	803	23	94	3	15
Arkansas	7,244	63	571	3,590	50
California	7,487	30	618	99	10
Colorado	3,734	24	1,906	16	52
Connecticut	1,146	22	159	45	20
Delaware	262	5	49	4	22
District of Columbia	13	0	2	0	15
Florida	4,197	41	1,094	327	35
Georgia	6,295	175	2,527	419	50
Hawaii	369	1	67	26	25
Idaho	2,053	4	686	0	34
Illinois	14,662	499	2,626	1,377	31
Indiana	10,438	138	3,234	2,433	56
Iowa	18,975	268	8,681	801	51
Kansas	15,046	437	8,404	282	61
Kentucky	7,587	65	942	74	14
Louisiana	8,401	49	1,310	3,391	57
Maine	1,351	9	110	194	23
Maryland	1,891	12	268	377	35
Massachusetts	1,207	70	435	30	46
Michigan	4,735	308	1,806	54	46
Minnesota	7,876	76	1,562	92	22
Mississippi	9,270	84	5,612	90	62

Missouri	15,095	253	3,012	75	22
Montana	2,334	4	631	596	53
Nebraska	11,001	171	8,072	159	76
Nevada	255	5	17	2	9
New Hampshire	1,335	38	656	3	52
New Jersey	1,775	42	591	29	37
New Mexico	571	5	156	9	30
New York	8,491	81	1,658	0	20
North Carolina	10,429	39	6,748	2	65
North Dakota	3,731	34	1,609	509	58
Ohio	16,825	150	5,620	1,134	41
Oklahoma	14,877	173	3,741	130	27
Oregon	2,816	9	340	57	14
Pennsylvania	11,179	178	3,057	933	37
Rhode Island	133	5	24	2	23
South Carolina	4,670	26	765	0	17
South Dakota	4,292	71	2,319	119	58
Tennessee	11,103	202	1,939	1,223	30
Texas	18,546	103	2,044	8	12
Utah	964	23	161	185	38
Vermont	1,364	13	151	0	12
Virginia	5,676	8	2,324	3	41
Washington	2,833	26	296	9	12
West Virginia	3,261	55	1,427	3	46
Wisconsin	6,608	53	1,100	5	18
Wyoming	942	10	217	319	58
Puerto Rico	794	4	11	0	2
Totals	304,948	4,271	92,375	24,861	40

Source: U.S. Department of Transportation, "Seventh Annual Report to Congress, Highway Bridge Replacement and Rehabilitation Program," Federal Highway Administration, Washington, D.C., 1986.

States with 50 percent or more of posted or should-be-posted bridges are Alabama, Arkansas, Colorado, Georgia, Indiana, Iowa, Kansas, Louisiana, Mississippi, Montana, Nebraska, New Hampshire, North Carolina, North Dakota, South Dakota, and Wyoming. States in the far West have the least problem in terms of total and percent of deficient and posted bridges.

Another indication of the condition of the local rural road system can be obtained from the need studies that are conducted in a few states. The need studies estimate the cost of an ultimate highway system. While an ultimate system is not likely to ever be funded, the studies provide an indication of the condition of the highway system. For example, the 1986–2005 twenty-year inventory investment needs in the Iowa county road system are estimated to be $10.4 billion (Iowa Department of Transportation 1987, 12). The projected twenty-year revenues for the Iowa county road system were estimated to be $5.6 billion; thus, there is an investment shortfall of $4.8 billion.

Local rural road and bridge maintenance and construction funds have been derived from three basic sources. State-highway user taxes are derived from excise taxes on motor fuels, motor vehicle registration fees, drivers' license fees, and use taxes on vehicles. Federal funds are derived from federal motor fuel and excise taxes and revenue sharing funds. Local funds are derived from property taxes levied on rural and urban property, road bonds and other miscellaneous funds.

The likelihood of realizing the projected $4.5 billion twenty-year revenues for the Iowa county road system is small for several reasons. First, the dramatic reductions in property valuations in rural areas since 1980 will reduce property tax valuations and, hence, property tax collections. State legislative bodies are reluctant to raise maximum property tax levies to allow for increased property tax collections. Second, local governments have already lost federal revenue-sharing funds (Smith 1987, 6). Third, there is a high probability that local governments will lose all federal aid funds, with the possible exception of bridge replacement funds, for the local rural road system (Smith 1987, 6). Fourth, there is increasing political pressure to reallocate road use tax funds from the local rural road system to the state and municipal road systems. In some states the local rural road system's share of road use tax funds is already small. If revenues continue to decline relative to investment needs, the local rural road systems will continue to deteriorate unless adjustments are made to reduce local rural road costs.

Relationship of Off-System Roads and Bridges to Rail Abandonment

It has been suggested that railroad abandonment is a major cause of the rural road and bridge problem. The logic used in the argument is that it is cheaper to build and maintain railroads than highways. For example, Shelby County, Iowa, for several years during the late 1970s and early 1980s, had no rail service. While rail abandonment does result in increased application of heavy-weight vehicles and increased damage caused by these vehicles, some of the costs of this damage are offset by increased taxes on vehicles and fuel. The argument that railroad abandonment is a major cause of the local road problem assumes all road traffic could be diverted to railroads. It is not possible for railroads to transport feed to hog, cattle, and chicken feeders, to deliver petroleum to farm tanks, to transport children to school, to deliver mail, to haul grain from fields to the local elevator, to haul milk or livestock from farms to the processing plants or to transport large farm equipment from farmsteads to fields. Thus, the local rural road system was an important transportation link before rail abandonment and the local rural traffic must be accommodated regardless of what happens to railroad branch lines.

Alternative Solutions

The local rural road and bridge problem is primarily a lack of funds to maintain and reconstruct the present system to accommodate the changing transportation needs of rural America. There are a number of alternative solutions to increase revenues or to reduce costs, as described below.

Continue to Present Sources and Tax Levels and the Current Size of the Local Rural Road and Bridge System

This alternative would mean that there would be no large increases in property or road use taxes to finance the reconstruction of the local rural road system. There have been motor fuel tax increases in many states in recent years. However, these have been offset in part by more fuel-efficient vehicles. In addition, the share of the road use tax funds going to the local rural road system will likely be offset in part by declining property tax collections as the decline in property tax valuation works its way through the tax system. Thus, this alternative would likely result in continued deterioration of the local rural road system. Counties and townships would continue to face increasing maintenance costs to repair existing surfaces and bridges. Some bridges would need to be closed without additional replacement funds. Perhaps more importantly, county and township governments could face increased exposure to large tort liability claims from damages resulting from deteriorating roads and bridges. Courts historically have been generous to these kinds of claims. This alternative is the one most likely to continue with some modifications.

Large Increases in State and Federal Funding

Potential sources of state funds include increased state or federal fuel taxes, increased state vehicle registration fees, funding from state and federal general funds, or an increasing share of the road use tax fund to the local rural road system. It is unlikely that the present political climate would permit raising the fuel and registration fees enough or to shift additional funds from state general funds to meet the increasing needs of the rural road system. At the present time, the federal government is attempting to reduce its role in financing local roads and bridges. However, the magnitude of the local rural road and bridge problem as well as the state and municipal road and stream system problems suggests that state governments may be forced to increase fuel taxes and to assume part of the cost of rebuilding the local rural bridges.

Improve Local Option Taxes Alone or with Bonding Authority for Local Rural Road and Bridge Funding

The local option taxes could be in the form of property, sales, fuel, excise, or other taxes. When levied alone, they would approximate user taxes because a significant portion of the traffic on local roads is local traffic. When these taxes are used to support bonding programs for capital improvements, the program becomes even more of a user tax. However, interest on the bonds increases the cost of rebuilding the system unless the inflation rate is greater than the interest rate.

Reduce the Minimum Reconstruction and Maintenance Standards on All Local Rural Roads and Bridges

The minimum standards for local rural roads and bridges are generally based on design guides published by the American Association of State Highway and Transportation Officials. In some cases road plans must be approved by state and federal agencies. Future reconstruction costs could be reduced by lowering the minimum design standards on low-volume, off-system rural roads. Costs could be cut by reducing the widths of rights-of-way and shoulders and bridges, by reducing the thickness of the pavement, and by reducing maximum grades. Lower minimum standards, on the other hand, could result in increased maintenance costs through greater erosion from steeper and more narrow ditches, faster deterioration of pavements and bridges, and reduced snow-storage capacities. This option would also increase vehicle operating costs for the traveling public.

Reduce the Size of the Local Rural Road System by Abandoning Some Road Segments that Serve No Property Accesses

The rectangular road grid of many local rural roads provides many property owners with up to four-way access to their homes, farmsteads, and other property. It is possible to maintain primary access to property with only one-way access. Some local rural roads could be eliminated from the system and still provide property access to all homes, farms, fields, and local businesses. However, reducing the number of rural roads will result in higher travel costs to the traveling public through longer travel distances. Thus, decisions to reduce the size of the rural road system must be evaluated in terms of the additional travel costs to the traveling public relative to the cost savings to the local governments providing the public road system. A recent Iowa study indicated that a small number of abandoned local rural roads in counties located near urban areas would yield maintenance and reconstruction cost savings that would be greater than the additional travel costs to the traveling public (Baumel et al. 1986). In rural counties a larger number of miles of local rural roads would produce net savings from road abandonment. These conclusions suggest that road abandonment can result in a reduction in net local road costs. However, any proposal to reduce the size of the local road system must be researched with care. We believe that there will be little effort to reduce the size of the local road system until programs are designed to relieve local government officials of the considerable political liability associated with road abandonment. One proposal to relieve elected government officials of the political liability and local governments of the financial liability is to establish appointed committees to develop and implement road abandonment proposals. Proposals to reduce local government financial liability include denying claims to an individual if the proposed road abandonment is a second access and placing a "cap" on damage claims.

Establish a Reduced Maintenance Classification on Selected "Area Service" Roads

Many low-volume road segments provide no property access or access only to farm fields. It is possible to significantly reduce maintenance on these area service roads and still provide access to farm fields. One estimate of the annual maintenance costs on these area service roads shown in Table 3.3 is $605 per mile of road.

The estimated maintenance costs on regularly maintained gravel roads ranges from about twenty-four hundred dollars to about four thousand dollars per mile per year, depending on the location and traffic levels on the road (Baumel et al. 1983, 52). The area service maintenance costs include no gravel resurfacing or snow removal. Thus, area service roads would eventually revert to dirt roads and would not be open in the winter. Therefore, these roads could not service households, farmsteads, or any other property that must have winter access by registered vehicles.

The Iowa analysis indicated a substantial net cost savings to counties over the additional cost to the traveling public from the area service option. However, there are some potential problems with this option. First, while the road surfaces would be downgraded over time, substantial local government investments would eventually be required on bridge reconstruction or on bridge replacement with low water crossings. Second, while the Iowa law exempts the county governments from liability from personal injury or property damage caused by the lower level of maintenance, the exemption has not been tested in the courts. Third, county boards of supervisors are reluctant to place many roads into the area service category because of the political implications.

Table 3.3 Estimated annual maintenance costs on
area service B roads

Type of annual service	Cost per mile
Blading, five times	$105
Signing	100
Culvert repairs and minor ditching	150
Culvert replacement	100
Major ditching	150
Snow removal	0
Surfacing	0
Total	$605

Establish a "Land Access" System

Another alternative to reducing local rural road costs is to establish a system of land-access roads. Land-access roads would remain under public jurisdiction but would not be open to public traffic. These roads, which would contain no residences, would provide access to farming operations only. All maintenance would be the responsibility of adjoining land owners. The level of maintenance would depend on the type of activity in the roads. For example, a road providing access only to fields could be allowed to revert to dirt, while a road serving a hog operation would need a gravel surface. All liability would be transferred to the adjoining land owners. However, the exclusion of public traffic could actually reduce liability from animal escape and vehicle accidents on public roads.

Elected local government officials would act as a review board to settle disputes among abutting owners over the level of maintenance and the distribution of the maintenance costs.

Most public roads have a sixty-foot right-of-way. However, land access roads may need only thirty-three feet of right-of-way. Thus, each abutting land owner would receive an additional sixteen feet of land along the land access road. Some roads could be returned to private ownership.

A 1976 editorial in the *Des Moines Register* states:

County roads that served dozens of farms 40 years ago may be serving only two or three farms today. Many roads that were

> once vital to a county's well-being have become, in effect, private roads although the county is responsible for their upkeep. Such roads no longer belong in the county road system.

While some observers believe that road abandonment is the fundamental answer to the lack of funds for rural road and bridge construction and maintenance, it often costs more to vacate a road than to keep it. District courts have tended to make large awards to landowners for the loss of public access. Many county engineers believe that only a very small number of local rural roads will be abandoned unless laws are changed to reduce damage claims for the action and to transfer the responsibility for maintenance and liability for publicly owned field access roads to the benefited property. The Iowa study compared public maintenance costs on low volume roads with private maintenance costs on public roads that had reverted to private drives (Baumel et al. 1986, 57). The private maintenance costs were substantially lower than the public maintenance costs.

The Iowa study also found that dead-end roads were prime candidates for conversion to private drives because these roads carry only traffic originally on or destined for residences, farms, and fields located on these roads. Thus, conversion of dead-end roads to private drives would result in no additional travel costs. Furthermore, private maintenance costs on these roads would likely be substantially lower than public maintenance costs. However, damage claims permitted by some state laws may be so large that the private drive option will likely be exercised only if these maximum damage claims are lowered.

Reduce and Enforce Weight Limits on Local Rural Roads and Place Weight and Width Limits on "Implements of Husbandry"

This alternative undoubtedly would reduce maintenance costs of existing roads and bridges. However, a reduction of current weight limits and placing weight and width limits on "implements of husbandry" would increase the costs of agricultural production and of moving these products to market. It would also create enforcement problems. There is a need to study the reconstruction and maintenance costs of increased weight limits versus the increased costs of agricultural production if lower weight limits were imposed.

Impose a Special Tax on Coal to Finance the Reconstruction and Maintenance of Coal-Hauling Roads

This tax, which could be imposed on each ton of coal mined, could be adjusted to cover the additional costs from increased coal traffic on some local rural roads and bridges.

Farmer Attitudes on Local Road and Bridge Problems

In 1980, Pioneer Hi-Bred International Incorporated—a seed company located in Des Moines—conducted a sixteen-state poll of farmers' attitudes on grain transportation (Baumel and Schornhorst 1983, 378). Questionnaires were distributed to about 99,000 Pioneer customers and almost 35,000 completed questionnaires were returned. While the sample was not randomly selected, the large number of responses provides useful information on farmer attitudes toward local rural roads and bridges.

One question asked farmers if the deterioration of county roads and bridges is a problem affecting their area in moving farm machinery or grain from the fields or to the elevator. Only 34 percent of the farmers responding indicated that it was a problem. The responses varied widely by states. Table 3.4 shows the responses by states compared to the number and percent of deficient bridges in 1980. The percentage of farmers believing that roads and bridges are a problem was low in many of the states, including Iowa, Nebraska, South Dakota, and Texas, that had the largest number and percent of deficient bridges. This suggests that farmers were not fully aware of the magnitude of the problem.

One question asked the respondents to rank six alternative solutions to the local rural road and bridge problem. The alternatives and responses are presented in Table 3.5. Reducing the size of the system, reducing or eliminating the agricultural motor fuel tax exemption, and imposing a county tax on real estate were the least preferred solutions. Almost one-third of the farmers were willing to try to live with the present system. The preferred solutions were increased federal or state funds for upgrading roads and bridges. Some states, including North Carolina, Virginia, West Virginia, and Delaware, have taken over the maintenance and rehabilitation of the county road system.

Table 3.4 Deficient off-federal-aid bridges and percentage of farmers who believe county roads and bridges are a problem

State	Deficient road and bridges		Percentage of farmers believing roads and bridges a problem
	Number	Percentage	
Colorado	187	32	26
Illinois	6,937	47	50
Indiana	8,476	75	54
Iowa	10,452	55	25
Kansas	6,579	53	48
Michigan	2,552	59	46
Minnesota	3,702	46	20
Missouri	10,413	84	59
Nebraska	9,439	81	32
North Dakota	2,537	68	34
Ohio	3,484	24	50
Oklahoma	3,507	62	61
South Dakota	2,162	68	19
Texas	11,514	65	28
Wisconsin	4,359	68	23

Source: Baumel, C. Phillip, and Eldo Schornhorst, "Local Rural Roads and Bridges: Current and Future Problems and Alternatives," Transportation Research Board, Low-Volume Roads: Third International Conference, Transportation Research Record 988, Washington, D.C., 1983.

Federal and state governments are attempting to shift the road maintenance and rehabilitation responsibility to local governments. But, agriculture and local governments are looking to the state and federal governments to assume a major role in the local road and bridge programs. One way out of this circular dilemma is for representatives of each group to attempt to define and agree on the role of each level of government—federal, state, and local—in dealing with the rural local road and bridge problem. Once these roles have been agreed on, each level of government can proceed with making choices from the above set of alternatives, none of which is easy.

An advisory panel to Pioneer Hi-Bred International, consisting of farmers and transportation specialists, made several recommendations for dealing with the local rural road and bridge problem. They suggested that with the reduction in the number of farmsteads, removing some roads from the county system should be feasible in order to properly maintain the remaining part of the system. Second, those whose

Table 3.5 Farmer responses to alternative solutions to problem of local rural roads and bridges

Alternative	Percentage of farmers		
	Agree	Disagree	Not sure
Upgrading key county roads and dropping others from system	18	50	20
Continue current program and reduce weight limits	31	42	27
Additional federal funds	57	18	14
Additional state funds	51	16	21
Reduce or eliminate agricultural motor-fuel tax exemption	22	54	14
Levy county tax on all real estate	12	58	18

Source: Baumel, C. Phillip, and Eldo Schornhorst, "Local Rural Roads and Bridges: Current and Future Problems and Alternatives," Transportation Research Board, Low-Volume Roads: Third International Conference, Transportation Research Record 988, Washington, D.C., 1983.

livelihoods depend on doing business with farmers should share in the cost of maintaining an efficient system of county roads. Third, reduction of weight limits in an effort to hang on to the current system is not a workable long-range solution. Fourth, local control over the setting of priorities and supervision of work should be maintained, regardless of the source of funds.

Conclusions

The local rural road and bridge problem is a lack of funds to reconstruct and maintain the present system to accommodate the changing transportation needs of rural America. This paper outlines several alternatives to either increase the funds for reconstructing this system or to downgrade or reduce the size of the system. The optimal solution to the problem is likely to require a combination of several of these alternatives. Selection of this combination of alternatives will require analyses of the benefits and costs of each option in areas within each state. In addition, enabling legislation will be required in many states to implement some of these alternatives.

References

Baumel, C. Phillip, Cathy A. Hamlett, and Gregory R. Pautsch. 1986. "The Economics of Reducing the County Road System: Three Case Studies in Iowa." National Technical Information Service, DOT/OST/P–34/86/035, Springfield, Virginia.

Baumel, C. Phillip, and Eldo Schornhorst. 1983. "Local Rural Roads and Bridges: Current and Future Problems and Alternatives." Transportation Research Board, Low-Volume Roads: Third International Conference, *Transportation Research Record* 988, Washington, D.C.

Chicoine, David L., and Norman Walzer. 1984. "Financing Rural Roads and Bridges." U.S. Department of Agriculture, Office of Transportation and Marketing, Washington, D.C.

Iowa Department of Transportation. 1987. "Quadrennial Need Study, Report of Highways, Roads and Streets for Study Years 1986 through 2005." Ames, Iowa.

Smith, Wesley D., P. E. 1987. "Presentation to the Transportation Committee Iowa House of Representatives, 72nd General Assembly." Hamilton County Engineer, Webster City, Iowa.

U.S. Department of Transportation. 1986. "Seventh Annual Report to Congress, Highway Bridge Replacement and Rehabilitation Program." Federal Highway Administration, Washington, D.C.

4

Financing Rural Roads and Bridges: Issues and Trends

David L. Chicoine
Norman Walzer
Steven C. Deller

Rural transportation arteries are the vital link between farmers, markets, and rural employment centers. Agriculture depends on the timely marketing of commodities and products and on purchased production inputs, which both must move over the rural road system. Access to off-farm jobs, which are of increasing importance in rural economies for members of farm families and other rural countryside residents, is over the rural road network. Yet the condition of this transportation infrastructure is cause for concern. Recent studies have disclosed disinvestment in rural low-volume roads. The costs of improving and upgrading major parts of the system far exceed resources available to responsible rural local governments under existing funding policies and improvement programs (e.g., Baumel and Schornhorst 1983; Chicoine and Walzer 1984; Baumel, Hamlett, and Pautsch 1986; and Walzer and Chicoine 1987).

Most discussions of the condition and adequacy of public infrastructure have focused on the supply of public assets in urban areas and on the aging interstate highway and connecting bridges (Choate and Walter 1981; NCPWI 1986). However, some efforts have focused specifically on infrastructure in rural areas (Reid and Sullivan 1984; Chicoine and Walzer 1986). While the national concern is with evaluation of infrastructure performance and condition of existing facilities, the more immediate issue in many rural areas is investment in new facilities (Ryan 1987).

Central to all discussions of public infrastructure are estimates of the cost of rehabilitation and required new investments. A limitation of infrastructure analyses is the approach to establishing needs and determining associated costs. Consequently, estimates of the costs of rehabilitating and investing in the public's capital vary widely, and there is increased questioning of the results of the plethora of studies (Peterson et al. 1986).

Rural economies have undergone a major restructuring in many states, resulting in increased unemployment, accelerated exodus from farming, and declines in the tax base and population (Jahr, Johnson, and Wimberley 1986). Particular concern is voiced about the ability of rural governments to provide roads and bridges, as well as other essential public services (Chicoine 1987).

This chapter describes variation in governmental arrangements for providing rural road systems and rural road finance by state. The rural low-volume road system in the United States is characterized by great diversity in decision-making authority and financing methods. Understanding this diversity is central to an evaluation of the performance of rural low-volume road systems, their finance, and state and local policy options to address shortcomings. Particular attention is paid to an analysis of the importance of governance and finance organization for rural low-volume road systems.

The chapter has three major sections plus a discussion of policy implications. The first section details the variations in rural low-volume road responsibilities among states. The size of the rural road network in the United States is discussed as well as interstate variations. The second section highlights financing methods with particular focus on linkages between the degree of decentralization in road authority and road finance. The importance of property taxes in financing rural low-volume road systems, the dependence of rural governments on shared state motor fuel taxes, and the methods used by state governments to distribute these revenues to rural road jurisdictions are emphasized.

Next, the implications of organizational structure for rural road services are investigated. The effects of the decentralization of the governmental structure on rural low-volume road employment are analyzed within a rural road employment model. The results show that employment is influenced by service prices and fragmented road authority. Finally, the results are summarized and policy implications are discussed.

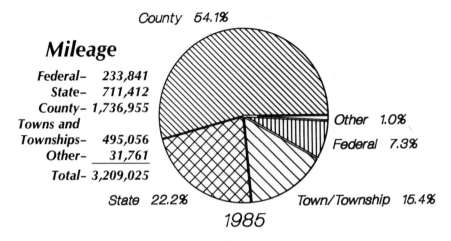

County 54.1%

Mileage

Federal–   233,841
State–   711,412
County– 1,736,955
Towns and
Townships–   495,056
Other–   31,761

Total– 3,209,025

State   22.2%

Other   1.0%

Federal   7.3%

Town/Township   15.4%

1985

Fig. 4.1. Rural road possibilities. (FHWA, Highway Statistics 1985, Washington, D.C.)

Rural Low-Volume Road Authority

The rural road system in the United States includes approximately 3.2 million miles of roads and highways plus thousands of connecting bridges. Nearly 22 percent of the mileage is the responsibility of state government and 7.3 percent is under federal jurisdiction. More than 60 percent of the rural road mileage is on county and town/township systems with county government responsible for over 50 percent of all miles (Figure 4.1). Of course, there are significant differences in the level of service and type of roads and highways maintained by states, the federal government, and county and town/township government.

The county and township systems are the farm-to-market roads bringing inputs to farms and ranches, farmers and ranchers to communities and off-farm jobs, and are the connecting roads between parcels of land and farms and ranches, local collectors, and state highways. In the Midwest and West these routes form the characteristic rectangular road grid that evolved from the township and range land survey. This survey established 640-acre land subdivisions and is the basis for section-line roads at one-mile intervals. Many of these roads have a loose aggregate surface, a narrow right-of-way, and carry fewer than fifty vehicles per day (Chicoine and Walzer 1984).

Responsibility for rural low-volume roads varies among states and relates to historical settlement patterns, early economic conditions, and government organizational preferences of initial settlers (Chicoine and Walzer 1985, chapter 2). The size of rural road networks within any state, of course, is determined by the area and resource endowment of the state. There are fewer miles of rural roads in each northeastern state than in each state in the Midwest, for example.

Organization of Rural Road Systems

All roads and highways outside municipal boundaries could be maintained and financed entirely by state government. Centralized state rural low-volume road authority and finance is one of the general configurations of rural low-volume road systems in the United States (Figure 4.2). Centralized road authority exists in Delaware, Alaska, Virginia, West Virginia, and North Carolina. (Two urban counties in Virginia have road and highway authority.)

In addition to state centralized responsibility in five states, seven states in the Northeast place rural low-volume road authority with town governments, a reflection of the dominance of the New England town in the local government structure in that region.

The third structure is overlapping road authority in county and town or township (in the Midwest) government. New York and New Jersey, in the Northeast, and most states in the Great Lakes region, the Corn Belt, and the Northern Plains have overlapping county and town/township road responsibilities (eleven states). Idaho has non-overlapping road responsibilities shared between county government and special function road districts. In the tiered, overlapping county-town/township systems, townships typically provide routes with lower service demands, and counties have responsibility for more heavily traveled connector roads.

Kansas, Nebraska, Missouri, and Illinois have some counties with overlapping road authority and other counties with road authority centralized in county government or a county-wide road district (Illinois). Three midwestern states (Indiana, Iowa, and Michigan) with centralized county rural low-volume road systems, removed rural road responsibility from township government in the past. For example, in 1884 legislation was adopted in Iowa authorizing consolidation of road functions at the county level and the levying of a property tax to finance a county road fund. There effectively are no township governments in Iowa today (Chicoine 1986).

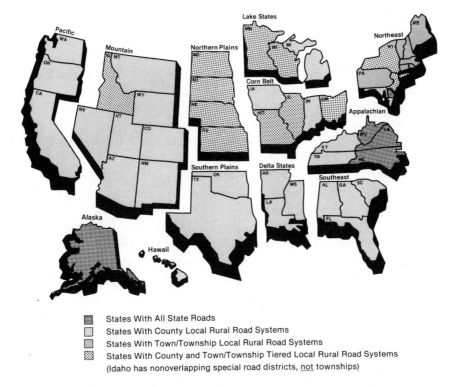

States With All State Roads
States With County Local Rural Road Systems
States With Town/Township Local Rural Road Systems
States With County and Town/Township Tiered Local Rural Road Systems
(Idaho has nonoverlapping special road districts, not townships)

Fig. 4.2. Jurisdiction authority for rural low-volume roads

The distribution of rural road mileage and other responsibilities varies significantly among states with overlapping systems. County responsibility for rural low-volume road mileage in the major county-township states ranges from 12 percent in North Dakota to 45 percent in New Jersey and Ohio (excluding the states with mixed systems). Other arrangements differ as well. In Ohio all bridges more than twenty feet in length are the responsibility of county government, even when they are located on township roads. In some states similar bridges are under township jurisdiction. In other states, townships have road responsibility but contract with county governments for most or all typical road maintenance and construction activities. Wisconsin is an example.

In the states with town systems and those with overlapping county-town/township systems, local road responsibilities are held by part-time citizen volunteer elected officials. In some cases the three or five member township board or commission administers the road program and manages or actually does all or most of the road work. In other states one person is elected to a town/township road supervisory office. In Illinois a township road district commissioner is elected every four years to administer and provide rural road services. A road master or overseer is elected in other states. In contrast, it is common for the principal road and highway administrator at the county level to be an appointed position held by a professional engineer. This is generally true for counties in overlapping county-town/township systems and for counties in county systems.

The fourth organization for rural low-volume roads is the county system. In two Appalachian states, the Delta states, the Southeast, the Southern Plains, the Mountain states, and the Pacific states, county government is responsible for all rural low-volume local roads and bridges. This pattern reflects the historically strong role of county government in southern states and the vastness of western regions which require a relatively more centralized local government organization (Chicoine and Walzer 1985, chapter 2).

Rural Road System Size by State

Table 4.1 describes rural low-volume local road systems by state and region. The first two columns show total miles of rural low-volume road and miles per 1,000 rural population. The population adjusted miles identify three general groupings of states. The first group includes most of the states in the Northeast and Appalachia. These states have the lowest road density—fewest miles of rural road per 1,000 rural people.

The second group is the Northern Plains states, Oklahoma, and the Mountain states with 100 or more miles of rural road per 1,000 rural people. The third group includes the states in the Corn Belt, the Lake states, and most southern states where miles of rural road per 1,000 rural people range between thirty and sixty. The many miles of rural low-volume road that need to be maintained at minimum safe travel standards, but directly serving a relatively small population, present financial and administrative challenges. Population and traffic counts may be poor indicators of agricultural and rural traffic demands in states with low road density.

The distribution of local rural road responsibilities by type of jurisdiction is also presented in Table 4.1. The regional patterns in road systems illustrated in Figure 4.1 are shown with added detail. The varia-

Table 4.1 Rural low-volume road responsibilities

| State by Region | Rural Road Mileage | | Distribution of Miles (percent) | | |
	Total	Per 1,000 Rural Population	State	County	Townships
Northeast					
Maine	10,981	8.3	0	0	100.0
New Hampshire	6,097	13.8	0	0	100.0
Vermont	9,662	28.5	0	0	100.0
Massachusetts	11,365	12.2	0	0	100.0
Rhode Island	1,427	11.6	0	0	100.0
Connecticut	6,703	10.2	0	0	100.0
New York	58,457	21.6	0	29.8	70.2
New Jersey	7,468	9.2	0	44.9	55.1
Pennsylvania	46,608	12.8	0[a]	0	100.0
Delaware	3,552	20.3	100.0	0	0
Maryland	11,173	13.5	0	100.0	0
Lake States					
Michigan	79,987	29.5	0	100.0	0
Wisconsin	79,248	47.0	0	24.6	75.4
Minnesota	99,216	73.5	0	44.0	56.0
Corn Belt					
Ohio	62,574	21.7	0	43.9	56.1
Indiana	64,233	32.7	0	100.0	0
Illinois	83,558	43.8	0	18.0	82.0
Iowa	88,890	73.8	0	100.0	0
Missouri	67,545	43.1	0	75.9	24.1
Northern Plains					
North Dakota	74,463	222.9	0	12.3	87.7
South Dakota	59,913	161.9	0	44.1	55.9
Nebraska	73,891	127.2	0	78.5	21.5
Kansas	111,190	141.3	0	70.7	29.3[b]
Appalachian					
Virginia[c]	49,422	27.2	100.0	0	0
West Virginia	30,107	24.2	100.0	0	0
North Carolina	69,559	22.7	100.0	0	0
Kentucky	36,838	20.5	0	100.0	0
Tennessee	33,324	18.3	0	100.0	0
Southeast					
South Carolina	18,915	13.2	0	100.0	0
Georgia	66,592	32.4	0	100.0	0
Florida	59,431	38.8	0	100.0	0
Alabama	57,884	37.2	0	100.0	0
Delta States					
Mississippi	54,755	41.3	0	100.0	0
Arkansas	49,243	44.5	0	100.0	0
Louisiana	28,235	21.4	0	100.0	0

Table 4.1 *continued*

State by Region	Rural Road Mileage		Distribution of Miles (percent)		
	Total	Per 1,000 Rural Population	State	County	Townships
Southern Plains					
Oklahoma	85,762	86.6	0	100.0	0
Texas	134,150	46.3	0	100.0	0
Mountain States					
Montana	53,595	144.8	0	100.0	0
Idaho	26,739	152.8	0	50.4	49.6d
Wyoming	13,684	78.2	0	100.0	0
Colorado	47,572	84.9	0	100.0	0
New Mexico	30,296	83.5	0	100.0	0
Arizona	24,724	56.3	0	100.0	0
Utah	19,939	87.5	0	100.0	0
Nevada	22,328	190.8	0	100.0	0
Pacific States					
Washington	38,167	34.8	0	100.0	0
Oregon	32,145	38.1	0	100.0	0
California	59,684	29.0	0	100.0	0
Alaska	9,980	68.8	100.0	0	0
Hawaii	1,672	12.9	0	100.0	0

aTwo urban counties in Pennsylvania have county road authority.
b695 of the 1367 Kansas townships have road authority. The remainder are in counties with county-unit road systems.
cTwo urban counties in Virginia have county road authority.
dIdaho has special road districts, now townships.
Source: Federal Highway Administration, *Highway Statistics—1985,* Washington, D.C.: U.S.DOT; 1982 Census of Government, *Governmental Organization,* GC82(1), Washington, D.C., U.S. Department of Commerce.

tion in road responsibilities in the states with county-town/township overlapping systems ranges from very decentralized in North Dakota, Illinois, Wisconsin, and New York, where towns or townships have jurisdiction over 70 percent of the rural road mileage, to Missouri and Nebraska, where townships are responsible for less than 25 percent of the miles of rural low-volume local roads in each state.

The number of rural road jurisdictions and average miles maintained per local government with road authority offer very distinct contrasts across states and regions. The average number of road miles per town/township, presented in Table 4.2, ranges from 17 miles per township in Pennsylvania to 50 miles per township in Missouri, and close to an average of 50 miles in Illinois, Wisconsin, North Dakota, and Kansas. For

Table 4.2 Number and average size of rural road jurisdictions by state

State by Region	Jurisdiction			
	County		Towns/Townships	
	Number	Average Miles	Number	Average Miles
Northeast				
Maine	0	0	475	23.1
New Hampshire	0	0	221	27.6
Vermont	0	0	237	40.8
Massachusetts	0	0	312	36.4
Rhode Island	0	0	31	46.0
Connecticut	0	0	149	45.0
New York	57	305.1	928	44.2
New Jersey	21	159.7	245	16.8
Pennsylvania	0*	0	1549	30.0
Delaware	state maintained			
Maryland	23	485.8	0	0
Lake States				
Michigan	83	963.7	0	0
Wisconsin	72	270.4	1269	47.1
Minnesota	87	502.0	1795	30.9
Corn Belt				
Ohio	88	312.1	1318	26.6
Indiana	91	671.0	0	0
Illinois	102	147.2	1434	47.8
Iowa	99	897.9	0	0
Missouri	114	449.6	325	50.1
Northern Plains				
North Dakota	53	172.7	1360	48.0
South Dakota	64	412.5	996	33.6
Nebraska	93	624.1	470	33.7
Kansas	105	748.8	695*	46.8
Appalachian				
Virginia*	state maintained			
West Virginia	state maintained			
North Carolina	state maintained			
Kentucky	119	309.6	0	0
Tennessee	94	354.5	0	0
Southeast				
South Carolina	46	400.2	0	0
Georgia	158	421.5	0	0
Florida	66	900.5	0	0
Alabama	67	893.9	0	0
Delta States				
Mississippi	82	636.4	0	0
Arkansas	75	656.6	0	0
Louisiana	62	455.4	0	0

Table 4.2 *continued*

State by Region	Jurisdiction			
	County		Towns/Townships	
	Number	Average Miles	Number	Average Miles
Southern Plains				
Oklahoma	77	1113.8	0	0
Texas	254	528.1	0	0
Mountain States				
Montana	54	972.4	0	0
Idaho	44	306.5	65*	204
Wyoming	91	150.4	0	0
Colorado	62	767.3	0	0
New Mexico	33	918.0	0	0
Arizona	14	1766.0	0	0
Utah	29	687.5	0	0
Nevada	16	1395.5	0	0
Pacific States				
Washington	39	926.4	0	0
Oregon	36	842.9	0	0
California	59	1011.6	0	0
Alaska		state maintained		
Hawaii	3	557.3	0	0

*Two urban counties in Pennsylvania and two urban counties in Virginia have county road authority. Of the 1,367 Kansas townships, 695 have road authority. The remainder are in counties with county-unit road systems. Idaho has special road districts, not townships.
Source: Federal Highway Administration, *Highway Statistics—1985*, Washington, D.C.: U.S.DOT; 1982 Census of Government, *Governmental Organization*, GC82(1), Washington, D.C., U.S. Department of Commerce.

counties in states with overlapping rural road systems, the average system ranges from 147 miles per county in Illinois to 624 miles per county in Nebraska. The range for states with county local rural road systems is from 150 miles per Wyoming county to 1,766 miles per Arizona county. Extensive federal land holdings in Wyoming likely account for the small average size. Of course, the averages mask variations within states.

The number of rural governments with road authority is large. A total of 14,349 towns and townships maintain rural roads and 2,732 counties have road authority. Thus, a total of 17,081 local governments provide rural low-volume roads. The average town/township is responsible for 38 miles of low-volume road. In the county-town/township states, the average county rural road network is 333 miles. In county states the average size is 728 miles per county.

Rural Low-Volume Road Finance

Organizational diversity in rural low-volume road authority and responsibility is paired with diversity in finance. Generally, support for rural road budgets comes from three major sources (Fig. 4.3). The most important, nationally, are shared motor fuel tax receipts and license fees from state government (33.7 percent), property tax revenues (21.1 percent), and appropriations from the general fund of towns/townships and counties (19 percent).

Two factors should be noted about the aggregate distribution of road receipts. The first is that property tax dependence of rural low-volume local roads is understated. General funds appropriated by counties and towns/townships for roads and bridges are often property tax revenues. Local sales taxes are another source of local government general funds in some states.

A second caveat is the failure of aggregate data to reflect the importance of federal general revenue sharing (GRS) in financing rural road budgets in some states and for some jurisdictions, particularly townships. Evidence is that prior to the abolition of GRS, an average of 13 percent of the road expenditures by midwest townships was financed by GRS, for example. In some states this percentage exceeded 20 (Walzer, Chicoine, and McWilliams 1987).

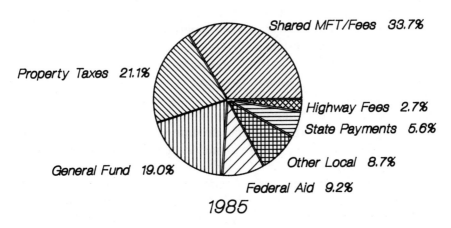

Fig. 4.3. County and township road receipts. (FHWA, Highway Statistics 1985, Washington, D.C.)

In the aggregate, rural road systems maintained by the more than 17,000 rural townships and counties are dependent, first, on local general taxation (48.8 percent), a large percentage being property taxes. Second is shared highway user taxes and fees from state government and other state grants-in-aid (39.3 percent). Third is direct federal aid (9.2 percent). Fourth is local highway and road user taxes and fees (2.7 percent) (FHWA 1986).

The heavy dependence on local revenues, in general, and property taxes, in particular, demonstrates the potential vulnerability of local rural road budgets to fiscal stress created by the poor financial conditions in farming, the general restructuring underway in rural economies in many regions of the United States, and the property tax relief policies adopted in many states. The extent and timing of the stress depends on the importance of agriculture in the property tax base, reassessment policies of state and local government, and the operating characteristics of the property tax. For example, policy requiring reassessments on a six-year cycle may not capture the poorly performing farm economy in the tax base for several years. This insulates rural governments in the immediate future and delays the fiscal impact until the next reassessment. Alternatively, property taxes operated without levy or rate limitations present only a political barrier to the rate increases necessary to compensate for a weakened or falling tax base (Chicoine 1987).

These complexities prevent strong general conclusions about the degree of fiscal stress that the local rural road system is or will be experiencing because of troubles on America's farms. In some states economic conditions and financing systems combine and seriously impact rural road budgets. In other states the structure of the financing system insulates road budgets from much of the economic adversity in agriculture. For example, the property tax dependence of Illinois township road districts combined with annual farmland reassessment policies and a system of legislated road tax rate limits present formidable budget challenges to rural low-volume local road budgets (Chicoine and Jacobs 1987).

On the other hand, limited use of property tax financing by Ohio townships and no rate or levy limits for Wisconsin townships limit the direct implications of a poorly performing farm economy for township rural road fiscal health in these two states. These differences in three midwestern states with similarly organized rural low-volume road systems demonstrate the diversity of conditions and the range of implications the weakened farm economy has for the rural transportation system.

Property Tax and Shared Motor Fuel Tax Dependence

Table 4.3 provides some insight into the potential implications of a changing property tax base for rural low-volume local road finance. Road budget support in the Northeast reflects the general heavy reliance on the property tax in financing local government in that region. Most general fund appropriations in these states are property tax financed. The exceptions are Maryland and Delaware.

There really is no pattern among states in the Lakes region, the Corn Belt, and the Northern Plains in rural low-volume local road finance. More than 50 percent of county and township road receipts are shared motor fuel taxes (MFT), license fees, and other state aid in Michigan, Ohio, Indiana, Illinois, Iowa, and North Dakota. In the other six states in heartland regions, local revenues are the single largest source of support. Similarly, dependence on MFT increased between 1977 and 1984 in about half the states and decreased in the other half in these regions.

Rural road finance in the heartland states ranges from centralized state support to almost financial independence. Jurisdictions in states with more centralized financing have less of the total costs of roads born locally and more paid by state taxpayers. On the other hand, road jurisdictions with little or no financial autonomy or local revenue raising authority are restricted in their ability to respond to service demands and have limited independence. Financially dependent road jurisdictions are more accurately viewed as agents of state government than as independent local governments.

The pattern of rural road receipts in the southern regions and the western regions also show very mixed financial arrangements. In the south, for example, more than 60 percent of local road revenues in Tennessee and Alabama are shared MFT receipts. Yet, in Georgia, Arkansas, and Louisiana local sources of funding are most important. Similar variations exist in the southwest, Mountain, and Pacific states. Some states have more centralized financing systems with shared fuel taxes being central, while other states combine revenues from property taxes, other local sources, and shared state monies. However, in all states, shared receipts from highway user taxes and fees are an important component of rural low-volume local road finance.

Table 4.3 Local rural road finance by state (percent)

	Revenue Source Distribution					Motor Fuel Tax Dependence	
	Local[a]		Intergovernmental				
			State		Federal		
State by Region	PT	GA	MFT	Other		1977	1984
Northeast							
Maine	0	53.8	29.3	2.1	14.8	12.7	29.3
New Hampshire	0	78.9	.4	2.2	18.4	33.6	.4
Vermont	53.2	4.5	33.3	0	9.1	23.0	33.3
Massachusetts	0	55.5	22.9	8.6	13.0	95.0	22.9
Rhode Island	0	40.6	5.4	0	54.0	9.4	5.4
Connecticut	0	53.6	29.6	0	16.8	44.8	29.6
New York	18.2	53.6	15.7	8.3	4.1	15.7	15.7
New Jersey[a]	0	92.9	0	.9	6.1	2.6	0
Pennsylvania	13.1	32.1	38.4	0	16.5	24.7	38.4
Delaware	NA						
Maryland	2.6	2.6	64.3	19.4	11.1	46.9	64.3
Lake States							
Michigan	2.1	19.8	54.2	11.5	12.4	84.4	54.2
Wisconsin	32.0	43.5	20.5	0	3.9	26.2	20.5
Minnesota	32.3	11.4	34.5	13.2	8.5	33.7	34.5
Corn Belt							
Ohio	2.4	2.9	91.1	.4	3.2	81.8	91.1
Indiana	14.1	4.9	71.2	5.6	4.2	72.7	71.2
Illinois	40.4	0	47.4	8.5	3.8	43.8	47.4
Iowa	23.7	3.8	46.8	14.8	10.9	41.2	46.8
Missouri	64.3	0	18.0	8.6	26.6	26.9	18.0
Northern Plains							
North Dakota	13.5	11.3	43.7	13.6	17.9	30.1	43.7
South Dakota	51.7	1.2	27.9	10.3	9.0	30.0	27.9
Nebraska	37.5	3.4	26.6	8.1	24.4	37.5	26.6
Kansas	70.0	0	23.2	2.0	25.2	17.1	23.2
Appalachian							
Virginia	NA						
West Virginia	NA						
North Carolina	NA						
Kentucky	3.0	25.6	51.8	10.9	8.7	22.6	51.8
Tennessee	30.3	.8	62.2	4.0	2.8	65.4	62.2
Southeast							
South Carolina	0	41.2	40.7	0	18.1	71.8	40.7
Georgia	0	84.2	5.1	.3	10.4	6.8	5.1
Florida	23.8	22.7	35.0	12.6	5.8	47.0	35.0
Alabama	19.1	3.8	67.0	.6	9.5	76.0	67.0
Delta States							
Mississippi	23.7	2.7	32.3	8.1	40.5	38.2	32.3
Arkansas	10.0	35.6	19.9	11.3	23.2	50.0	19.9
Louisiana	17.8	27.6	28.4	13.6	12.4	17.5	28.4

Table 4.3 *continued*

State by Region	Local[a]		Intergovernmental State	Other	Federal	Motor Fuel Tax Dependence 1977	1984
	PT	GA	MFT	Other		1977	1984
Southern Plains							
Oklahoma	Missing						
Texas	75.7	3.0	16.8	0	4.5	19.6	16.8
Mountain States							
Montana	61.1	1.9	28.6	0	8.4	26.5	28.6
Idaho	31.7	9.4	44.0	5.6	9.2	46.2	44.0
Wyoming	0	9.1	33.6	4.8	52.4	48.6	33.6
Colorado	37.8	6.1	34.3	12.4	9.4	49.6	34.3
New Mexico	.8	24.6	48.8	0	25.7	58.8	48.8
Arizona	6.3	4.3	73.5	7.7	8.2	53.8	73.5
Utah	0	63.9	35.5	0	.6	35.6	35.5
Nevada	26.2	50.3	16.2	0	7.3	49.2	16.2
Pacific States							
Washington	44.3	2.4	33.7	2.9	16.7	42.8	33.7
Oregon	1.1	.3	44.2	.5	53.8	29.7	44.2
California	5.7	19.5	54.3	2.0	18.5	75.1	54.3
Alaska	NA						
Hawaii	2.3	3.6	74.2	.4	19.5	59.9	74.2

[a]Data estimated by FHWA. MFT distribution information indicates New Jersey counties and townships receive a share of state collected taxes. These receipts may be included in the General Fund Appropriation (GA).
Source: Federal Highway Administration, *Highway Statistics—1985,* Washington, D.C.: U.S.DOT.

Motor Fuel Tax Rates and Rate Changes

Table 4.4 presents information on motor fuel tax rates by state, rate changes between 1977 and 1986, and the last year in which rates were changed. The financial health of state MFT funds is a major determinant of the level of state aid supporting county and town/township rural road spending. Frequently, these jurisdictions receive a fixed percentage of MFT receipts shared among eligible units based on a formula. For example, Minnesota counties get 29 percent of the MFT receipts, Arkansas counties get 15 percent, and Illinois township road districts receive 15.89 percent (FHWA 1986). Higher fuel tax rates and more receipts lead directly to increased state funding for county or town/township roads and highways.

On 1 January 1987, the average state gasoline tax was 13.3 cents per gallon, in addition to the federal rate of 9.0 cents per gallon. In 1986

Table 4.4 Motor fuel tax rates by state

State by Region	Percent Tax Rate Change 1977–86	Last Year of Rate Increase	Tax Rate January 1987 (¢/gallon)
Northeast			
Maine	55.6	83	14.0
New Hampshire	40.0	81	14.0
Vermont	44.4	83	13.0
Massachusetts	29.4	83	11.0*
Rhode Island	30.0	83	15.0*
Connecticut	54.5	85	17.0
New York	0.0	72	8.0
New Jersey*	0.0	72	8.0
Pennsylvania	33.3	83	12.0
Delaware	18.2	81	13.0
Maryland	50.0	83	13.5*
Lake States			
Michigan	66.7	84	15.0*
Wisconsin	150.0	85	17.5*
Minnesota	88.9	84	17.0
Corn Belt			
Ohio	71.4	83	12.0
Indiana	75.0	85	14.0
Illinois	73.3	85	13.0
Iowa	128.6	85	16.0
Missouri	0.0	87	7.0
Northern Plains			
North Dakota	62.5	83	13.0
South Dakota	62.5	81	13.0
Nebraska	91.6	85	18.2*
Kansas	37.5	84	11.0*
Appalachian			
Virginia	94.4	80	17.5
West Virginia	23.5	78	15.35*
North Carolina	72.2	81	15.5*
Kentucky	66.6	86	15.0*
Tennessee	142.9	85	17.0
Southeast			
South Carolina	44.4	81	13.0
Georgia	0.0	71	7.5
Florida	5.6	73	9.7*
Alabama	57.1	84	13.0
Delta States			
Mississippi	0.0	73	9.0
Arkansas	58.8	85	13.5
Louisiana	100.0	84	16.0
Southern Plains			
Oklahoma	53.8	85	10.0
Texas	200.0	84	15.0

Table 4.4   *continued*

State by Region	Percent Tax Rate Change 1977–86	Last Year of Rate Increase	Tax Rate January 1987 (¢/gallon)
Mountain States			
Montana	112.5	83	17.0
Idaho	52.6	83	14.5
Wyoming	0.0	76	8.0
Colorado	157.1	83	18.0
New Mexico	57.1	83	11.0
Arizona	100.0	84	16.0
Utah	100.0	84	14.0
Nevada	116.6	85	13.0
Pacific States			
Washington	63.6	84	18.0
Oregon	71.4	85	12.0
California	28.6	83	9.0
Alaska	0.0	61	8.0
Hawaii	29.4	85	11.0

*1977 national average was 7.8¢; 1986 national average is 13¢. Florida dropped their rate from 9.7¢ to 4.0¢ in 1986. PT = property taxes; GA = general fund appropriations; MFT = State Motor Fuel Tax shared receipts. After 1 January 1987 the MFT in Missouri was increased to 11¢. Tax on diesel fuel is higher in 7 states and lower in 7 states than the gasoline tax, and the tax on gasohol is lower in 17 states (no tax in New Jersey, New Mexico, and Alaska). Variable tax expressed in cents per gallon. Florida has a 4¢/gal. tax plus 5% levy on the retail average price with a 5.7¢/gal. floor on the variable levy adding to 9.7¢/gal.
Source: Federal Highway Administration, *Highway Statistics—1985,* Washington, D.C.: U.S.DOT.

eight states increased motor fuel taxes. These increases come on top of increases in thirty-four states in 1981, eighteen states in 1982, twenty-seven states in 1983, and fifteen states in 1984 (HUF 1987).

A limitation of the per gallon MFT is that receipts depend on fuel usage. Higher gasoline prices and more fuel efficient cars and trucks decreased motor fuel use in the early 1980s triggering frequent rate increases to protect the fiscal health of state road funds. Some states also responded and adopted a variable motor fuel tax, sometimes in combination with the per gallon levy. The receipts from variable levies weakened during the downturn in fuel prices in the middle 1980s, again stressing state road and highway funds and causing additional rounds of rate increases (HUF 1987).

The importance of the history of state MFT rate increases for rural low-volume road finance is that frequent and large rate increases during the 1980s in many states may prevent additional rate increases to target funds for improvements in rural low-volume road systems. This may limit increases in state revenues to finance general upgrading and targeted programs such as bridge rehabilitation and replacement programs. Local road budgets stressed because of poorly performing farm property tax bases may not be relieved with additional state road monies from future rate increases. Reallocation of current state MFT receipts with more funds to jurisdictions with weakened local fiscal capacity is an alternative to rate increases. Reallocations, however, will be resisted by jurisdictions that stand to lose state aid.

Motor Fuel Tax Distribution Formulas

Characteristics of state motor fuel tax distribution formulas for counties, cities, and towns/townships are presented in Table 4.5. The general factors identified to distribute MFT receipts to local governments are needs, miles of road, equality among eligible units, population, and several other determinants, including assessed valuation, area, vehicle miles traveled, and value of farm products sold. Most state distribution formulas use more than one factor to determine the road grant-in-aid to local governments. There are a few exceptions, however, including county road aid in New York, Illinois, and Hawaii, and township road aid in Illinois and Ohio.

Of the specific factors listed, the most popular is road mileage. In twenty-one states the miles of roads maintained or the percentage of all county roads in a county are used in determining MFT distributions. Twelve states use roads under township jurisdiction to allocate MFT receipts among towns/townships. Population is included in the distribution formula for counties in nineteen states and for towns/townships in seven states. In some states total county population is used; in others just the population outside incorporated places is considered. Population is the most frequent factor used by states in distributing MFT receipts among incorporated communities. Vehicle registrations rank second, followed by equal distribution among eligible cities.

Among other factors used by states, county area is used most frequently. States using county area in allocating MFT receipts include Arkansas, Florida, Tennessee, Kentucky, and South Carolina in the South, Oklahoma, Montana, and Wyoming in the West, and Iowa in the Corn Belt. Area and miles of road both measure need that is not reflected in vehicle travel and favor more sparsely populated jurisdictions with low road density and lightly traveled roads.

There are several unique features operating in a number of states. For

Table 4.5 State motor fuel tax distribution formulas

State by Region	Counties						Cities						Townships					
	Needs	Mileage	Equal	Veh. Reg.	Pop.	Other[a]	Needs	Mileage	Equal	Veh. Reg.	Pop.	Other[a]	Needs	Mileage	Equal	Veh. Reg.	Pop.	Other[a]
Northeast																		
Maine	NCR							Y			Y	Y		Y			Y	Y
New Hampshire	NCR							Y			Y	Y		Y			Y	Y
Vermont	NCR											Y						Y
Massachusetts	NCR							Y		Y	Y	Y		Y		Y	Y	
Rhode Island	NCR							Y			Y	Y		Y			Y	
Connecticut	NCR							Y			Y			Y			Y	
New York		Y				Y						Y						Y
New Jersey	NCR			Y								Y						Y
Pennsylvania	NCR							Y			Y			Y			Y	
Delaware	NCR							Y			Y		NT					
Maryland		Y	Y	Y					Y	Y		Y	NT					
Lake States																		
Michigan		Y	Y	Y	Y			Y			Y		NTR					
Wisconsin		Y	Y		Y			Y						Y				Y
Minnesota	Y	Y	Y	Y		Y	Y			Y	Y	Y		Y				
Corn Belt																		
Ohio	Y	Y	Y	Y		Y				Y	Y			Y				
Indiana			Y	Y		Y					Y		NTR					
Illinois	Y			Y							Y			Y				
Iowa	Y					Y					Y		NT					
Missouri		Y				Y					Y		none reported					

Table 4.5 continued

State by Region	Counties Needs	Counties Mileage	Counties Equal	Counties Veh. Reg.	Counties Pop.	Counties Other[a]	Cities Needs	Cities Mileage	Cities Equal	Cities Veh. Reg.	Cities Pop.	Cities Other[a]	Townships Needs	Townships Mileage	Townships Equal	Townships Veh. Reg.	Townships Pop.	Townships Other[a]
Northern Plains																		
North Dakota		Y		Y	Y	Y					Y			Y				
South Dakota		Y		Y	Y	Y					Y			Y		Y	Y	
Nebraska				Y	Y			Y		Y	Y		none reported					
Kansas			Y	Y		Y		Y		Y	Y		cntys share w/ twps					
Appalachian																		
Virginia	NCR						none reported	Y			Y		NT					
West Virginia	NCR										Y		NT					
North Carolina	NCR							Y			Y		NT					
Kentucky		Y	Y		Y	Y					Y		NT					
Tennessee		Y	Y		Y	Y					Y		NT					
Southeast																		
South Carolina		Y		Y	Y	Y								NT				
Georgia		Y		Y	Y	Y						Y		NT				
Florida				Y	Y	Y				Y	Y			NT				
Alabama			Y	Y	Y					Y	Y			NT				
Delta States																		
Mississippi				Y	Y	Y	none reported			Y	Y							
Arkansas			Y	Y	Y	Y					Y			NT				
Louisiana				Y	Y	Y								NT				

Southern Plains								
Oklahoma	Y		Y	Y		Y		NT
Texas		Y	Y	Y				NT
Mountain States								
Montana	Y		Y	Y	Y	Y		NT
Idaho	Y	Y	Y			Y		Yᵇ
Wyoming	Y		Y	Y		Y	Y	NT
Colorado	Y		Y	Y	Y			NT
New Mexico	Y	Y	Y		Y			NT
Arizona		Y		Yᶜ				NT
Utah	Y		Y	Y	Y	Y	Y	NT
Nevada	Y		Y	Y		Y	Y	NT
Pacific States								
Washington	Y		Y	Y	Y	Y		NT
Oregon		Y				Y		NT
California	Y	Y	Y		Y Y Y	Y		NT
Alaska				Y	NCR			NT
Hawaii				Y				NT

[a] Other includes relative sales, area, revenue raising ability, amount specified by law, past spending, vehicle miles traveled, block grants, miles of rural mail routes, property taxes, assessed value, value of farm products sold, and previous aid.

[b] Idaho has special districts with road authority, not townships. Counties may share MFT receipts with road districts.

NCR = no county roads; NT = no town/township government; NTR = no township roads.

[c] Arizona counties receive 20 percent of MFT receipts distributed to each county by the ratio of total sales of fuel within the county to total statewide sales.

Source: Federal Highway Administration, Highway Taxes and Fees: How They are Collected and Distributed, Washington, D.C.: U.S.DOT (March 1986).

example, the value of farm products sold in a county is considered in Nebraska. Michigan reimburses counties for snow-plowing expenses and for the salary of the county professional highway engineer. Arizona, Florida, and Louisiana distribute MFT receipts, in part, on point of purchase. In some states the distribution is a tiered process with initial distributions to county areas, and these funds are then allocated between all local road jurisdictions in the county. For example, in North Dakota the county area allotment is determined by vehicle registrations. Of this total, 73 percent is paid to county governments and 27 percent to municipal governments in the county distributed by city population.

In Nevada, county area MFT funds are distributed between county governments and municipalities based on relative property tax bases inside and outside corporate boundaries. The one-cent MFT collected for the township road fund in North Dakota is not refundable for off-road vehicle use and is distributed among townships based on population and road miles. In Kansas, no less than 25 percent of shared MFT funds are statutorily required to be spent on rural mail and school bus routes.

Diversity in Rural Road Finance

Higher state motor fuel tax rates will affect rural road jurisdictions in the various states differently. There is little evidence of any pattern of rural low-volume road finance among states and across regions nor is there evidence that MFT distribution formulas in neighboring states provide the same level of state subsidy to local low-volume road systems. The variations in approaches indicate that a policy effectively addressing needs in one state may be of little consequence in another.

A finance system in which state aid is combined with local resources provides incentives for local road officials, farmers, and other rural low-volume road users to favor more centralized financing methods. For example, by raising state highway user taxes and fees and/or increasing the receipts shared with local governments, the cost of needed rehabilitation, new investments, and higher maintenance outlays paid locally is minimized (Chicoine and Walzer 1984; Walzer and Chicoine 1987).

Factors used to distribute MFT receipts to rural road jurisdictions favoring rural areas include area, miles of road, and equal distribution among units. Rural road authorities fare poorly when receipts are allocated by population, vehicle registrations, and point of fuel sale. There may be little relationship between these latter attributes and the size of the rural road network that local road officials are trying to maintain at minimum safe travel standards. Most states include several factors. The weighing of factors in formula calculations is critical for rural low-volume local road finance.

Implications of Rural Road System Organizational Differences

The implications of variation in governmental organization on the provision of rural low-volume local road services are examined using a public employment model of rural road services estimated with state level data (Bahl, Burkhead, and Jump 1980; Bahl, Gustely, and Wasylenko 1978; Ehrenberg 1973). Positive effects of alternative governmental structures and financial arrangements on local public sector budget outcomes and expenditure behavior have been investigated most often by adapting reduced form expenditure models to take into account governance and finance organizational differences (Dilorenzo 1983; Martin 1980; Mehay 1984; Wagner and Weber 1975). A few studies reported comparative analysis of local government consolidation efforts following voter approval of reorganization plans (Gustley 1977; Cook 1973).

Most empirical investigations, however, have focused on verifying conceptual propositions on the merits of centralized/consolidated versus decentralized/fragmented governmental arrangements. Responsiveness (consumer efficiency), administrative efficiencies, and scale economies have been central issues. Generally, areas served by integrated, centralized governance systems have been observed to have higher expenditures, other factors being equal. The normative conclusion drawn from this evidence is that centralized local governmental arrangements increase spending because of bureaucratic inefficiencies. These inefficiencies overshadow any economies of scope and scale that may be realized with more centralized governmental arrangements and a more efficient provision of services.

The limited evidence on scale economies in local rural road provision suggests larger jurisdictions may have lower per unit costs (Fox 1980). In the Midwest, the least cost size rural road system under township jurisdiction has been shown to be about eighty miles, or about twice the size of the typical town/township road system in the United States and the Midwest (thirty-eight and forty miles) (Chicoine, Walzer, and Deller 1987).

The rationale for using public employment, or in this case rural road employment, as an objective measure of rural low-volume local roads is that road services can be represented by the number of persons employed. This then reflects collective preferences for rural road activities (Bahl, Burkhead, and Jump 1980, chapter 4).

Local rural road employment is specified as a function of the cost of a road employee, income and intergovernmental aid, and organization of the rural road system. Specifically, the model can be represented, following Ehrenberg (1973), as:

$$RE_j = f(WAGE_j, INC_j, AID_j, ORG_j) \qquad (1)$$

where RE is the rural road employment per thousand miles of local low-volume road in state j, WAGE is the average cost of a rural road employee measured as the ratio of total road payroll of road jurisdictions to the number of hours worked by full-time equivalent employees in state j (data are for the month of October), INC is per capita income in the jth state, and ORG_j is a measure of the governmental organization of the rural low-volume local road system in state j.

Rural road employment is expected to be negatively related to the cost of employees and positively related to the level of intergovernmental aid, other factors being equal. More road aid suggests a lower cost of road services to local taxpayers and more of the cost paid by state taxpayers. If more fragmented and smaller rural road systems, such as those in town systems and overlapping county-town/township systems, are relatively more responsive to individual demands for services, then higher rural road employment, as a measure of rural road services, may be associated with measures of the organization of rural road governance. However, this result is not unambiguously distinguishable from a supply-cost explanation for a positive relationship between rural road employment and governmental structure. The claim could be made that small, fragmented overlapping systems are inefficient and duplicative, resulting in higher employment and increasing service costs.

The two measures of rural road governmental structure used are rural road units per 1,000 miles of rural low-volume road in a state (ORG_1) and county road employment as a percent of total county and town/township road employment in the state (ORG_2). Employment is the number of full-time equivalent highway employees reported by county and town/township government in the 1982 Census of Government. The determinants of rural road employment per thousand miles of road

Table 4.6 Estimates of rural road employment model

Variable	OLS		Box-Cox	
	Model A	Model B	Model A	Model B
Average hourly wage (WAGE)	−24.801 (1.83)**	−28.321 (1.84)**	−1.256 (2.46)*	−0.945 (2.47)*
Per capita income (INC)	.048 (3.93)*	.044 (2.94)*	4.616 (3.13)*	5.28 (3.17)*
State and federal aid/1000 miles (AID)	9.808 (1.85)**	26.310 (5.95)*	0.448 (6.04)*	0.392 (7.47)*
Gov't structure units/1000 miles (ORG$_1$)	2.738 (4.01)*	—	.095 (1.56)**	—
percent county road employ (ORG$_2$)	—	−1.202 (1.99)**	—	−.176 (3.88)*
Constant	−337.73	−171.75	−24.87	−22.36
R^{-2}	.66	.56	.57	.67
F	21.63	14.73	15.33	22.72
N	45	45	45	45
λ		−.08	−.14	
λ confidence internal		(.38,−.35)	(.30,−.60)	

Note: Absolute value of *t* statistics are in parenthesis; dependent variable is rural road jobs per 1,000 miles of rural road.
*significant at the .05 level
**significant at the .10 level

estimated across states are presented in Table 4.6. Only states with local rural road systems are included in the analysis.

The model was estimated in linear form with ordinary least squares (OLS) and using a Box-Cox transformation testing for functional form. The Box-Cox flexible non-linear specification allows the data to determine the appropriate functional form. Model A includes governmental units per thousand miles of road (ORG$_1$) as the measure of rural road organization, and Model B includes percentage of county road employment (ORG$_2$) as the measure of governmental structure. The maximum likelihood estimates of the Box-Cox transformation indicate the relationship estimated is nonlinear. Because of the transformation of the data, an exact interpretation of the coefficients from the Box-Cox estimates is difficult. Since the estimates of the Box-Cox transformations are consistent with the linear OLS estimates (and can be interpreted as elasticities), the discussion focuses on the OLS estimates.

In general, the model performed reasonably well. The average wage rate was inversely related to the level of road employment. On average, states where wages were one dollar per hour higher than average are associated with road employment of twenty-four to twenty-eight employees per 1,000 miles less than average. The average wage was $7.73 per hour. States with above average per capita income have above average rural road employment. This is as expected, reflecting the higher demand for road services associated with higher incomes. More road aid from the federal and state government is associated with higher levels of road employment. This suggests that there is relatively higher rural road employment in states with more centralized financing as reflected in aid per 1,000 miles of rural roads.

The coefficient on the number of rural road governmental units per 1,000 miles (ORG_1) suggests that, on average, states where the number of governments per 1,000 miles are above average by one unit are associated with road employment about three FTEs per 1,000 miles of road above average. Also, the coefficient on percent county road employment (ORG_2) suggests, on average, states with percent of county road employment one percent above average are associated with an average of 1.2 rural road employees per 1,000 miles below average.

The results of the governmental structure measures are consistent and indicate that in states with more units of rural road jurisdictions (a fragmented, decentralized organization) road employment is higher per 1,000 miles of road, and in states where the percent of road workers employed by county governments is higher (the more centralized the rural road system) there are fewer road employees per 1,000 miles of rural road. One conclusion from this preliminary cross state analysis is that efficiencies (fewer employees per thousand miles) may be gained with the reorganization of local rural road systems into more centralized systems. One weakness of this analysis is the failure to account for differences in local fiscal capacity. The diversity in financing methods makes overcoming this limitation complicated.

One difficulty in analyzing the performance of the local public sector is accounting for differences in service quality and quantity (Chicoine and Walzer 1985). This shortcoming must be recognized in interpreting the results of the cross state rural road employment model. Service differences may account, in part, for the results. However, generally, a more centralized rural road governmental organization is associated with larger road jurisdictions. Thus the findings of the cross state analysis of rural road employment are consistent with intrastate investigations of efficiencies in rural low-volume road services (Fox 1980; Chicoine, Walzer, and Deller 1987). These results suggest policies encouraging jurisdictional consolidation or cooperation to capture available economies warrant consideration in states with small road units and decentralized rural low-volume road authority. In addition to reorganization, these policies should encourage innovative and creative delivery systems such as contracting-out, joint purchasing programs, the sharing of specialized personnel and equipment, cooperative approaches to improved management, and so forth. There is opportunity for horizontal cooperation between neighboring like jurisdictions and vertical cooperation between county (or the state) governments and subcounty towns/townships in overlapping systems.

The investigation of the implications of governmental organization for local rural road services suggests additional, more detailed analysis of the differences in the organization of rural road systems and their financing is needed to provide a better foundation for evaluating rural road services and the costs of rehabilitation and new investments. These investigations should pay particular attention to variations in the organization and financing of systems and the implications of these variations for rural low-volume local road services and the estimated costs of upgrading.

Summary and Policy Implications

The descriptions and analyses in this chapter demonstrated the organizational and financing differences characterizing the rural low-volume local road system in the United States. While the many miles of local roads provide all or part of the same bundle of services to farmers, ranchers, and other residents of rural America, the governance structure through which service preferences are expressed and roads are provided and the revenue systems used to finance services vary from state to state. Organizationally, rural low-volume roads are provided under four general structures—centralized state systems, county government systems, overlapping county-town/township systems, and decentralized town systems. The administration of rural road systems varies from professional appointed engineers to elected citizen part-time road officials. Average mileage per responsible jurisdiction ranges from under forty to more than 1,000.

Rural road systems are financed through a combination of local revenues, which are mostly property taxes in many states, and state-shared motor fuel taxes. The dependence on shared state-highway user taxes and fees varies from state to state, but the financing of rural low-volume local roads is a state/local partnership in all states with a local system. The implications of the poorly performing farm economy for rural road finance vary from state to state depending on the importance of the farm economy and the farm property tax base, the use of property taxation in rural road finance, reassessment policies, and the operating characteristics of the property tax. More fiscal stress is likely to be experienced in the heartland states, where property tax financing is common and the farm economy is facing significant restructuring.

Mileage and area are factors used in state shared motor fuel tax formulas that benefit rural jurisdictions. Indicators of road demand such as population, fuel sales, and motor vehicle registrations may not reflect agricultural and rural traffic road demand and the need for state road aid. State motor fuel tax increases during the past five years may limit opportunities for significantly higher state shared revenues to finance general improvements on rural road systems and for targeted assistance programs such as bridge rehabilitation and replacement.

Alternative revenue sources, such as local option user taxes or fees, including wheel taxes or registration fees, or the use of general tax sources, like the sales tax, may provide local governments needed revenue flexibility. A limitation of these revenue options in very rural and agriculturally dependent road jurisdictions is that they typically have very thin bases. Sparce populations, few vehicles, and limited retail sales, for example, severely limit the revenue that can be raised at reasonable rates. The elimination of all or part of off-road fuel tax refunds, while not popular with the farm sector, may need to be reviewed in some states if these revenues could be targeted to upgrading the local rural road system.

There is need to evaluate the governance and administrative organization for providing rural road services in many states. Preliminary evidence suggests that less fragmented organizations or more interjurisdictional cooperation should be considered. Alternate approaches to reorganization vary from jurisdictional consolidation, such as took place in Iowa at the turn of the century, to contracting for services, to vertical and horizontal cooperation in road projects, equipment and professional service acquisition and input purchases, to road closures and managed service reductions under "primitive" road programs.

It is evident that a significant increase in spending above current levels is required to improve rural low-volume local road services and reach standards implicit in many transportation infrastructure studies. Financing this level of spending within the current state/local government partnership approach will require nonmarginal revenue additions or substantial reallocations of currently available highway and road funds, which may not be realistic in most states. The prudent (and realistic) approach will likely be balanced incrementalism combining some revenue-enhancing policies, both state and local, with improved performance through reorganization and improved administration where warranted. Moving toward a safe, adequate, and affordable rural low-volume local road system will require as much variation in approach as there is variation in organization and finance in the rural road system. Flexibility to respond to local demands and preferences for financing systems should be retained as alternatives are considered.

References

Bahl, Roy W., Jesse Burkhead, and Bernard Jump, Jr., eds. 1980. *Public Employment and State and Local Government Finance*. Cambridge, MA: Ballinger Publishing Co.

Bahl, Roy W., Richard D. Gustley, and Michael J. Wasylenko. 1978. "The Determinants of Local Government Police Expenditures: A Public Employment Approach." *National Tax Journal* 31 (March): 67–79.

Baumel, C. Phillip, Cathy A. Hamlett, and Gregory R. Pautsch. 1986. *The Economics of Reducing the County Road System: Three Case Studies in Iowa*, DOT/OST/P–34/86/035, Washington, D.C.: USDOT.

Baumel, C. Phillip, and Eldo Schornhorst. 1983. "Local Rural Roads and Bridges: Current and Future Problems and Alternatives." *Transportation Research Record* 898: 374–78.

Chicoine, David L. 1986. "Infrastructure and Agriculture: Interdependencies With a Focus on Local Roads in the North Central States." In *Interdependencies of Agriculture and Rural Communities in the 21st Century*, Peter Korsching and Judith Gildner, eds., Ames, IA: Iowa State University Press, 141–64.

Chicoine, David L. 1987. "Issues and Implications of the Financial Crisis in Agriculture: The State/Local Government Finance Dimension." *Agricultural Finance Review* 47 (Special Issue): 62–71.

Chicoine, David L., and James Jacobs. 1987. "Evidence on The Property Tax Base of Illinois Road Districts." *Illinois County and Township Official* 47 (June): 14–16.

Chicoine, David L., and Norman Walzer. 1984. *Financing Rural Roads and Bridges in the Midwest*. Office of Transportation, Washington, D.C.: USDA.

Chicoine, David L., and Norman Walzer. 1985. *Governmental Structure and Local Public Finance*. Boston: Oelgeschlager, Gunn and Hain, Inc.

Chicoine, David L., and Norman Walzer, eds. 1986. *Financing Local Infrastructure in Non-Metropolitan Areas*. New York: Praeger, Inc.

Chicoine, David L., Norman Walzer, and Steven C. Deller. 1987. "Efficiencies in Local Transportation Systems: A Cost Analysis of Low-Volume Roads in the U.S." University of Illinois, memo.

Choate, Pat, and Susan Walter. 1981. *America in Ruins*. Washington, D.C.: Council of State Planning Agencies.

Cook, Gail C. A. 1973. "Effect of Metropolitan Government on Resource Allocation: The Case of Education in Toronto." *National Tax Journal* 26 (December): 585–90.

Dilorenzo, Thomas J. 1983. "Economic Competition and Political Competition: An Empirical Note." *Public Choice* 40 (2): 203–9.

Ehrenberg, Ronald G. 1973. "The Demand for State and Local Government Employees." *American Economic Review* 63 (June): 366–79.

FHWA (Federal Highway Administration). 1986. *Highway Taxes and Fees: How They are Collected and Distributed*. Washington, D.C.: FHWA.

Fox, William F., Jr. 1980. *Size Economies in Local Government Services: A Review*. RDRR 22, Economic Research Service, Washington, D.C.: USDA.

Gustley, Richard D. 1977. "The Allocation and Distributional Impacts of Governmental Consolidation: The Dade County Experience." *Urban Affairs* 12 (3): 349–64.

HUF (Highway Users Federation). 1987. "Editor's Resource." Washington, D.C.: HUF.

Jahr, Dale, Jerry W. Johnson, and Ronald C. Wimberley, eds. 1986. *New Dimensions in Rural Policy: Building Upon Our Heritage*. Joint Economic Committee, Washington, D.C.: Government Printing Office.

Martin, Delores Tremewan. 1980. "Entry Restrictions and Expenditure Effects in the Local Government Market." *Annals of Regional Science* 14 (14): 12–22.

Mehan, Stephen L. 1984. "The Effect of Governmental Structure on Special District Expenditures." *Public Choice* 44 (2): 339–48.

NCPWI (National Council on Public Works Improvements). 1986. *The Nation's Public Works: Defining the Issues* Report to the President and the Congress, Washington, D.C.: NCPWI.

Peterson, George E. et al. 1986. *Infrastructure Needs Studies: A Critique*. Washington, D.C.: The Urban Institute.

Reid, J. Norman, and Patrick J. Sullivan. 1984. "Rural Infrastructure: How Much? How Good?" *Rural Development Perspective* 1 (October): 9–13.

Ryan, Barry. 1987. "Estimates of Wastewater Treatment Capital Requirements in Rural America." AGES861218. Economic Research Service, Washington, D.C.: USDA.

Wagner, Richard E., and Warren E. Weber. 1975. "Competition, Monopoly and the Organization of Government in Metropolitan Areas." *Journal of Law and Economics* 18 (3): 661–84.

Walzer, Norman, and David L. Chicoine. 1987. *County Roads and Bridges: Finance and Administration*. Office of Transportation, Washington, D.C.: USDA.

Walzer, Norman, David L. Chicoine, and Ruth T. McWilliams. 1987. "Rebuilding Rural Roads and Bridges." *Rural Development Perspectives* 3 (February): 15–20.

5

Deregulated Agricultural Transportation: Problems and Issues

James C. Cornelius

Transportation of agricultural products throughout the United States has undergone significant changes since 1980 as the result of deregulation. The term deregulation is not entirely accurate in this case, since there are still numerous areas of government regulation in the transportation industry. That is, transportation is not now "unregulated." Deregulation refers to the context of the regulatory environment prior to 1980, compared to the post-1980 period.

The U.S. government's involvement in transportation regulation is composed of two general aspects, safety regulations and economic regulations. Safety regulations are designed to protect both the individual and society from unsafe transportation practices. Speed limits, weight limits, and flight plans are typical examples of safety regulations in transportation.

Economic regulation is not so concise in either its intent or scope, but is designed to influence the transportation industry's performance through various economic sanctions. National legislation to deregulate transportation has been concerned primarily with relaxing the economic regulations imposed upon various carrier modes (i.e., railroads, airlines, motor and barge carriers) involved in interstate commerce. During the 1980s, carriers have been given increased flexibility in determining transportation rates, service, and the ability to enter or exit the transportation industry. The results of such deregulation have had direct effects on the producers, shippers, carriers, and consumers of many agricultural commodities. In addition, the secondary impacts of deregulation have spread to other areas of the rural economy.

Transportation deregulation applies primarily to the carrier industries, which influences the various manufacturing and service sectors who rely upon transportation. Thus, transportation deregulation has had impacts on industries in addition to agriculture, including passenger transportation on commercial airlines and railroads and other raw and manufactured goods sectors. In this chapter, however, the focus will be on examining the issues and problems in agriculture arising from transportation deregulation.

Historical Perspective

In order to appreciate the consequences of deregulation, it is necessary to first understand the regulatory environment that existed prior to the enactment of transportation deregulation in 1980. Access to transportation has long been recognized as one of the key elements governing agricultural and economic development of a region. Economic development and prosperity in the United States during the nineteenth century was due in part to the expansion of transportation facilities (railroads, inland waterways, roads, and ports) to facilitate the movement of people and commerce.

By the late 1880s, the railroads offered an effective means of transporting agricultural commodities across the developing nation, and in so doing enhanced interregional trade and development. But the concentration of transportation market power in the hands of relatively few railroads led to the exploitation of farmers and other shippers in some instances. The Granger movement, representative of farm interests, was the driving force behind legislation to control railroads. After a thirteen-year struggle in Congress, federal control of the railroads was enacted in 1887 with the Act of Regulate Commerce, now known as the Interstate Commerce Act (Sampson and Farris 1971). This act is important insofar as it established a precedent that regarded transportation as a public utility, with an obligation of service to the general public at reasonable prices (Farmer 1964).

In the 100 years since this initial act, subsequent legislation has added to, amended, and in some cases reduced, federal regulations of the railroads, as well as added other carrier modes (i.e., motor carrier, water carrier, and airlines) to the realm of federal and state transportation regulation. Following the depression, government control over transportation in terms of both safety and economic concerns became more comprehensive and increasingly influenced the economic performance of some carrier groups. This change was due to stringent requirements on rate setting procedures, restricted access to transportation markets, service requirements, and strict control over certain business activities such as mergers, abandonments, and equipment ownership.

One notable exception in the trend toward deregulation of transportation during this time was the explicit exemption of motor carriers of agricultural commodities from economic regulation. This exemption was written into the Motor Carrier Act of 1935 and has remained in effect since (Farmer 1964). As a result, motor carriers of raw agricultural products have always been exempt from economic regulations in interstate commerce. Many states, however, have established economic regulation over intrastate truck transportation.

During the 1970s, agricultural transportation problems escalated due to the sudden increase in export sales of farm commodities, significantly higher fuel costs, and a shortage of rail cars. Existing economic regulation of carriers seemed to aggravate transportation problems, and pressures to deregulate transportation became a priority concern at the national level. Again, the implications of deregulation extended beyond the agricultural sector, touching all those industries and services that rely upon the movement of goods and services.

Following tentative steps to reform the rail industry (the Railroad Revitalization and Regulatory Reform Act of 1976), meaningful deregulation of the transportation industry was accomplished with the Staggers Rail Act of 1980 and the Motor Carrier Act of 1980 (USDA 1982). The intended result of this combined legislation, as well as similar deregulation of the U.S. airline industry in 1979 and the Inland Waterways Revenue Act of 1978, was to place more reliance on allocation of transportation resources through the free market mechanism rather than government regulation.

Subsequent transportation legislation, such as the Surface Transportation Act of 1982 and the Waterways Resources Development Act of 1986, have pushed further into the complexities of the market allocation mechanism by establishing a basis for the imposition of "user fees" affecting highway and waterway users.

The implementation of transportation deregulation has not necessarily been a unanimous decision. Rural areas, including remote agricultural producers, are concerned about service and rates. Carriers worry about inter- and intramodal competition, consumers are concerned about the cost of delivered products, and travelers in general are suspicious of uncertain, volatile fares. Now, having accrued several years of experience with the deregulation of agricultural transportation, it is possible to draw some conclusions regarding the apparent efficacy of this policy change and to reevaluate the concerns that existed in the early 1980s.

Ongoing Concerns About Transportation Deregulation

The impact of deregulated agricultural transportation has not been uniform across all affected groups. The most dramatic changes have occurred in the sectors influenced by rail transportation, but with significant impacts for other modes as well. The benefits in many cases have been in the area of greater efficiency of operation, often due to the economies of size associated with better utilization of equipment. The trade-off has been in the area of service to smaller, less efficient shippers who face reduced service, often at a higher rate. The potential market power of railroads remains a concern to many, particularly for shippers with no other transportation alternatives.

Adjustments, inequities, and losses resulting from deregulation have not run their course. The competitive market forces extract a toll on identifiable groups of shippers, producers, and carriers, while the benefits are spread across society as a whole. The agricultural economy has responded relatively quickly to the market environment created through transportation deregulation; possibly a reflection of the inherent market orientation and competitiveness of many agricultural sectors. The issue has progressed beyond philosophically adapting to transportation deregulation; today's challenge is efficiently operating and responding to the incentives created by a deregulated market environment.

Surviving and benefiting from deregulation requires a two-tiered approach for educational and technical assistance. The first objective is to understand the expectations associated with transportation deregulation, which includes having a working understanding of the rate-making mechanism, service obligations, the transportation infrastructure, competition among carriers, and the resulting consequences for agricultural shippers and rural economies in general. The second, and more active, role is assisting in the efficient responses to the economic incentives. Priority educational opportunities in this regard for both shippers and carriers include assistance in efforts such as organizing shipper cooperatives, establishing and negotiating contract rates, improving capacity utilization, or calculating least-cost route design. The response to the incentives created through transportation deregulation also includes the negative or painful adjustments to change. Dealing with loss of service through consequences such as rail line abandonment, or adjusting to higher freight rates demonstrates that not all of the consequences of deregulation have been benign.

Assessing the Impacts of Transportation Deregulation

The major focus of deregulation has been to allow the allocation of transportation services to occur under a more natural, market-based system. It is therefore appropriate to assess the performance of deregulation in light of traditional market-performance indicators, in this case features such as freight rates, efficiency of operation, and services provided.

Rate Structure

Transportation deregulation has allowed carriers, particularly railroads, increased flexibility in adjusting rates, in recognition that the demand for transportation services is not unlike the demand for other goods and services; that is, the demand for transportation increase as rates are lowered and vice versa. The responsiveness of transportation demand to changes in rates (the price elasticity of demand for transportation) varies by commodity, region, and degree of competition (Wilson 1982; Miklius, Casavant, and Garrod 1976). Agricultural producers in remote inland regions may be totally dependent on a single rail carrier so that their demand for transportation is relatively insensitive to rate changes. Alternatively, producers and shippers who have several competing carriers available are likely to be much more responsive to changes in transportation rates. By allowing carriers increased flexibility in establishing rate structures, a competitive market equilibrium is more likely, ultimately benefiting shippers and consumers. Alternatively, carriers who enjoy monopoly powers due to lack of competition (the so-called market dominance situation) may be able to use their rate-making powers to extract higher than necessary returns from shippers. Deregulation has been most effective in ensuring equitable rates and service where there is potential competition among and between carriers but has yet to satisfactorily address the question of shippers captive to a single carrier.

In many segments of freight transportation, rate structures have grown out of a traditional concept called "value of service rate making" (VOSRM). Under VOSRM, the transportation rate is directly proportional to the value of the commodity being transported. Low-valued commodities have low rates, and high-valued commodities have high rates, other factors being equal. Although natural competitive forces within the transportation industry have eroded VOSRM practices over time, deregulation has tried to focus the rate-making procedure on a cost and efficiency basis in a way that is more consistent with an efficient economic allocation, whereby goods and services (in this case the transportation service) are priced at their marginal cost. In this manner, cost-saving technologies developed by carriers can be passed along to shippers, leading to an overall enhancement of the marketing system.

Unit Trains

There is ample evidence that the rate structures afforded railroads through deregulation have achieved some of the benefits as described above. One example is the rise in importance of "unit trains" or "fast trains," whereby railroads have passed along the efficiencies associated with improved technology by offering shippers low rates for larger volume shipments. Under the unit train concept, railroads may offer grain elevators successively lower "multicar" rates depending upon the volume (number of carloads) of grain being shipped. A single rail car of grain shipped from central Montana to a west coast export terminal might be billed at forty-five dollars per metric ton, whereas a unit train shipment of fifty-two cars of grain can be shipped for as low as twenty-five dollars per metric ton. Proportional discounts may be available for three, ten, or twenty six-car shipments. The railroad is able to offer a lower multicar rate due to the cost savings in switching and handling achieved through the shipment of an entire train load of grain from one origination point to a single destination point. Cost simulations based on trainload shipments in Northwest Kansas estimated potential savings to the total system of 10.5 percent (Chow, Babcock, and Sorenson 1986). Similar cost efficiencies have been passed along as lower rates in other agricultural sectors as well, especially those with bulky, semi-perishable commodities transported over relatively long distances.

Peak Load Demand

A recurrent problem in agricultural transportation is the "peak load" demand for transportation services during certain times of the year. For example, shippers' demands for truck transportation of perishable fresh fruits peak during the summer and subside during the winter months. For an individual trucker, it would likely prove uneconomical to operate a truck tractor and refrigerated van for only two or three months of the year. Thus, the problem becomes one of providing transportation services for relatively brief yet intense transportation demand periods. To some extent, this problem can be addressed by a large, transitory motor-carrier fleet that is able to move from peak demand to peak demand across the nation, thus providing more consistent, year-around employment for carriers.

A second option to the peak-load demand problem is the implementation of demand-sensitive rates. This solution recognizes the role of prices—transportation rates in this situation—in allocating scarce resources over the short term. Historically, truck rates for fresh produce have been demand sensitive; a motor carrier can respond to those shippers willing to bid truck transportation services away from lower priority demands. Motor carriers of raw and unprocessed agricultural commodities have this rate flexibility because they are largely exempt from economic regulation in interstate commerce. Although the peak-load demand problem has not been completely solved under a deregulated economic environment, the marketplace has provided a workable, economic solution.

Rate Flexibility

One of the objectives of railroad deregulation has been to impart more flexibility into rate making. Prior to deregulation, the rate-making procedure was characterized by agreements made by carriers' rate bureaus petitioning the Interstate Commerce Commission (ICC) for authorization to change rates. Lengthy time lags and the regulatory procedures necessary to change rates greatly reduce the sensitivity of transportation services in this economic environment, often to the disadvantage of both carriers and shippers. Transportation deregulation has relaxed many of the rate-making procedures followed by railroads, although there are still explicit procedures for affecting rate changes. The greater flexibility in establishing rates has allowed railroads the opportunity to constructively set rates in accordance with demand, costs, and competition with other carriers.

Increased rate flexibility has had some structural impacts on the underlying merchandising pattern of some agricultural commodities, in that transportation costs, particularly for rail, can no longer be considered fixed as had been the case prior to deregulation. With increased uncertainty over transportation costs, merchandising for forward delivery or sale must account for the possibility of higher or lower rates, and this may show up in terms of a "risk premium" on forward market transactions.

Captive Shippers

Increased rate and service flexibility under deregulation has raised the most concern on the part of "captive shippers." Captive shippers are defined as those individuals who are solely dependent upon a single carrier, often the railroad, for transportation service. In this case, the carrier may be considered to have a monopoly that could lead to arbitrary, unfair pricing for the transportation service. Extensive discussion including litigation has attempted to effectively define captive shippers or conditions of "market dominance."

The issue is easier to define conceptually than practically. For example, when are railroads and motor carriers competitive, thus defusing a market-dominance situation, and when are motor carriers an ineffective alternative to railroads? The issue remains a controversy in policy decisions, perhaps because there has been little recent documented evidence of rate abuse by carriers in the case of captive shippers or market dominance. Nonetheless, the concern over their potential monopoly, first recognized by the Grangers one hundred years ago, remains a sensitive issue in many remote agricultural areas.

Contract Rates

An important rate-making procedure associated with transportation-deregulation is the use of contract rates. Like multicar rates discussed earlier, contract rates are not solely the result of deregulation. In both cases, however, the deregulated rate-making procedure has facilitated the widespread use of these practices. As the term implies, contract rates are the result of contracts between the carrier and shipper at predetermined rates for a special level of service.

Railroad contracting rules were specifically legislated in the Staggers Rail Act (Johnson 1983; Seaver 1983). Contracting can work for the benefit of both the carrier and the shipper, although there is ongoing concern that contract rates tend to favor larger volume shippers, to the exclusion of smaller ones. That is, larger shippers can guarantee larger volume in return for favorable rates and services. Since the implementation of the Staggers Act in 1980, contract rates have become common in agricultural rail transportation, particularly for bulky, semi-perishable commodities such as grains.

While contract rates have become increasingly important in rail transportation, this procedure has become one of the more controversial issues in transportation deregulation. The debate centers on disclosure of rates and contract terms. Generally, the terms of the contract are not publicly released either by the railroad or the shipper, and under deregulation railroads are no longer required to disclose all rate information. The lack of rate disclosure is perceived to benefit large shippers who have the ability to negotiate lower rates because they ship larger volumes of traffic. The terms of a contract may be sensitive to disclosure where there is active competition among carriers. Rail carriers have downplayed the role of contract rates to discriminate against small shippers beyond the inherent advantage of economies of size passed along to larger shippers. Numerous local cases have been investigated in an effort to obtain disclosure of contract rates, while at least one rail carrier has indicated an intention to faze out contracts on grain shipments. The latter action, with a reversion to traffic-based rates including volume incentives, represents one possible compromise in this area.

User Fees

User fees is a term applied generally to the charges made against carriers whose transportation service relies in part upon publicly provided facilities, such as highways and improved navigable waterways. An important structural difference between railroads on one hand and motor and barge carriers on the other is ownership of the transportation network. Railroads generally own and maintain their own transportation network system, while motor carriers rely upon publicly funded roads, and barge operators rely upon publicly funded lock systems and dredged waterway systems.

One of the tenets of transportation deregulation is that the carrier industries should not receive undue economic subsidization from the public sector at the expense of other, competing modes. User fees are one of the means available to assess carriers the public cost of providing the transportation network. This charge might be in the form of a toll or a tax on fuel or freight. One of the difficulties in the user fee concept is the accounting procedure for determining the user fee charge (Casavant, Mehringer, and Meyer). The national highway system and inland waterways are multiple use networks, extending to a wide range of users and public objectives. Motor carriers and waterway users are concerned that user fees may undermine their competitive position with railroads, to the extent the user fees are reflected in increased transportation rates.

The problems encountered in equitably assessing user fees has slowed the implementation of this concept. In most instances, the user fee is assessed in terms of federal taxes on diesel fuel used by commercial vehicles and vessels on publicly provided transportation networks.

Freight Rate Levels in Agricultural Transportation

The increased ability of carriers, railroad in particular, to adjust transportation rates in accordance with both demand and cost of service has been one of the major components of transportation deregulation. Advances in transportation service and technology, along with revived economic health of the nation's railroads, are often cited as the positive results of deregulation, but concerns still exist over the potential of carriers to exploit captive shippers or discriminate against small shippers.

There is evidence that freight rates in general have moderated following deregulation, though this also reflects exogenous variables besides deregulation, such as the decline in world petroleum prices. The index of transportation costs as a component of all food marketing costs increased 57 percent between 1978 and 1981, but rose only 13 percent between 1981 and 1986. The period just after enactment of transportation deregulation actually witnessed a sharp increase in transportation rates; the rail freight rate index jumped 22 percent between 1980 and 1982. The rail rate index rose only about 8 percent between 1982 and 1986 however (USDA 1987).

An important conclusion regarding the influence of deregulation on freight rates is that rates have not necessarily decreased, nor should they be expected to uniformly decline. Rather, lower rates are likely where deregulation has resulted in increased operating efficiencies. For example, average freight rates on wheat moving from the Central Plains to Gulf ports have steadily declined since 1981. This is partly the result of lower multicar and contract rates that reflect cost savings by railroads. Not all rates are being reduced, however. User fee charges, or surcharges assessed by railroads on low density lines, may lead to increases in some rates structures. Both of these scenarios are consistent with a market-based allocation of the resource.

Transportation Service

Transportation rates for agricultural commodities are only one component of deregulation. The service provided, covering attributes such as frequency of service, transit time, technology, and related features, is of equal or greater concern in the shipment of some commodities. Consider, for example, the situation that developed in rail freight prior to deregulation in the late 1970s. In that case, a shortage of rail cars relative to grain transportation demands led to an awkward system of rationing by the railroads in servicing rural shippers. Rail rates were effectively controlled by the rate-making procedures overseen by the Interstate Commerce Commission, such that available rail service could not be allocated on the basis of rates. Thus, even though the rate structure may have been acceptable, service was not adequate to meet demand.

Experience with deregulation has shown a responsiveness on the part of carriers to provide service in accordance with demand. A key rationing device has been the increased flexibility of the rate structure. In addition, technological advancements on the part of carriers, such as unit trains or trailer on flat car (TOFC) combinations complement the service provided. Relaxation of the exempt status of motor carriers of agricultural commodities has broadened the categories of products that may be hauled under the exempt status, leading to more efficient utilization of capacity, which may show up as either lower rates or improved service.

Service has also been adversely affected under deregulation, especially in the case of abandonments or decreased service where carriers have been given more freedom in determining service networks. The heart of the service issue is whether or not carriers have an obligation to serve the public, or if this service is provided solely in response to effective demand. Under the original definition of public service, carriers were envisioned to have a "common carriage" obligation, meaning that producers or shippers in any location had a right to access the transportation system. In some cases, this included service at a subsidized rate, relative to the actual cost of providing the service. Remote, high-cost shippers were often subsidized by other shippers and consumers on higher density transportation routes.

The "cross subsidization" of some shippers by others has been altered under transportation deregulation, such that both groups—the high-cost shippers and the low-cost shippers—now pay closer to the actual cost of receiving the service. Remote agricultural producing regions, with high-cost transportation access, have experienced declining service in this regard, particularly for rail and air transportation. Truck transportation of agricultural commodities in interstate commerce has always been exempt from economic regulation, so the impacts of deregulation are less dramatic.

Motor carriers are somewhat more dependent upon backhaul potentials in determining cost of service and therefore rates, due to higher variable costs relative to railroads. Attracting truck transportation into rural areas may be enhanced if truckers are able to broaden the category of available backhauls. In some cases, such as the transportation of fresh potatoes out of south central Idaho, there is simply not enough backhaul potential to attract the number of truckers necessary to transport the potato crop by truck. In this situation rail carriers have provided alternative service, utilizing some of the same cost-base efficiencies utilized in grain transportation, to fill the transportation demand. Rail transportation of potatoes may not be quite as fast or desirable as truck transportation, but availability of service and competitive rates have made rail transportation a viable alternative, particularly for long distance hauls to eastern markets.

Competition Among Carriers

While transportation deregulation has had significant impacts on producers and shippers, as discussed above, the policy change has also directly influenced the nature of competition among the alternative carrier modes. Competition among carriers, or lack of it, depends upon several variables. First, the distance of transport may well dictate what type of carriers are involved. Relatively short-distance hauls of less than fifty miles are almost exclusively the domain of trucks. Because of the comparative ease of entry into the trucking industry, combined with an extensive highway network, competition among truckers is fairly active. The potential of these carriers to charge excessive rates is limited. Some truckers would argue that there is too much competition among motor carriers, and "cutthroat" rates are below their operating costs.

Both railroad and barge companies have higher overhead costs than motor carriers and rely on longer distance hauls to spread these fixed costs. In terms of fuel costs, rail and barge transport is relatively cheaper than trucking. Thus, in the intermediate to long-distance hauls, rail and barge service, if available, is less costly than comparable trucking rates. There is no precise distance at which rail transportation becomes cheaper than trucking, but at distances beyond 200 miles, competition begins to favor railroads over trucks, depending upon backhaul opportunity for trucks and shipment volume for rails.

The competition among carriers on distances beyond two or three hundred miles is often strongest between inland waterway carriers and railroads. Barge transport may be the least expensive in terms of moving a given tonnage over a given distance, but barge transport is dependent upon access to a navigable river, and is somewhat limited in service for perishable agricultural commodities. Where intermodal competition does not exist, intramodal competition must be relied upon to insure equitable rates and service.

An important concern over competition among carriers centers on those remote, isolated producers and shippers that are dependent upon a single railroad for agricultural transportation. Truck or truck/barge transport may not pose effective price competition with the railroads, especially where the truck portion exceeds two or three hundred miles. The plight of producers in isolated regions is not a new problem. Access to markets is an important factor in determining competitive advantage among regions. Economic variables such as land values, crops grown, or returns to producers are directly related to transport costs.

Generally, the closer the shipper to a market, or alternative transportation modes, the more rate competition among carriers (MacDonald 1987). Research has evaluated the competitiveness between competing grain carriers in the Pacific Northwest in terms of sensitivity of rate change (Logsdon et al. 1982). A 10 percent increase in rail rates was estimated to cause railroads to lose nearly 8 percent of their wheat volume to truck/barge competition. Alternatively, a 10 percent reduction in rail rates would be expected to increase the railroad's share of the grain traffic by nearly 15 percent. These estimates provide an explanation for the increased rate competition between rail and truck/barge carriers along the Columbia-Snake system following deregulation. By offering rate discounts for multicar shipment, railroads have been able to regain a sizeable portion of the grain traffic lost to truck or truck/barge alternatives in the 1970s.

In contrast, economic analyses of North Dakota and Kansas grain transportation demand document the precarious position of remote, inland grain shipping areas. These findings suggest that a railroad serving captive shippers could expect to pass along substantial rate increases without losing any appreciable shipping volume (Chow, Babcock, and Sorenson 1986; Wilson 1982).

In the years following the Staggers Act, rail service to grain shippers in many regions appears to have improved. The decline in grain exports during this same period, however, has lessened the demand for shipping services. This has heightened competition among carriers for available freight volume, probably to the benefit of shippers and producers. Thus, the long-term impacts of deregulation could change in the event of significant increase in the demand for transportation services due to a resurgence in U.S. grain exports.

Structural Changes in the Transportation Infrastructure

As shippers, carriers, and consumers adjust to the explicit changes in transportation brought about by deregulation, more subtle changes also are occurring in the marketing system. Such changes are apparent in the location of production and processing of agricultural commodities. The influence of cost-based transportation rates has directly influenced the competitive position of various producing regions in the United States.

The location of fruit and vegetable production, for example, appears to have been gradually changing, partially in response to transportation deregulation. West Coast states have been a major producing region of many fruits and vegetables, shipping these products across the United States to major consuming regions in the East. During the past fifteen years, there has been an increase in production of selected fruits and vegetables in the North Central and Northeast states (Hamm 1987). Adjustments in freight rates to a cost basis, improved equipment utilization, and more freedom in establishing rates has provided an economic incentive to move production areas closer to consuming areas on the east coast, despite generally lower yields compared to west coast productivity (USDA 1985). Such changes in regional competitive advantage are not solely the result of changes in shipping costs, but competitive transportation rates have been an important factor in shifting some agricultural production closer to consuming regions.

Structural changes also have occurred in response to new transportation technology that has been enhanced by deregulation. The evolution of the current grain handling system in the United States, whereby local production is channeled into regional "subterminal" elevators for shipment in unit trains to terminal markets has been encouraged through railroad deregulation allowing more flexibility in establishing rates and service. By comparison, the technological development of boxed beef (itself unrelated to transportation deregulation), may ultimately lead to changes in the beef feeding and processing industry, as truck shipment of frozen boxed beef is lower cost and more efficient than the shipment of carcasses.

Rural Economic Development

The primary impacts of transportation deregulation on agriculture relate to the cost, service, and competitive changes borne by the producers, shippers, carriers, and consumers directly involved. Lower rates might increase returns to shippers or producers, providing economic benefit to a particular group of individuals. Similarly, a loss of rail service might increase shipping costs, with resulting lower returns to producers. These primary impacts, both good and bad, will in turn lead to changes in profitability, crop production patterns, acreage, and product form.

A secondary group of impacts resulting from transportation deregulation may be imposed on other parties not directly involved with agricultural transportation. For example, the impact on rural roads and bridges due to changing transportation patterns is a serious concern to other rural residents who rely upon these roads for the provision of nonagricultural transportation such as providing busing for school children, fire and police services, or personal vehicle use. The decline in economic activity associated with a loss of transportation service will similarly impact businesses besides agricultural firms in rural communities. If agricultural transportation comprises part of "critical mass" necessary to sustain economic activity in rural areas, the losses or gains attributable to changing transportation considerations may affect the entire community.

As with many of the changes in agricultural transportation, the impacts upon rural areas may not be totally the result of transportation deregulation. Still, the provision of market-oriented transportation services, and a deemphasis of public service or common carriage obligations will add to a community's responsibility in bearing the costs of changes in transportation.

Summary of Major Problems and Issues Relating to the Deregulation of Agricultural Transportation

Several issues have been identified that have arisen, in part, as a result of transportation deregulation. Adverse and favorable consequences may arise from the same point, depending upon the circumstances. The following summary of issues represents ongoing concerns in agricultural transportation that are related to deregulation. The concept of public-service obligation in providing transportation service has given way to a philosophy of market-oriented service based on willingness and ability to pay. The potential market power of some carriers is a concern to shippers, especially those shippers relying upon a single carrier. Alternatively, deregulation has led to increased competition among and between carriers in some markets. Railroad abandonment or reduced frequency of service has adversely impacted shippers in isolated regions. The use of confidential contract rates by railroads concerns many small shippers who feel larger shippers may be receiving preferential treatment by carriers. Deregulation has brought about change in the transportation infrastructure, including the attendant marketing system. Changes in the transportation service brought on by deregulation often lead to secondary economic impacts on rural areas.

These topics are not ranked in any order of priority. There is some overlapping among these issues, since they may arise from common underlying causes. A number of specific issues can further be attached to these summary points depending upon the context and situation. Generally, the costs or losses associated with transportation deregulation often fall on identifiable groups, whereas the benefits are spread across the wider population.

There have been adverse impacts due to transportation deregulation, but many of the intended improvements in the economic efficiency appear to have been realized. As a result, one of the challenges for educators is to help various groups adjust to specific, adverse consequences of deregulation, while providing the broad-based education program that will allow shippers, carriers, and consumers to take advantage of the economic incentives that exist in this business environment.

Conclusions

Deregulation of agricultural transportation has led to some significant changes in allocation patterns of this service resource. Initially, both shippers and carriers coped with new way of doing business in the transition period between a regulated and relatively deregulated market place.

Now, with more than five years' experience in deregulated transportation markets, this transition is nearing completion. There appears to be a general acceptance of the consequences of economic deregulation of transportation, but concerns still exist. Paramount in this regard are unresolved differences over the role of public intervention in transportation in order to insure a competitive market environment that penalizes neither shipper nor carrier.

The benefits from deregulation have come about largely as a result of increased economic efficiency in the provision of transportation services due to new flexibility on the part of carriers in adjusting to demand. While deregulation has resulted in some encouraging improvements relative to previous market environment, it has come at the expense of some identifiable groups who have borne disproportionate costs in terms of loss of service or higher rates.

The increased reliance on a market-oriented allocation of transportation service to agriculture has lessened the need for governmental involvement in the areas of rate making, provision of service, and organization of the transportation industries. Nevertheless, there are problems and issues regarding deregulated agricultural transportation that pose challenges for educators. Many of the educational and technical assistance needs address business decisions necessary in the marketplace, which is a departure from the regulation-based educational programs appropriate in the past.

References

Casavant, K., J. Mehringer, and N. Meyer. N.d. "Waterway User Fees and Wheat Transportation in the Pacific Northwest." PNW 30, Washington State University.

Chow, M. H., N. W. Babcock, and L. O. Sorenson. 1986. "Analysis of Structural Changes in a Grain Logistic System: Trainload Facilities and Intermodal Competition in Northwest Kansas." *Agribusiness* 2 (Fall): 279–92.

Farmer, R. N. 1964. "The Case for Unregulated Truck Transportation." *J. Farm Econ.* 46: 398–409.

Hamm, S. R. 1987. "Trends in the U.S. Processing Vegetable Industry." *Vegetable Situation and Outlook.* Economic Research Service, Washington, D.C.

Logsdon, C., K. Casavant, R. Mittelhammer, and L. Rogers. 1982. "An Economic Analysis of the Demand for Truck–Barge Transportation of Pacific Northwest Wheat." Research Bulletin XB0924, Washington State University Agricultural Research Center.

Johnson, M. A. 1983. "Contracting for Railroad Freight Service." Transportation Deregulation and Agriculture Series Publication WRDC17. Western Rural Development Center, Oregon State University.

MacDonald, J. M. 1967. "Competition and Rail Rates for the Shipment of Corn, Soybeans, and Wheat." *R and J of Econ.* 18 (Spring): 151–63.

Miklius, W., K. Casavant, and P. Garrod. 1976. "Estimation of Demand for Transportation of Agricultural Commodities." *American J. of Agric. Econ.* 58 (May): 217–23.

Sampson, R. J., and M. T. Farris. 1971. *Domestic Transportation: Practice, Theory and Policy,* 2nd ed. Boston: Houghton Mifflin Co.

Seaver, S. K. 1983. "The Staggers Rail Act." Transportation Deregulation and Agriculture Series Publication WRDC16. Western Rural Development Center, Oregon State University.

U.S. Department of Agriculture. 1982. "An Assessment of the Impacts on Agriculture of the Staggers Rail Act and Motor Carriers Act of 1980." Office of Transportation, Washington, D.C.

U.S. Department of Agriculture. 1985. *Vegetables*. Crop Reporting Board. Washington, D.C.

U.S. Department of Agriculture. 1987 and earlier. *Agricultural Outlook*. Washington, D.C.

Wilson, W. W. 1982. "Estimation of Demand Elasticities for Transportation Modes in Grain Transportation." Agricultural Economics Report No. 159, Dept. of Agric. Econ., North Dakota State University.

Part III

Transportation's Contribution
to
Rural Economic Development

6

The Effect of Transportation Service on the Location of Manufacturing Plants in Nonmetropolitan and Small Metropolitan Communities

Frank M. Goode
Steven E. Hastings

The objective of this chapter is to discuss from both a theoretical and empirical perspective the effect of transportation services on a community's ability to attract manufacturing plants. The next section contains a discussion of the evolution of industrial location theory and highlights the role of transportation services in each of the theories. Section III presents the results of an econometric study designed to identify the factors associated with the location of new manufacturing plants in nonmetropolitan and small metropolitan communities in the Northeastern states.

The Role of Transportation Services in Prominent Industrial Location Theories

Theoretically, transportation services and their costs have frequently been considered an important factor in the location decisions for manufacturing plants. Virtually every prominent location theory of the twentieth century has addressed the role of transportation. In this section, the treatment of transportation in the theories of Weber, Losch, and Greenhut is discussed and compared.

Weber's Least-Cost Model

Alfred Weber is generally considered to be the first economist to develop a rigorous and systematic theory of industrial location. Weber's theory was based on three assumptions: that inputs for the production process are located at selected points in space; that the market for the product is located in urban centers and their locations are fixed; and that all of the labor required is available at a fixed price and is located at specific points in space.

Given these assumptions, Weber argued that the optimum location for a plant is where production costs are minimized. Weber identified three cost factors that must be used to identify the minimum cost location: transportation costs, labor costs, and agglomeration factors. Transportation costs are the costs associated with transporting inputs to the plant and distributing the product to the market. Labor costs are "wages and salaries which are paid out in the course of the production process" (Weber 1929, 95). Agglomeration factors are associated with industrial concentration and include cost reductions due to the proximity of auxiliary industries.

Weber believed that transportation costs were the dominant factor in determining the least-cost location. Labor costs and agglomerations factors only "distort the transportation network and shift it to certain other points" (Weber 1929, 35). In essence, Weber believed that a plant would locate at the site where transportation costs were a minimum. If there was no labor available at the site, the plant might be located in a community near the minimum-transportation-cost site. However, it was not unreasonable to expect labor to resettle at the minimum-transportation-cost site. Thus, labor costs were viewed as having only a modest impact on the optimum plant location. Similarly, Weber acknowledged that there are cost advantages for a plant located near other plants from which it purchases inputs or to whom it sells outputs. According to Weber, these cost advantages were modest in comparison with transportation cost and could have only a marginal impact on determining the optimum plant site.

Thus, in Weber's view, transportation networks were the dominant determinant of industrial location. Considering the industrial structure and the transportation systems in industrialized countries in the late nineteenth and early twentieth centuries, Weber's theory was a reasonably accurate explanation of the spatial distribution of economic activity. Early industrial development in the United States was concentrated in industries that relied on natural resource inputs such as iron and textiles. The transportation system was primarily water-based and the major markets were on the East Coast. In this environment, transportation cost dictated the location of resource-based industries. For example, the location of iron foundries was dictated by the coexistence of iron ore, timber, and a river large enough to transport the finished product to the East Coast markets. In essence, it was so expensive to transport iron ore and timber more than a few miles that iron foundries were located very near the resources. Labor costs and agglomeration factors had little influence on the location of iron foundries.

Losch's Revenue Maximization Model

Writing several decades later, August Losch criticized "Weber's and all other attempts at a systematic and valid location theory" (Losch 1954, 29). Losch's model stressed that the optimum site was one that maximized revenue rather than minimized costs. These two theorists reached polar conclusions primarily because they were based on different assumptions. Weber assumed that inputs were located at selected locations, while Losch assumed they were uniformly distributed over space. The most important difference between them was that Weber assumed a transportation network comprised of a limited number of trunk routes such as rivers, and Losch assumed an all-encompassing network (Losch 1954, 69). In the extreme, Weber assumed a world where the only transportation was along major rivers; Losch assumed any good could be transported on a straight line route between *any* origin and destination, and transportation rates did not vary over space.

Losch's assumptions that all inputs including labor were uniformly distributed over space amounted to an implicit assumption that the cost of production is equal at all points in space. Thus, the optimum site was where revenues were maximized. Since Losch assumed that markets were uniformly distributed over space, maximizing revenues was accomplished by controlling the largest possible market area.

The size of the market area was determined by transportation cost and the location of other firms producing the same product. The outer boundary of the market area occurs where the price of the product (cost of producing the product plus the transportation cost associated with delivering the product to the market) is more than the consumer is willing to pay. If the cost of producing a commodity is five dollars and the transportation cost is one dollar per mile and if the consumers will not pay more than ten dollars for the commodity, the maximum market area will be a circle with a radius of five miles. The price to a consumer six miles from the producer would be five dollars (production cost) plus six dollars for transportation cost. This is the largest market area (and maximum revenue) that a firm can hope to achieve. A firm may find a site that provides such a maximum market area and for a time realize considerable profits. However, the consumers near the boundary are paying high prices for the product because of the high cost of transportation. Losch argues the competing firms realize that they can capture those consumers if they operated a plant closer to the consumers than the current producer; that is, if the competing firms are closer the transportation cost and thus the price to those consumers is lower. Competing firms will be established if they can capture a market area that will generate revenues sufficient to cover cost.

According to Losch the end result of this process is a uniform distribution of producers over space. Each producer will control a market that is just large enough to generate the revenues necessary to cover costs. The essence of the Losch model is that producers will be spatially distributed in such a way that the cost of transporting the output to consumers is minimized. Thus, transportation costs are the central focus of Losch's theory.

Losch's theory predicts a uniform distribution, while Weber's theory predicts a seemingly random distribution of producers along major transportation routes. In order to understand the influence of transportation on the present and future geographical distribution of economic activity, it is useful to understand why the industrial location theories of Weber and Losch lead to such different predictions regarding the spatial distribution of producers.

The major reason that the theories of Weber and Losch were so different was because they were attempting to explain the phenomena of industrial location in two very different worlds. There were three important factors that differentiate the worlds of Weber and Losch, namely, transportation, technology, and energy.

When Losch's work was published, industrialized countries had highly developed rail and highway systems. The technology used in many manufacturing processes had recently changed, and the new production methods required a different set of inputs. New technologies for iron and steel production used coal rather than wood. New and more mobile energy forms, such as electricity and petroleum, were generally available.

The interaction of these three factors had a profound impact on the location of economic activity. The early iron industry relied almost exclusively on water transportation to deliver the product to the market. Usually there was a large city at the mouth of the river; thus, for all practical purposes the iron foundry had a single market. This situation was consistent with Weber's assumption regarding concentrated markets. The rail and highway systems that were in place by 1950 made it possible for an iron foundry to serve customers nationwide. Thus, Losch's assumption of geographically dispersed markets was consistent with the world of the mid-twentieth century.

The development of new and mobile energy forms affected the locational patterns of many industries. For example, most of the early textile industry in the United States was concentrated along waterways that provided power for the mills. The near-universal availability of petroleum-based energy and electricity resulted in the textile industry becoming one of the most "footloose" industries. Weber's assumption that inputs were available at a few specific locations was a realistic assumption when water power was important. However, Losch's assumption that inputs are uniformly distributed is consistent with the fact that petroleum and electrical energy are widely available at reasonably uniform prices.

Thus, the theories of Weber and Losch yield very different predictions regarding the geographical distribution of economic activity because the theories are based on very different assumptions. In general, Weber's assumptions are consistent with the conditions existing in the nineteenth century and Losch's are consistent with those of the mid-twentieth century.

Greenhut's Profit-Maximization Model

Although the theories of Weber and Losch were based on very different assumptions and lead to very different conclusions, current location theory is essentially a synthesis of their work. In fact, Greenhut argues that both the Weber and Losch models are special cases of the more general model he developed (Greenhut 1956, 97–98). The Greenhut model was designed to include "both variable costs and flexible demand within a single system of thought" (Greenhut 1956, 96). Actually, the Greenhut model included six basic location factors, namely, transportation costs, production costs, revenue or demand, agglomeration economies, revenue-enhancing factors, and personal considerations.

Greenhut's consideration of transportation and production costs was similar to the Weber approach. Greenhut identified four types of production costs, land, labor, capital, and tax rates. Industries that have perishable or bulky inputs or outputs will tend to base their location decision on transportation costs. Greenhut suggests that the Weber model fits these industries. If an industry's inputs are perishable or bulky, that industry will tend to locate near the source of the supply of inputs; otherwise they will tend to locate near the markets. Spatial variations in production costs may distort the minimum-transportation-cost location somewhat. For example, the minimum transportation cost for a plant might be in an urban center near its market. However, tax rates and land and labor prices may be significantly higher in the urban center than in a rural community twenty miles from the center. If the plant, by locating in the rural community, can save enough on production costs to cover increased transportation costs, it will locate in the rural community.

Greenhut's treatment of revenue or demand factors was similar to that presented by Losch. Greenhut suggests that a firm may first choose an aggregate market area based on total sales. That is, the firm understands that it can capture only a small part of the total market, but it will prefer a market area that has a high sales volume to a market with a low sales volume. For example, a textile plant producing cold-weather garments would locate in Minneapolis rather than Miami. After the plant has selected an aggregate market area, the decision of where to locate within that area is made using a process similar to that described by Losch. First, those making the location decision will identify all potential locations within the aggregate market area and determine the revenue that can be generated at each location. In the Losch model the location with the largest revenue will be selected, but Greenhut suggests that the costs as well as revenues at each location must be considered. In Weber's model the location with the minimum cost would be selected. However, Greenhut argues that the location where net revenues (revenue minus cost) are maximized is the location that will be selected. This location may not be either the revenue maximization nor the cost-minimization location.

In the case of the cold-weather garment manufacturing, the revenue-maximizing location may be in the southern suburbs of Minneapolis. Suppose that ten miles south of Minneapolis there is a rural community, and the price of land and labor and tax rates are significantly lower than in suburban Minneapolis. Further suppose that a company has a plant in the rural community that produces the insulation material that is used in cold-weather garments. Production costs would be considerably lower in the rural community, but because there are fewer people per square mile, revenues would also be lower. If moving from suburban Minneapolis decreases costs more than revenue, then net revenues will be greater in the rural community. Thus, one of Greenhut's major contributions was synthesizing the Weber and Losch models into a more comprehensive and reasonable model of industrial location.

In addition to the synthesis, Greenhut recognized that some industries are subject to agglomeration effects. The essence of agglomeration effects is that specialized cost or revenue considerations cause plants to concentrate at a single location rather than being spatially dispersed, each having its separate market area. For example, a plant may locate near an input supplier, not only because it reduces transportation, but because the plant can maintain a smaller inventory of the input; that is, to insure continuous production a plant maintains an inventory of inputs. However, if the plant is near the supplier, the inventory can be replenished promptly, thereby reducing the need to maintain large input inventories. Further, if there are economies of size in the production of the input, several plants that use the input may locate near the supplier to take advantage of these economies (lower input prices) as well as lower transportation cost and inventory requirements. An example of agglomeration effects on revenue are shopping centers. A shopping center may contain several shoe stores all competing directly with one another. However, given consumer behavior, shoe stores find they will sell more shoes if they concentrate at a single location than if they are dispersed, each having its own market area.

Finally, Greenhut was the first to suggest that there may be many locations that will provide approximately equal profits, and the choice among these locations will be based on personal considerations. This aspect of Greenhut's theory may be particularly relevant in studying rural industrial location. The dramatic growth of the manufacturing sector in rural areas from 1940 to 1980 is clear evidence that rural locations are profitable. It is conceivable, however, that many rural communities have not experienced growth, not because they are unprofitable locations, but because they do not have the amenities that plant managers find personally desirable. In essence, several rural communities may be profitable locations for a plant, but the community that is selected may be the one that has a good school system, nice parks, and adequate public services.

Thus, modern location theory suggests that site selection involves a process of balancing cost and revenue considerations. On the cost side, transportation costs, tax rates, labor and land costs, intermediate inputs, and agglomeration effects must be considered. On the revenue side, the number and location of those purchasing the product (be they consumers or other plants), the location of competing firms, and the existence of agglomeration effects must be taken into account. If net revenue is equal at several alternative sites, then community amenities may be the determining factor. An empirical study designed to identify the role of these factors in the location of industry in rural and small metropolitan communities in the Northeast is discussed below.

An Empirical Investigation of the Effect of Transportation Services on The Location of Manufacturing Industries in the Northeastern United States

The study reported in this section was designed to investigate the effect of a set of social and economic variables on the location of various types of manufacturing industries in rural and small metropolitan communities in the Northeast. Only the variables associated with transportation are discussed in this chapter. A complete list of the variables used in the study is provided in the Appendix.

The Study Area and the Units of Analysis

The study area included the New England, mid-Atlantic, and southern Atlantic states and Virginia. The units of analysis used in the study were all rural and small metropolitan communities in the study area.

A community was defined as a Census place and all surrounding Minor Civil Divisions or Census County Divisions whose population centroid was within five miles of the population centroid of the Census place. Rural communities were communities whose center (Census place) was not in a Metropolitan Statistical Area (MSA). Small metropolitan communities were MSA centers whose population was one hundred thousand or less. There were 730 rural communities and 368 small metropolitan communities.

The Dependent Variable and the Industries Studied

This study used regression analysis to identify the factors associated with the industrial location. The dependent variable used in the regression models was a dichotomous variable that had a value of one if the community attracted a new plant during the period 1970–78 and a value of the variable was zero if there was no new plant. The data for this variable were obtained from the Duns Market Indicators (DMI) file.

A regression model was estimated for each industry included in the study. Table 6.1 contains a brief descriptive title for each of the "aggregate industries" included in the study. Every four-digit Standard Industrial Class (SIC) industry in the manufacturing sector is included in one of the sixty-nine industries. Four-digit industries with similar input coefficients (from the National Input-Output Study) were combined to form one of the "aggregate industries."

The Transportation Variables

Distance to Road. This variable measured the road distance between a community and the nearest non-limited-access state or federal paved road. The hypothesis was that communities that are near paved highways would have lower transportation costs than communities that are not near these types of highways. The regression parameters for this variable are expected to be negative.

Distance to Limited-Access Four-Lane Highways. This variable measured the road distance from the community to the nearest limited-access four-lane highway. Generally, this variable reflects the distance to an Interstate Highway. The hypothesis and expected signs are similar to the previous variable.

Number of Rail Lines. This variable measured the number of railway

Table 6.1 Summary of Regression Results for Nonmetropolitan Communities*

Industry	Railroads	Airlines	Distance to 4-Lane Highway	Distance to 2-Lane Highway	Market
Meat Packing Plants	·	P	·	·	·
Poultry and Dairy Processing	P	·	·	·	N
Fish and Canned Specialties	·	·	P	·	N
Grain and Seed Processing	·	·	·	·	P
Miscellaneous Foods	P	·	·	·	·
Tobacco	·	·	·	·	·
Broadwoven Fabric	·	·	·	·	N
Narrow Fabric	·	·	·	·	N
Miscellaneous Textiles	·	·	·	·	·
Fabricated Textile Products	·	·	·	·	·
Logging	·	·	P	N	P
Sawmills	·	P	P	·	N
Hardwood Flooring	·	·	·	·	N
Specialized Sawmills	·	·	·	·	N
Wood Furniture	·	·	·	·	N
Wood Veneer and Containers	P	P	·	·	N
Miscellaneous Wood Products	·	P	·	·	·
Metal Household Furniture	·	·	·	·	·
Metal Office Furniture	·	P	·	N	·
Paper Mills	·	P	·	·	·
Paper Containers	·	·	N	·	·
Newspaper Publishing	·	N	·	·	·
Periodical Publishing	·	·	·	·	·
Book Publishing	·	·	·	·	N
Binding and Card Printing	·	·	·	N	N
Commercial Printing	·	P	N	·	·
Agricultural and Industrial Chemicals	·	·	·	·	N

Industry					
Plastics		N			
Drugs	N				N
Refined Petroleum	P			N	
Tires	P			P	
Leather Products	N				
Glass and Glassware	N				
Stone and Clay Products					
Concrete Block and Brick					
Other Concrete Products			P		
Ready Mix Concrete	N	N		N	
Gray Iron Foundries					
Lead Smelting					
Zinc Smelting					
Aluminum Foundries					
Metal Bolts and Wire					
Nonferrous Smelting					
Copper Wire					
Cutlery and Hand Tools	N				
Heating and Plumbing Fixtures	Z				
Structural Metal	Z		N	P	P
Coating and Engraving	Z			N	
Miscellaneous Metal Products	Z				
Engines	P				
Mobile Homes and Campers	Z		P		
Construction Equipment	N	P			
Machine Tools and Dies	N				N
Special Industrial Equipment					
General Industrial Equipment	Z				
Service Machines	Z		N		
Radio, TV, Telephones				N	
Household Appliances	N				
Electronic Components	N				
Motor Vehicles	P				

Table 6.1 *continued*

Industry	Railroads	Airlines	Distance to 4-Lane Highway	Distance to 2-Lane Highway	Market
Measuring Instruments					
Jewelry and Musical Instruments	P				N
Burial Caskets					N
Sporting Goods		P			N
Advertising Signs		P			N
Miscellaneous Manufacturing					N
Apparel					

*"P" indicates a positive coefficient that was significantly different from zero at the 10% level. "N" indicates a significant negative coefficient.

lines that had operating stations in a community. This variable was designed to reflect the availability and quality of rail service in a community. The hypothesis was that certain industries are dependent on rail service and would locate only in communities where the service was available. The regression parameters for this variable are expected to be positive.

Number of Airlines. This variable measures the number of airlines that have scheduled stops in the community. The rationale for this variable is that industries require air transportation not so much for their products but for their personnel. For example, a corporation may not locate a branch plant in a community that does not have air service because it is inconvenient for corporate executives to visit the plant. The regression parameters on this variable are expected to be positive.

Potential Net Input Availability (PNIA). This variable was defined as follows:

$$PNIA_j = \sum_{i=1}^{n} \frac{P_i - C_i}{T_{ij}}$$

where

$PNIA_j$ is the potential net input availability in community j;

N is the number of communities within 300 miles of community j;

P_i is the production of the input in community i;

C_i is the consumption of the input in community i;

T_{ij} is the cost of transporting the input from community i to community j.

In essence, this variable reflects whether community j is located in an area with a surplus or deficit supply of the input. For a more detailed discussion of the variable, see Hastings (1982). The regression parameters for this variable are expected to be positive.

Market Access. This variable was defined as follows:

$$MA_j = \sum_{i=1}^{n} \frac{C_i - P_i}{T_{ij}}$$

where

MA$_j$ is the market access for firms in community j;

N, C$_i$, P$_i$, and T$_j$ are as defined for the PNIA variable.

This variable reflects whether or not community j is in a region where there is an excess demand for the product. When this variable is positive there is an excess demand. For a more detailed discussion of this variable, see Goode (1986). There are two hypotheses concerning the sign of the coefficients for the variable. If the plants in an industry respond to agglomeration effects and concentrate spatially, then the signs of the coefficients are expected to be negative. That is, if the plants concentrate, they will be expected to locate in an area that has an excess supply (negative excess demand). If the plants tend to disperse spatially, each having its market area, then plants would be expected to locate where there is an excess demand, and the signs on the coefficients will be positive. The following section provides a summary of the empirical findings.

Empirical Results

Two models were estimated for each industry. One of the models used nonmetropolitan communities as the unit of observation, and the other model used metropolitan communities as the unit of observation. Two models were estimated because it was hypothesized that the factors associated with industrial location in rural communities would not be the same as those associated with location in small metropolitan communities. The partial results shown in Table 6.1 clearly indicate that this was the case. Accordingly, the empirical results for the nonmetropolitan communities will be discussed first followed by a discussion of the results for metropolitan communities.

Empirical Results for Nonmetro Communities

Rail Service. The results in Table 6.1 indicate that rail service was an important location factor for only a few industries. However, the results were basically as hypothesized. That is, industrial location for five of the industries was positively associated with the availability of rail service. Intuitively, the results appear reasonable. Rail service was positively associated with food processing and wood products industries. Many food processing plants in the Northeast depend upon the delivery of raw materials by rail from the Midwest. The wood products industry also relies upon rail service for delivery of products to market areas. Thus, in general the availability of rail service in rural communities has a positive influence on the community's ability to attract industries.

Air Service. The information in Table 6.1 shows that industrial location for nine of the industries is positively associated with air service and that location in five of the industries is negatively associated with air service. Several of the industries for which industrial location was positively associated with air service are known to be characterized by large firms with multiple branch plants. Thus, the hypothesis that air service is important for branch plant location is supported by the empirical results. On the other hand, it is not at all clear why the location of certain industries should be negatively associated with air service. However, in general, it does appear that the availability of air service in rural communities is a positive influence on industrial location.

Distance to Limited-Access Highway. Industrial location for five industries was positively associated with proximity to limited-access highways and four industries were negatively associated with distance to these highways. Although these results are not as hypothesized, they are not unprecedented. Other studies have shown that interstate highway construction did not stimulate economic development in the counties in which the interstate highway was located, but stimulated economic development in counties adjacent to the interstate counties. Thus, the results here are consistent with the finding that proximity to a limited-access highway is not a dominant industrial location factor for rural communities.

Access to State or Federal Paved Roads. Access to paved roads has an impact on rural economic development similar to that of rail service. The coefficient on this variable was significant in only six of the models but it had a negative sign in five of the six models. The consistency of these results would suggest that the economic development of rural communities is impeded by the lack of access to paved roads.

Market Access. Perhaps the most surprising finding of the study was the dominant role played by agglomeration effects. The market variable was a significant location factor for thirty-five of the industries. For twenty-nine of the industries, industrial location was negatively associated with the market variable. These results clearly suggest that plants in these industries are tending to concentrate geographically.

Empirical Results for Small Metropolitan Communities

Rail Service. The information in Table 6.2 suggests that rail service is positively associated with industrial location in small metropolitan communities. Industrial location in nine of the industries was positively associated with the availability of rail service. Again, however, industrial location in four of the industries was negatively associated with the availability of rail service. The industries for which industrial location was positively associated with availability of rail service are generally known to be heavy users of rail freight. For example, meat packing plants and ready-mix concrete operations rely heavily on rail service to deliver their inputs. Large furniture items such as desks and large television sets are frequently shipped by rail. Thus, the findings suggest that rail service is in general a positive influence on economic development in small metropolitan communities.

Air Service. The results shown in Table 6.2 concerning the role of air service on the location of industry are ambiguous. Industrial location in eleven of the industries was positively associated with air service and ten of the industries show a negative association. It may be that most small metropolitan communities have airport facilities even if they do not have scheduled airline service. If so, corporate flights can be made to most of the small metro communities even though there is no scheduled air service. In any case, the results do not suggest a strong association between airline service and the economic development of small metropolitan communities.

Distance to Limited-Access Highways. Apparently limited-access highways are more important to the economic development of small metropolitan communities than was the case for nonmetropolitan communities. Industrial location in six of the industries was negatively associated with distance to limited-access highways, and only one was positively associated with access to these highways. Thus, it appears that proximity to these limited-access highways is a positive influence on the location of industries in small metropolitan communities.

Distance to State or Federal Paved Roads. Essentially all of the small metropolitan communities were no more than two miles from a state or federal paved road. Thus, the variable had no discriminating power and was removed from the model.

Market Access. As was the case with nonmetropolitan communities, agglomeration economies appear to play a very important role in the

Table 6.2 Summary of Regression Results for Small Metropolitan Communities*

Industry	Railroads	Airlines	Distance to 4-Lane Highway	Distance to 2-Lane Highway	Market
Meat Packing Plants	P				N
Poultry and Dairy Processing		N			N
Fish and Canned Specialities					
Grain and Seed Processing		N			
Miscellaneous Foods					
Tobacco		P			
Broadwoven Fabric					N
Narrow Fabric	P				
Miscellaneous Textiles					N
Fabricated Textile Products	P				
Logging					
Sawmills					P
Hardwood Flooring					
Specialized Sawmills			P		
Wood Furniture		N			
Wood Veneer and Containers		P			N
Miscellaneous Wood Products	P	N			N
Metal Household Furniture		P			N
Metal Office Furniture					N
Paper Mills					
Paper Containers					
Newspaper Publishing					N
Periodical Publishing					
Book Publishing					
Binding and Card Printing					N
Commercial Printing					N
Agricultural and Industrial Chemicals			N		

Table 6.2 *continued*

Industry	Railroads	Airlines	Distance to 4-Lane Highway	Distance to 2-Lane Highway	Market
Plastics					N
Drugs	N				P
Refined Petroleum	P				
Tires	P				N
Leather Products		P			N
Glass and Glassware		N			N
Stone and Clay Products					
Concrete Block and Brick					
Other Concrete Products					
Ready Mix Concrete	P				N
Gray Iron Foundries					
Lead Smelting					
Zinc Smelting					N
Aluminum Foundries					
Metal Bolts and Wire					N
Nonferrous Smelting		P			
Copper Wire		P			
Cutlery and Hand Tools		P			
Heating and Plumbing Fixtures		P			

Table 6.2 *continued*

Industry	Railroads	Airlines	Distance to 4-Lane Highway	Distance to 2-Lane Highway	Market
Structural Metal	N				N
Coating and Engraving			N		N
Miscellaneous Metal Products					N
Engines					N
Mobile Homes and Campers		P	N		
Construction Equipment	P				N
Machine Tools and Dies		P			N
Special Industrial Equipment		P			N
General Industrial Equipment		N			N
Service Machines		N	N		N
Radio, TV, Telephones	P	N			
Household Appliances	N	N			N
Electronic Components		N			P
Motor Vehicles					N
Measuring Instruments	N				
Jewelry and Musical Instruments		N			N
Burial Caskets		N			
Sporting Goods		P			
Advertising Signs			N		
Miscellaneous Manufacturing			N		
Apparel					

*"P" indicates a positive coefficient that was significantly different from zero at the 10% level. "N" indicates a significant negative coefficient.

location of industry in small metropolitan communities. The market variable was significant in the regression models for thirty of the industries. In twenty-seven of those industries, the location of plants was negatively associated with the market variable. Again, this figure indicates a strong tendency for plants to concentrate in space rather than disperse and control their individual market areas.

Summary of Empirical Findings

In general, rail service consistently had a positive influence on industrial location in both nonmetropolitan and small metropolitan communities. As would be expected, industries that have either bulky inputs or outputs tended to be most influenced by the availability of rail service.

The availability of air service appears to be more important in nonmetropolitan communities than it was in small metropolitan communities. Again, it may be that the major impact of air service on industrial location is to provide corporate executives with access to branch plants. Thus, a variable that measures access to airports would be preferable to the air service variable used in this study.

Proximity to limited-access highways was not an important location factor for nonmetropolitan communities, but it did exhibit a consistent pattern of being positively associated with industrial location in small metropolitan communities. Conversely, access to paved roads is consistently associated with industrial location in nonmetropolitan communities but not small metropolitan communities.

Agglomeration economies play an important role in the location of many industries in both nonmetropolitan and metropolitan communities. The precise reason for the regional concentration on certain industries is unclear; however, the results of the study suggest the need for additional study of the role of agglomeration economics on the location of industry in rural communities.

Policy Implications

The policy implications that follow from these results are reasonably straightforward. Communities seeking to attract new industries should make whatever efforts are possible to maintain rail service. In some instances, communities have been successful in restoring rail service that had been discontinued. Nonmetropolitan communities may consider the feasibility of establishing regional air service. In many instances, county governments have provided the financial assistance and organizational skills required to construct and operate airports. Nonmetropolitan communities should devote some of their efforts to improving access roads. A quality highway providing the rural community with access to the interstate system has a positive influence on industrial location in nonmetropolitan communities.

In general, the concept of agglomeration economies is not well defined; however, the results of this study would certainly imply that the industrial recruitment efforts in both small metropolitan and nonmetropolitan communities should focus on industries that are doing well in the region. Almost none of the industries considered in this study showed any indication of being market oriented.

In essence, the results of this study support the conventional wisdom that improving transportation services tends to have a positive influence on the community's ability to attract new industry. Also, the conventional approach of focusing industrial recruitment programs on industries that are locating in the general area has merit.

References

Goode, Frank. 1986. "The Efficacy of More Refined Demand Variables." *Growth and Change* 17 (1): 66–75.

Greenhut, M. L. 1956. *Plant Location in Theory and Practice.* Chapel Hill: The University of North Carolina Press.

Hastings, Steven E., and Frank M. Goode. 1982. "An Input Supply Approach: Improved Measures of Industrial Location Factors." *Growth and Change* 13 (0): 25–31.

Losch, August. 1954. *The Economics of Location.* New Haven: Yale University Press.

Weber, Alfred. 1929. *Theory of the Location of Industries.* Chicago: University of Chicago Press.

Appendix: Variables Included in Regression Models

Proportion of the population that is nonwhite
Proportion of year-round houses with public sewer
Proportion of the population with 16 or more years employment in manufacturing
Proportion of the population living in same county as in 1975 for 5 or more years
Proportion of the population less than 18 yrs old

Proportion of the population 25 years or older with college degree

Proportion of the population that is urban

Proportion of the population 65 or more years old

Male labor force participation rate (civilian)

Female labor force participation rate (civilian)

Proportion of year-round houses that are vacant

Males 16 or older working 27 or more weeks in 1979 as proportion of males who worked in 1979

Females 16 or older working 27 or more weeks in 1979 as proportion of females who worked in 1979

Community population

Per capita income of persons

Number of railroads serving community

Number of airlines serving community

Number of hospital beds

Distance to interstate highway

Distance to primary road

One if in New England; 0 otherwise

One if in Mid-Atlantic; 0 otherwise

Proportion of the population that is in college

Distance to nearest SMSA

Community's state tax per capita

Local and county tax per capita

Potential net input availability (PNIA) for Forestry

PNIA for Energy exploration

PNIA for Iron Mining

PNIA for Petroleum Drilling

PNIA for Petroleum Refining

PNIA for Electricity and Gas Utilities

7

Effective Transportation Management at the Firm Level

James Beierlein

The need for firms to better manage their own transportation activities is often overlooked. A poorly managed transportation operation can offset the cost advantages offered by a rural location, greatly reduce a firm's profits, and diminish its competitiveness in distant markets.

This chapter will outline some of the basic steps a firm must take to ensure the efficient operation of its transportation system. This process must begin with the top managers of the firm adopting the proper perspective toward the market, transportation, and the role that transportation can play in the overall success of the firm. Once these steps have been taken, it is necessary to apply the same management procedures used in other areas of the business to transportation in order to carry out the proper planning, organizing, controlling, and directing of the transportation function. If it is run effectively, transportation can be a major contributor to the success of the firm.

Developing the Proper Perspective Toward the Market

Many firms take what is called a *production approach* toward the market where the production process is the central activity of the firm. Under the production approach the firm first decides what to produce and then tries to sell it. When this approach is employed, all other activities, including transportation, are seen as extensions of the production process.

The production approach to the market works best in markets where demand for the product is significantly greater than the available supply. The managers of the firm usually find themselves concentrating on how to produce the most product for the lowest cost, which often leads to transportation being thought of as the part of the production process that handles the physical movement of items in and out of the plant. Thus, the proper management objective is the minimization of total transportation costs.

The production approach to the market has served this country well for many years, particularly in the years after World War II when greater technical efficiency in manufacturing permitted the rapid satisfaction of consumers' seemingly endless demand for goods and services. Eventually, however, the supply of most products exceeded the demand and changed the nature of the market for most products. Now consumers could choose the goods they wanted from a number of competing producers. Consumers then began to buy only those products that best fit their particular needs and no longer had to settle for just what they could find. Many firms have adopted this more consumer-need oriented approach to the market. This new approach is referred to as the market approach.

Under the *market approach* there is a significant change in the way the firm views the market. Planning begins with an examination of consumer needs and then seeks to develop products that can be profitably produced to meet those needs. The market approach is almost exactly opposite to the production approach because the consumer need is identified first, and then the product is produced to fill it.

In this new market situation, the profitability of a firm rests more with its ability to successfully satisfy consumer needs than on its ability to be an efficient producer. Thus, the long run success of the firm requires that satisfaction of consumer needs be at the center of all the firm's actions.

Developing the Business Plan

A critical ingredient in the success of many firms is the presence of a sound business plan. The top managers of the firm explain in writing exactly how they are going to make their business a success. The business plan should have sections that address each of the four basic functions of management: planning, organizing, controlling, and directing.

Planning

The first step in developing a sound business plan is to define as precisely as possible the firm's purpose and objectives. The *purpose* defines what consumer needs the firm is going to fill. The *objective* tells how the firm is going to fill those consumer needs better, faster, cheaper, and more completely than any of its competitors. The objective is what gives the firm its competitive edge in the marketplace and causes consumers to buy from this firm rather than from someone else.

In the definition of its purpose and objectives the firm must staunchly establish the concept that the profitable satisfaction of consumer needs is the central purpose of the firm. In addition, once these have been clearly defined, they must be pursued publicly, relentlessly, and enthusiastically so that all employees and consumers know what they are and can accept the firm's motives as genuine and worthwhile.

Organizing

Once the planning stage has been completed, top management must develop an organizational structure that will permit the firm to efficiently reach the goals set in planning. This step normally requires careful work to ensure that the organization is able to carry out its intentions on schedule.

Without continuous and vigorous leadership in this area firms find themselves focusing more on satisfying the needs of their employees and owners than on meeting the needs of their customers. This focus often leads to the production of products that are either easy to make or technically interesting to the firm rather than those that fill a consumer need. Successful firms resist this tendency. They have a strong and continuing external focus to their business that helps keep them constantly aware of changes in consumer needs and of more profitable ways to meet them.

From this definition of the firm's purpose and objectives, the owners should be able to identify its critical tasks. *Critical tasks* are those tasks that must be done well for the firm to accomplish its purpose or, if done poorly, will cause the firm to fail. Once the critical tasks have been identified, an organizational structure needs to be designed to see that these critical tasks are allowed to function smoothly and that they are not subordinated to any other activities within the firm. Critical tasks must be given priority since they are the ones that give the firm its competitive edge in the marketplace.

The success of many firms in rural areas is heavily dependent upon the ability to produce *and* ship products to distant markets at a cost below that of competitors. For this reason transportation is a critical task to these firms. As such it should be given priority in the firm's organizational structure, since if it does not operate effectively it can more than wipe out whatever production cost savings that might come from operating in a rural area and may cause the firm to fail. Thus, the proper functioning of the firm's transportation system is critical to the success of a rurally located business that sells to distant markets.

Controlling

Once the plans and organizational structure are established, top management must develop the controls and feedback mechanisms necessary to measure the firm's progress toward the purpose and the objectives established in planning. It is at this stage that the forms and other measures of individual, department, and company performance are devised.

In terms of the management of transportation activities, controlling means developing procedures to establish transportation cost standards and ways to monitor them so they remain within the limits prescribed in its business plan. These limits should be seen as guidelines rather than as a rigid set of rules, since the overriding concern is still the profitable satisfaction of consumer needs. There may be times when an increase in overall profits may require an increase in physical distribution costs. For example, the use of air freight to give a customer faster delivery may increase transportation cost, but if it leads to capturing a large long-term contract with a high profit margin, it may help the firm accomplish its overall profit objective.

The first step in the controlling process is to institute a sound recordkeeping system so the firm will know what its transportation costs are and whether it is performing as expected. Such information is vital to a firm if it is to survive and reach its corporate objectives.

Directing

This final component of the business plan is where all the plans, organizational structure, and control mechanisms are synthesized to make an actual, successful operating business. When this procedure is followed, the result should be a firm that has as its central purpose the profitable satisfaction of consumer needs, a firm in which everyone shares a common vision of what the firm is to do and how it is to accomplish it. When these tasks are completed, the managers of the firm can turn their attention to developing the proper marketing mix of *product*, *price*, *place*, and *promotion* that will permit it to successfully accomplish its purpose and objectives.

Developing a Successful Marketing Mix

Transportation management plays an important role in the overall success of any firm. Transportation is part of the place portion of each product's marketing mix. The place portion of the marketing mix includes all those activities that ensure that the right product, carrying the right price, given the right promotion is in the right place so that consumers can conveniently acquire it.

The successful accomplishment of the place portion of the marketing mix requires the establishment of two separate systems. First, a strong system of middlemen must be established who will efficiently overcome the conflicting needs of producers and consumers, and who will give the firm's products a high level of attention. Second, a strong physical distribution network must be established that can move the firm's products quickly and efficiently to the consumer.

For the physical distribution system to be of value to the firm in developing a successful marketing mix for a product, the system must be viewed from a marketing perspective and not as an extension of the production process. It is the consumers' view of the situation that affects the demand for the product. Consumers wish to know all about the product, what its final price is, and where they can obtain it. They weigh all of these factors in deciding whether or not to purchase the product. All of these factors must be appealing to the consumer for the sale to take place. Thus, the physical distribution system must be an integral part of the place portion of each product's marketing mix.

The proper objective for the firm with respect to place is to determine the most convenient placement of the product for the consumer that maximizes the profits of the firm. Therefore, physical distribution must be under the control of the marketing department and include control of inventory levels, selection of transportation modes (e.g., rail versus truck versus ship), and location of plants, warehouses, and retail stores. Each plays a part in the overall physical and technical efficiency of the firm and its ability to profitably satisfy the needs of consumers. Such matters must be addressed as part of the firm's overall business plan and each product's marketing mix. Merely minimizing physical distribution costs may not be sufficient if it does not lead to higher consumer satisfaction and higher overall profits for the firm.

Managing the Physical Distribution System

The next step in improving the management of the physical distribution system is to develop a sound recordkeeping system that covers all of the firm's transportation activities. The management of transportation system can be separated into two parts. The first part is an analysis of the flow of materials in and products out of the plant. The second part is control of transportation costs for company-owned vehicles.

Analysis of Material and Product Flows

The first step in better managing the physical distribution system is an analysis of the flow of materials in and products out of the plant. The goal of this effort is to determine if any patterns exist in these flows and if they could be arranged more efficiently (e.g., combine loads, use lower cost shippers, and so forth). This type of analysis can also include the use of computerized vehicle routing and scheduling. Such analysis normally focuses on answering the following six questions:

What is moved in or out of the plant?

When or how often is it moved?

Where does it come from or where does it go?

How much is moved?

How is it moved?

What does it cost to move it?

Analysis of the answers to these six questions can greatly assist a firm in seeing and understanding the transportation aspect of its business. When these data are combined with detailed sales records, it should be possible to place the product in all the right places and at all the right times. The important distinction is that consumer preferences determine the placement and timing of deliveries, not the production manager. Goods are made available for sale when consumers are ready to buy, not when producers feel like offering them. The distinction is important and can often be the difference between economic survival and failure.

Vehicle Use and Cost Records

The second part of the analysis is performed when the firm owns or leases vehicles and has the opportunity to establish detailed records of vehicle use and cost. This information can be valuable in establishing proper preventative maintenance schedules for company-owned vehicles. Using low-cost computer or simple forms, it is possible to quickly determine the basic elements of the cost of transportation for the firm (e.g., cost per mile by type of vehicle, repair cost per vehicle, and so forth).

Rapid feedback to the firm and drivers can help the firm identify the most efficient or reckless drivers in the fleet, which vehicles are the most efficient to operate, and so forth. Armed with this type of data, the transportation manager has a better chance of operating his fleet in the most efficient manner possible. The effective management of the firm's transportation function can be instrumental in helping it accomplish its corporate objectives and ensure its financial survival.

Use of Computerized Vehicle Routing

Advances in computer technology have made it possible for individual firms to use computerized vehicle routing. One of the more successful and most utilized programs in this area is ROUTE, offered by Milton Hallberg at The Pennsylvania State University. If a firm has a good recordkeeping system of vehicle costs and customer demands, it is possible to quickly schedule deliveries and route vehicles to a large number of customers with a savings in route miles of 10 to 30 percent.

This type of computer-generated vehicle routing would be useful for any firm that operates a single truck or a fleet of vehicles from a single warehouse or manufacturing plant. For the system to function, the company must know: the location of each customer, the approximate time needed to make a delivery at each stop, what types of vehicles can service each stop, the cost of operating each type of delivery vehicle used by the firm, and the number of delivery vehicles available by type (e.g., van versus tractor trailer, and so forth).

While computerized vehicle routing can lead to significant savings, the real value of the computerized routing system lies in its ability to analyze various business options related to transportation. For example, it was possible to determine answers to the following types of questions:

How much extra does it cost the firm to meet all the delivery time restrictions imposed upon it by its customers?

Is it better to pay overtime or to place additional vehicles on the delivery routes?

What is the additional cost of adding one more customer to the delivery route?

The use of computerized vehicle routing is now within the grasp of most businesses. It provides its users with a quick and easy way to more efficiently operate their transportation systems.

Use of Backhauls

Recent changes in trucking regulations have increased the opportunities to employ backhauling. Backhauling involves locating and carrying a load in a vehicle that would otherwise be running empty. A normal situation is for a truck to carry a load to a destination and then return empty to the plant. Unfortunately, it costs the firm almost as much to operate that vehicle empty as full, and there are significant transportation revenues that can be obtained from locating a load to carry back to the plant. Once again a computer program has been developed to perform an economic analysis of the feasibility of such actions.

The essence of the program is to determine if the revenues (or avoided costs) of picking up the backhaul load exceed the additional costs of hauling that load. If they do, the excess revenue can be applied to reduce the costs of making the original delivery, thereby lowering the firm's overall transportation costs. Backhauling provides a firm with a way to reduce the estimated 40 percent of all truck mileage each year that is covered without a paying load. Some analysts feel that a firm can expect to backhaul between 10 and 25 percent of the total tonnage carried each year.

In addition to these direct benefits, there are at least two indirect benefits from backhauling. First, the firm's use of its own drivers and vehicles for pick-ups saves its suppliers the cost of transportation. Second, the firm gains greater control over the timing of the receipt of inputs and shipment of products, which can lead to greater inventory savings and further add to the firm's profits.

Managing Fleet Costs

There are a variety of methods ranging from very simple to very complex that can be employed in managing fleet costs. In practice, the simplest methods are often the best.

One of the simplest procedures is to establish a log for each vehicle in which all the repairs and maintenance are recorded along with the date, mileage, and cost of each item. These data form the nucleus of a fleet cost program.

In addition to these data, a daily log of vehicle operating expenses should be kept. This log would record beginning and ending mileage each day, the name of the drivers, routes driven, fuel purchases, and all other direct expenses associated with the vehicle.

The data in these two logs gives the transportation manager all the information he needs to determine when to schedule vehicles for preventive maintenance items such as coolant replacement, oil changes, lubrications, and so forth using the manufacturer's recommended service internals. It can also help him determine which vehicles are the most efficient to operate, which drivers are the most expensive to have operating the firm's vehicles, when a vehicle should be replaced, or whether it is better to lease vehicles rather than own them. If the firm operates a large fleet, these records can also be adapted to determine that servicing facilities are operating efficiently and whether the number of breakdowns is at a minimum.

The management of the transportation function in a firm requires the same level of attention and skill that is devoted to any other area of the business. These lessons are particularly important to firms in rural areas where poor management of the transportation activity can exceed any cost advantage a rural location offers. The procedures highlighted here are ones that firms needs to pursue more vigorously if they are to succeed.

Conclusions

The effective management of transportation in a firm in a rural area is a critical task. The profitable operation of firms in these areas depends heavily on the ability to efficiently receive the inputs and ship their markets to distant markets. However, for transportation to contribute to the accomplishment of the firm's overall profitability, transportation must be considered as part of the firm's overall marketing mix of product, price, place, and promotion developed for each product. For this reason transportation must be under the control of the marketing department and not the production department. This practice will ensure that its value as a marketing tool is fully utilized.

Once these steps have been established, the firm can begin to better manage this vital activity. These efforts can take two directions. First, the flow of products into and out of the firm can be analyzed in order to identify areas where greater efficiencies can be found. Such efforts can include the use of computerized vehicle routing and scheduling. However, managers must not be become so focused on minimizing the cost of transportation that they lose sight of its role as a marketing tool and its impact on overall corporate profits. Second, transportation management can also focus on the effective control of vehicle repairs and maintenance costs.

Regardless of what is done, it is important that firms in rural areas remember that transportation is a marketing tool and a critical task that the firm must perform well to keep its competitive edge in the market. Through better management of its transportation function a rural firm can retain this edge and flourish.

References

Beierlein, James G. 1981. "Estimating the Economic Feasibility of Backhauls in Food Distribution Using a Programmable Calculator," AERS #154, Department of Agricultural Economics and Rural Sociology, The Pennsylvania State University.

Hallberg, M. C., and J. G. Beierlein. 1983. "Multi-Stop Route Design and Distribution System Analysis for a Wholesale Food Distributing Firm." In *Planning and Decision in Agribusiness: Principles and Experiences*, edited by C. H. Hanf and G. Schieffer, 265–79. Elsevier Scientific Publishing Company.

Part IV

Transportation's Contribution
to
Rural Quality of Life

8

Passenger Transportation Problems in Rural Areas

Alice E. Kidder

Demand for Passenger Transportation in Rural Areas

Passenger transportation needs in rural areas are primarily met by private vehicles. During the day, parking lots near interstate interchanges fill with vehicles as carpools and vanpools are formed to travel long distances more efficiently.

The growth of private vehicle ownership has led to a decline in the service outreach of the privately owned public transportation suppliers: cutbacks in service by intercity bus operators, the decline of the taxis in rural areas, and the virtual disappearance of commuter trains in rural areas attest to the dominance of the automotive age.

As women have increasingly entered the labor market in the last twenty years, the number of families owning two or more cars has risen. Rural areas are growing in population and jobs, and for those rural areas that offer economic opportunities, there is considerable personal mobility: company-based carpooling and vanpooling programs, multiple-car families, and a good used car market.

Nevertheless, despite these hopeful signs, there are still many important segments of the rural population that need other forms of transportation and for whom mobility is an important goal as yet not achieved. These groups include:

- the frail elderly;
- youth below the driving age;

- the physically challenged;

- persons without cars or other vehicles because of low income;

- persons who during the day have no access to a vehicle (housewives in one-car families; persons whose cars are not functioning);

- persons who do not have a valid driver's license;

- persons who may have access to a car but who fear to drive or who prefer not to drive long distances;

- persons whose mental capacities do not match driving requirements; and

- persons in families where the number of individuals with travel demands exceeds the number of vehicles available.

The demand for rural passenger transportation comes less from the general public and more from special submarkets such as those listed above. The demand for mobility in rural areas is therefore distinct from the urban public transportation in a number of important ways. First, the demand is less efficiently located. Rather than living along a few corridors with high levels of repeated demands, rural residents may be scattered over a wide area, with very low density of population. Some rural areas, such as those along a narrow valley in Appalachia, may lend themselves to fixed route, fixed schedule service; however, most areas require a demand-responsive service. The transit dependent are less likely to be predominantly low-income and more likely to have physical limitations that require a higher level of personal attention in solving their mobility problems. The demand tends to be sporadic since trips are not repeated as often as in urban areas. In urban areas an important portion of the transit demand comes from the repetitive journey to work. In rural areas more people use their own or other cars to get to work, and the public transportation needs are more for shopping, appointments, and recreation. Finally, the travel demands are organization-related. Trips are more likely to be made for a single trip purpose such as attending a place of worship, visiting a relative, seeing a physician, getting a meal at a congregate site, or attending college, for example. In urban areas, the CBD attracts riders to public transit where multiple trip purposes are simultaneously accomplished. Therefore, it is less easy in urban areas to identify the origin and destination links in the public transportation chain; public support for urban transit comes from a realization that the consolidation of trip purposes is cost-effective, energy-saving, and congestive-relieving. By comparison the demand for rural transportation is characterized by infrequency of demand; high cost per-person-trip which itself is an outgrowth of lack of consolidation; trips with longer mileage; and longer empty fronthauls or backhauls. There is some evidence that the numbers of trips per person is lower in rural areas (Burkhardt and Millar 1976).

The remoteness of some rural areas from urban centers raises the cost of providing for the mobility needs of those who are low income, who may need to reach key offices, such as employment agencies, employers, welfare offices, housing assistance, health centers, and other human service programs. The dispersion of the population hampers the effective outreach of many federal and state programs such as Head Start, nutrition programs for the elderly, private industry council employment training programs, and other national services. Students without cars may find difficulties in regular attendance at technical institutes, community colleges, or local four-year colleges. The response of the agencies and organizations is frequently the arrangement for private systems based out of the organization. The proliferation of vehicles standing idle because they are used not in the cooperation *among* organizations but rather for narrow, private purposes constitutes a waste of resources potentially available to provide needed services in rural areas.

Supply of Rural Passenger Transportation Service

The nature of the demand for rural transportation is such that it cannot, for the most part, be met with conventional, fixed-route, fixed-schedule service common to urban transportation. High costs require that special funding be available to defray the higher expenses of low-density travel demand. Rural areas may not have the economic base to support the higher cost out of public funds. Therefore, those privately provided services that do survive are those that cater to a particular submarket such as taxi service to rural areas adjacent to shopping centers, intercity transportation on rural areas that serve as corridors between two or more major cities, or charter service to cater to special groups, such as out-of-town trips for the elderly.

Some rural areas have succeeded in developing a public funding for augmented passenger mobility. Early demonstration projects have sometimes used Section 18 funding to maintain a public transportation. Some state-supported programs serve rural areas across the board. For example, in Missouri, OATS, and in Delaware, DART, have provided a high level of service to rural areas (Wallin and Kidder 1986).

There are widely varied funding sources, many based upon human service agency budgets that are not specifically earmarked for transportation but that can be used for this purpose if the planning and budget decisions are taken in this direction. (See the appendix for a list of sources.) Such a complicated chain of decision making that has to lock in place funds to support a transportation program year after year is very difficult to build and sustain. Turfism or competition among human service agencies often prevents coordination of human service agency transportation. To combat these inefficiencies in the provision of transportation some states, Wisconsin and Florida for example, have mandated coordination, and some states have facilitated that process by reviewing any human service agency budget line item for transportation to see whether the service might be provided by the regional transit program. North Carolina is a good example of the latter approach.

Other publicly funded transportation programs for rural areas grow out of a regional transportation authority. Franklin County in Massachusetts has evolved such a program from its state allocation for public transportation. Statewide rural programs, such as OATS in Missouri, have taken money from many public sources to build a broad network for mobility in rural areas. The problem with reliance upon the regional transit authority is that most are based in larger cities and see rural transportation service largely as a feeder line into the CBD. By contrast rural residents, particularly the transit-dependent ones, go only very occasionally to the CBD and have more local mobility needs to get to a dentist's office, or to a local hospital, to a meal site, or to a place of worship.

To summarize the most typical of rural situations, supply of transportation services is fragmented and uncoordinated. The private sector for-profit operators have withdrawn most service, except for occasional highpriced taxi rides, which must be called from a nearby town. Many rural areas have lost all train and intercity bus service. A large amount of public money is in fact being spent to provide selected human service agency clients in some rural areas with a high level of service (Kidder 1978). But these services are dependent upon unpredictable levels of annual funding out of human service agency budgets. Faced with the twin dilemmas of little cash support and the presence of many transportation needs, volunteer groups have gathered to provide service with their personal vehicles. This kind of informal ride-sharing is most successful in rural communities that have community awareness of needs. In many of today's rural communities, the two or three wage-earner family leaves few adults except younger retirees available to provide this service. Some organizations such as Green Thumb, FISH, Voluntary Action Centers, and RSVP have local branches from which volunteers can be drawn.

Rural areas generally have much lower levels of service and consequently more unmet needs for essential mobility than do their urban counterparts, where demand-responsive systems operate to provide life-equipped vans under the auspices of the local transit authority or as a human service outreach. To cope with these problems, agencies typically ration service by strict definitions of eligibility, limitations on trip purposes, and requirements for twenty-four or forty-eight hour advance notice. The next section describes some successful programs and ways to benefit from their local application.

Roles of the Government: Federal, State, and Local

Federal Assistance

Sections 16(b)(2) and 18 of the Surface Transportation Association Act offer important sources of financial assistance to rural areas. The first source provides states with money on a matching basis to purchase vehicles on behalf of nonprofit institutions, such as human service agencies. Some states, like Massachusetts, have instituted a volume purchase plan, with the benefits of dealer discounts adding an important element in cost reduction. The Section 18 funds provide a level of support for operating or capital costs of generalized public transportation service in nonurbanized areas.

Both Sections 16 and 18 are administered by the Urban Mass Transportation Administration (UMTA) within the U.S. Department of Transportation. UMTA has ten regional offices throughout the country. Funds are formula allocated to each of the states, where the state department of transportation puts together a proposal to spend the funds. These state agencies in turn typically have a proposal period in which they will receive proposals from local groups, such as councils on aging, United Way agencies, or other nonprofit organizations. Some states reserve the use of Section 18 funds to the regional transportation authorities.[1]

Section 18 funds are helpful in sustaining a limited number of rural passenger transportation programs, but the size of each state's allotment is small, on the average of $2–3 million annually, so that not all rural areas of a state can be equally well served. In some cases the states ration the limited allocation by requiring extension plans or by favoring fixed route systems. In other cases the program is used to finance paratransit or brokerage programs for some of the rural areas. In still other cases a matching funds program will support a fraction of locally funded transit.

Section 16(b)(2) offers funds to match funds used to purchase vehicles for human service and related nonprofit organizations. The federal share of assistance is 80 percent. This money can be used to purchase not only vehicles but also related items such as radio dispatching equipment. Many rural areas have multiple agencies that have received such assistance: councils on aging, mental health centers, vocational rehabilitation programs, private industry councils, and similar programs that need to offer pickup and dropoff services to participants.

Only about one-third of federal financial support for rural public transportation comes from U.S.DOT Urban Mass Transportation sources. Though less visible, a more important funding mechanism comes from the score or more of human service agency operating budgets. To support client mobility, drivers are hired out of personnel budgets, gasoline is purchased from supply line items, and maintenance of vehicles comes out of overhead allotments. Much of the federal aid is combined with state and local funds and cannot easily be rounded up to build a coordinated network of service. Efficiency minded leadership is necessary to identify and coordinate the use of these different program sources. For information on how to accomplish these efficiencies and improved service, workshops are available, and the U.S.DOT Office of Technology Sharing offers free publications. The U.S.DOT also finances research and a series of universities offer technical assistance. By 1988 there will be one university in each federal region with responsibility for transportation research and outreach. In addition to financial assistance, the federal government provides training opportunities and technical assistance to key personnel in rural areas. For information on current program availability, call the U.S.DOT Urban Mass Transportation Administration regional office.

State Assistance

The states vary considerably in their approach to rural transportation. Some states, like Delaware, Maryland, and New Jersey have experimented with fixing responsibility for rural transit operations on the state administration. Other states do not differentiate between urban and rural transportation, providing funds to both areas by formulas that typically reflect population, matching local funds, or other criteria that reduce the rural share.

A number of states try to regulate the proliferation of individual rural transportation programs with an eye to creating a regional network. North Carolina, for example, does not permit an individual human service agency to apply for a 16(b)(2) vehicle unless the regional transit program has certified it is unable to give the service requested. States such as Minnesota have set up a monitoring program to chart the productivity statistics of rural as well as urban systems, offering some technical assistance to systems intent on improving. Many states supplement federal assistance with additional state funds to cover planning, capital, and operating costs of rural programs.

Many states also regulate entry and exit of private, for-profit common carrier service and may have elements of price (rate) regulation and safety regulation as well. Increasingly, however, the move to deregulate has gained momentum. Intercity bus companies have used their new option to drop uneconomic service, particularly in rural areas. Rural residents can still frequently file complaints about service inadequacy with motor carrier bureaus in the state capital.

State governments have close association with many substate entities:

sharing revenue with counties, creating regional transit authorities, and planning jointly with regional planning agencies. The substate level is frequently charged with responsibility for needs assessments, alternatives analysis, and long-range planning. The rural (or exurban) perspective can shape the future transportation planning process at this level, if citizens appear at public hearings on long-range transportation plans. States, for example, allow regional control over funding for elder programs through Area Agencies on Aging. Their discretionary budgets can support some aspects of rural transportation development if the local planning process identifies this issue as an important need. The regional office will publicize the time and place at which public hearings on goal setting occur.

Under the New Federalism, state governments are given a prominent role in control over federal funds spent within the state. The governor's office should be contacted to see what funds for rural transportation are in the budget being proposed to the state legislature.

Local Assistance

The local government for rural areas may consist of many small jurisdictions, such as towns in New England, or it may consist of a countywide government or even a metropolitan planning region of which the rural area is a part. Local government is the place to begin when seeking for assistance in developing mobility programs for rural areas. Some counties have voted funds to support local systems. Some, as in New York state, are required to match state and federal funds. Counties frequently derive their revenues from state appropriations. Other forms of government depend upon property tax revenue. Both sources are hard pressed to cover current programs, and it may be difficult to secure the local aid for transportation programs.

As an alternative, some local government agencies have set up brokerage systems to make the fund stretch farther. Others have turned to in-kind services (the donation of vehicle maintenance services or free parking or office space) as a way of making the local contribution.

Local governments can provide the initiative for interagency agreements, for drafting new proposals for service, and for needs assessments. Unfortunately, the supply of available professionals to begin such programs is not always available in rural areas. The urban planners frequently are unaware of local rural needs and, without the assistance of knowledgeable local officials funding opportunities, can be overlooked. Many states are offering free programs of technical assistance to overcome these problems, and this area of education is important for cooperative extension outreach.

Opportunities for Educators and Technical Assistance Providers to Overcome Problems Identified

Organization of the Supply Side Through Brokerage

If one organization locally can take the lead in identifying available vehicles, drivers (volunteer or paid), maintenance facilities, and communications needed to perform transportation services, then other agencies can contribute by relinquishing control over vehicles and substituting fees for client services. The transportation broker then assembles the information about available services (human service agency programs, taxis, carpools, charter bus operations, public transit scheduled services, and so forth) and either consolidates the program into a working whole, as for example OATS in Missouri, or conveys the information about multiple programs to interested parties.

The brokerage program involves arranging for the payments between agencies for services rendered, prioritizing use of the available vehicles consistent with regulatory requirements, and providing information to the public. The brokerage program should accomplish many goals at once: eliminating duplication of trips, increasing the number of persons per vehicle, promoting volume purchases at discounts, and increasing the available consumer information.

The broker will find the myriad sources of demand in housing projects for the elderly, nursing homes, hospital complexes, community and four-year colleges, medical offices and health maintenance organizations, shopping centers, and recreational facilities. Frail elderly living alone are also in need of transport. Meals on Wheels, which takes food *to* the elderly, mobile libraries, and home health aides all need transportation to the elderly, as well. Sometimes these functions can be combined. Head State programs, senior centers, daycare projects, employment and training programs, and nutrition sites all need transportation for participants. The broker must identify these sources of support which can cover the operating expenses of the system. Some government documents are available to help.[2] Bringing together the supply of services, both public and private, and offering them to the general public or selected human service clients is not an easy task. It requires the support of one or more organizations offering the overhead necessary to organize. The tasks involved in organization include:

- inventorying available services identifying how they ration available supply of transportation facilities;

- identifying sources of payment such as federal and state subsidies, human service agency fees for transportation of clients, fares, donations by civic groups, and sources of in-kind contributions;

- developing a cost-effective method to perform the critical functions: telephone requests, scheduling and routing of vehicles, maintenance of vehicles; and

- generating local support for the continuation of public funding to this organization.

Since these tasks require a good knowledge of local institutions, leadership to perform these tasks must develop or emerge locally. Identification of and training of potential leaders is a critical challenge.

Empowering the Broker

The organizational costs are the most severe restrictions on growth. Once the organization has been achieved, the costs of continuing can be borne by the combination of funding and by assessment of fares.

What are the attributes of rural systems which have been successful in establishing a brokerage operation? First, the broker has the authority to set priorities on service. Unless agencies are willing to trust the broker to assign priorities in the case of conflicts, the long-term future of the program is in doubt. Funding from some of the sources less well served is withdrawn, and the shrinking of operating funds still further diminishes the opportunities to give service. Second, the broker has access to backup resources. As funding waxes and wanes from some constituent organizations, the broker must have access to alternatives, such as locally voted town appropriations. Third, the broker is meeting critical needs. Competition for public support is keen, particularly in rural areas where service delivery tends to be more costly than in urban areas. Sporadic use of equipment, frivolous trips, or neglect of critical needs will bring down a service in the eyes of the public.

Financing Rural Public Transportation Brokerage

One or more local organizations must commit the initial resources to staff a position where one person is responsible for organizing the brokerage system. There are many ways of accomplishing this task. The state department of transportation could fund a program of demonstrations, with the monies used to pay the organizing staff for a limited period of time. This approach has been tried in Massachusetts with some success. One lead human service agency or consortium of agencies could fund a staff position or earmark an existing staff position for the brokerage organizer. Kentucky has used the approach by designating one agency per area to play this role. It has set up its funding of the 16(b)(2) program to channel most funds through a lead agency designated by the governor. Local initiatives supported by Easter Seals, the United Way, or other private funding organizations can develop the brokerage organization by declaring this a funding campaign priority. A local level of government, such as a county or township, may decide to sponsor such an organization, devoting its resources to paying for a coordinator.

Once the initial overhead costs of pulling together the brokerage organization have been met, then the funding of rural public transportation becomes a matter of identifying who among the users has support either from their own funds, or from human service agency budgets. The broker can add up the trips per month and develop a billing procedure which draws funds from a variety of sources. It is important to build up a reserve to cover expenses when public agencies are in the down phase of a funding cycle.

Budgeting and Managing a Local Transportation Program

The budgeting process needs careful attention. Organizations that take on the responsibility of actual service provision must protect against rising costs, diminishing service quality, and inadequate service levels. Even if the service is given by a taxi company or other for-profit group, budgeting realistically is important to protect against future loss of service through bankruptcy.

Table 8.1 Planned expenditures for a
hypothetical rural system

	Expenditure
VEHICLE OPERATIONS	
Driver salary	$7,000
Dispatcher salary	1,000
Fringe benefits	4,070
Fuel and oil	3,400
Tubes and tires	820
Vehicle insurance	3,210
Vehicle depreciation	7,760
Vehicle license, registration, tax	400
Vehicle storage facility rental	1,000
Total	$28,660
MAINTENANCE	
Mechanic salary	$1,200
Mechanic aide salary	700
Fringe benefits	500
Materials and supplies	400
Telephone	350
Office rental	700
Utilities	250
Office equipment rental	200
Miscellaneous	150
Total	$4,450
TOTAL EXPENSE	$33,110

Note: Governmental regulations treat the issue of de-
preciation of capital or local share of capital costs in
various ways. These costs may or may not be required
of the local agency.
Source: Material prepared by S. Rosenblum.

Table 8.1 offers an example of the planned expenditures for a rural
transportation system. Since the scale of operations differs so widely, it
is impossible to give a typical budget. Studies have shown that costs per
client trip have ranged between one dollar and 15 dollars, depending
upon the severity of cost control, the degree of consolidation of trips,
and many other efficiency-related factors. Ways to control costs include: scheduling in advance to consolidate trips; operating on a route-
deviation but relatively repetitive pattern, so that van availability
becomes regularized; using volunteer drivers (Wallin 1986);[3] volume

purchasing of tires, gas, and vehicles; sharing space with other organizations; consistent use of preventive maintenance; shaping demand to be consistent with service through discounts for offpeak service; and negotiating for better insurance rates, or coming in under a local government policy. Increasing the pool of eligible users by developing charter services at attractive rates, for use at designated times, or by identifying new areas to which persons wish to travel may bring in more fares. However, if the goal of the program is to serve the mobility needs of those on restricted incomes, it is better to find revenue from other sources.

Identifying more sponsoring agencies can be of value, but only where the service can easily be expanded to handle the new requirements. It is tempting to add new service when a new organization requests it, but if this additional set of tasks strains relations with the founding organizations the public relations losses can be serious. Over time the organization providing service may coax out single or multiple vehicles which are underutilized by the other agencies, particularly when those agencies feel the pinch of high operating costs. Political accountability is the key. Since local areas vary tremendously in needs and service levels, it is important to understand the local political budgeting processes before attempting the costly organizational requirements of expanded rural mobility. The outstanding successes of some areas should serve as a model for those who want to improve mobility to rural residents.

Notes

1. Lo Dagerman, "Transportation Brokerage: Experiences from Bennington, Vermont" (1984), Paper prepared for Brandeis/Babson College Workshop on Passenger Transportation in Rural Massachusetts. Available from Office of Sponsored Research, Babson College, Babson Park, MA 02157. See also *ACCESS: Brokering Paratransit Services to the Elderly and Handicapped in Allegheny County, PA*, UMTA Technical Assistance Program, Final Report, December 1984, and *LISTS: Transportation Brokerage for the Elderly and Handicapped in Lancaster, PA*, UMTA Technical Assistance Program, Final Report, June 1984.

2. To find out how your state's funds are administered, call the transit division of the state department of transportation.

3. See Theodore O. Wallin, "Volunteer Based Transportation System" (1986), Urban Mass Transportation Administration. See numerous "how to" publications of U.S.DOT, such as "Implementing Driver Selection and Training for Human Service Agencies: Administrator's Guidelines," U.S.DOT, May 1980, and "A

Manual of Procedures to Apportion Costs of Rural Public Transportation Among Participating Towns and Human Service Agencies," NTIS, 1982.

References

Burkhardt, Jon E., and William W. Millar. 1976. "Estimating Cost of Providing Rural Transportation Service." *Transportation Research Record* 578: 8–15.
Evak, Daniel J. 1982. "An Information Systems Manual for Human Service Transportation Systems." Commonwealth of Pennsylvania, The Transportation Accounting Consortium, *A Model Standard Chart of Accounts for Rural and Specialized Transportation Providers*.
Kidder, Alice E. 1986. "Manual of Operations for Volunteer-Based Transportation Programs." Urban Mass Transportation Administration.
Kidder, Alice E. 1978. *Sources of Non-Federal Support for Public Transportation in Non-urbanized Areas*. National Technical Information Service, PB 284–410.
Walther, Erskine S. 1983. *State and Local Financing of Public Transit Systems*. Urban Mass Transportation Administration.
Wallin, Theodore O., and Alice E. Kidder. 1986. "Volunteer Based Transportation Programs," UMTA.

Appendix: Financing of Rural Passenger Transportation

SOURCES State and Federal

U.S.DOT Sources:
16(b)(2) UMTA funds for purchase of vehicles for nonprofit agencies
Section 18 funds of U.S.DOT Surface Transportation Assistance Act (UMTA)
Capital funds from Surface Transportation Assistance Act
Park and Ride facilities
Planning funds for rural areas
State appropriations for public transportation
State appropriations earmarked for rural areas
Revenue sharing funds

Health and Human Services Sources (HHS):
Funds for elder programs, including funds administered through the Area Agencies on Aging
Medicaid
Mental Health
Mental Retardation
Services and Commissions for the Blind

Housing and Urban Development (HUB):
  Community Development Funding
  Block Grant Funds

Private Sources:
  United Way
  Easter Seals
  Red Cross
  Traveller's Aid
  Civic groups such as Kiwanis, Lions, and Rotary
  Health Foundations (Kidney, Epilepsy, Cancer, etc.)

Educational Activities:
  School buses chartered for special services
  Community and four-year colleges may assess students for transportation through student fees
  Evening extension service classes and other adult education programs may offer transportation to students

Local Funds:
  Local taxes appropriated by local governments
  Local matching funds for aging, childcare, or other human service programs
  Donations
  Volunteers (donating time as clerical, drivers, dispatch, etc.)
  Volunteer fundraising (bake sales, carwashes, yardsales)
  Voluntary donations to a town fund

In-kind Contributions from Local Agencies:
  Vocational Schools (technical centers may provide low-cost maintenance of vehicles)
  Vehicle maintenance by town or county
  Dispatcher by police or town communications center
  Management by Council on Aging staff, by Community Development staff, or by other professional within human service agencies
  Volunteer drivers from RSVP, Green Thumb, Voluntary Action Centers, etc.
  Special reduced rates on volume purchase of gasoline
  Planning and survey work performed by local colleges and universities

9

Movement of Hazardous Materials in Rural America

Eugene R. Russell, Sr.

Great quantities of hazardous materials (hazmat) are transported through, over, or under almost every community in the United States daily. These include fuels, solvents, lubricants, compressed gases, corrosive chemicals, and toxic, flammable, radioactive, or explosive substances. These materials are vital to the American economy and must be transported.

Hazmat transportation is a large and growing segment of the transportation industry. Special concern is addressed to safety in the transportation of hazmat because of the potential for fires, explosions, groundwater contamination, and toxic effects to human health if hazmat are inadvertently released.

Hazmat are defined in the Hazardous Materials Transportation Act and in Title 49 of the Code of Federal Regulation (1984) as materials or substances in a form or quantity that the Secretary of Transportation has found to pose unreasonable risks to health and safety or property. Over 2,400 substances have been identified as hazardous materials. Shipments of these materials in specified quantities must carry warning labels (placards) and their transportation must conform to U.S. Department of Transportation (U.S.DOT), state, and local regulations.

U.S.DOT estimates indicate that about four billion tons of hazardous materials are shipped each year.* However, this estimate is uncertain because there are no complete data on hazardous material shipments at either the national, state, or local levels. Shipment of these vast quantities of hazardous materials is vital to the economy of the United States, but careful regulation is needed to protect the public health and safety.

Between 30 and 50 percent of the four billion tons of hazardous materials shipped annually move by highway (National Transportation Safety Board 1981; Transportation Research Board 1983). Virtually all of these highway shipments are carried by trucks. U.S.DOT estimates that 5 to 15 percent of all trucks on the road at any given time carry hazardous materials. Furthermore, it is estimated that there are about 10,700 shippers and 11,700 carriers involved in highway transportation, and there may be more than 400,000 trucks that regularly transport hazardous materials (National Transportation Safety Board 1981). Thus, the safety of hazardous material transportation by highway is a large-scale, truck safety management problem.

The demand for these materials and the need to transport them will continue to grow with U.S. industry. Given the present concern for the environment, a comprehensive program to minimize the dangers is needed, particularly in transport, where unsuspecting and unprepared populations can be subject to injury, death, or large financial losses.

Much emphasis on hazmat problems has been on urban places, particularly larger ones. This emphasis has been at the expense of the smaller urban and rural places, as well as the totally rural areas. In recent years the needs of these communities have been recognized, and some research has been conducted and programs have been implemented to help them. However, most studies are directed at larger cities and densely populated areas where the consequences of an incident are generally greater. Even good research and published reports that are applicable to rural areas, or could be adapted, are slow to filter down.

Hazardous materials education programs are particularly needed in smaller communities whose police and fire departments are not trained to handle tanker spills, explosions, or fires. Their lack of training can be dangerous both to themselves and to their community. The problems from a hazmat accident can easily be complicated by improvised approaches. There are hundreds of materials that represent high or even

*National Transportation Safety Board 1981; Transportation Research Board 1983; Abkowitz and List 1986; Office of Technology Assessment 1986.

unreasonable risk when not treated properly. The intrinsic hazards can be amplified by changing or adverse conditions that occur in transport accidents. Container head pressure and certain chemical combinations can greatly increase the hazard. Some substances can become unpredictable or more dangerous from the impact received in an accident.

Communities need to be able to estimate risks. They need to know the types and amounts of materials they are exposed to, and they need to understand potential dangers. They also need to have knowledge of the proper source of expert information for any category of hazardous material. They need training programs to acquaint personnel with necessary information. They need a response plan for emergencies. Lastly, particularly in small communities, they need to know how to develop an organizational structure for an emergency response program.

Magnitude of the Problem

General

There is no complete data base on hazmat shipments in the United States at national, state, or local levels; however, various estimates are available. The National Transportation Safety Board (NTSB) stated in a 1981 report that the U.S. Department of Transportation estimated that at least 4 billion tons and 218 million ton-miles of hazardous materials are shipped each year. At least 250,000 shipments of hazardous materials (bulk and nonbulk) are made every day. Hazmat transportation involves about 10,700 shippers and 11,700 carriers, and at least 400,000 trucks regularly transport these materials. In addition, between 5 and 15 percent of all trucks on the road at any given time carry hazardous materials.

Recent estimates by the Office of Technology Assessment (OTA) of the U.S. Congress (1986; Abkowitz and List 1986) provide more detail on the estimated quantities of hazmat shipped in 1982. These data, shown in Table 9.1, estimate that 59.8 percent of all hazmat by weight are transported by highway; although, because of the relatively long distances involved in rail, water, and air shipments, the highway mode accounts for only 11.9 percent of the ton-miles of hazardous materials shipped. The totals estimated by OTA for tons and ton-miles of hazardous materials shipped are substantially lower than the U.S.DOT estimates shown above, reflecting uncertainty in the available data.

Table 9.1 Estimated transportation of hazardous materials by mode in 1982

Mode	Number of Vehicles or Vessels Used for Hazmat Transportation	Tons of Cargo Transported	Ton-Miles (millions)
Truck	337,000 dry freight or flatbed 130,000 cargo tanks	927,000,000 (59.8%)	93,600 (11.9ᵉ
Rail	115,600 tank cars	73,000,000 (4.7%)	53,000 (6.7%
Waterborne	4,909 tanker barges	549,000,000 (35.4%)	636,500 (81.2⁹
Air	3,772 commercial planes	285,000 (0.01%)	459 (0.06⁹
	Total	1,549,285,000	783,559

ᵃBased on 1983 data.
Note: 1 mile = 1.609 km, 1 ton = 907.2 kg
Source: Office of Technology Assessment.

Accidents and Incidents

Accident data bases contain reports of traffic accidents obtained either from police reports, from motorist or motor carrier reports, or from independent follow-up investigations. Each data entry in an accident data base documents the characteristics of a particular accident or accident-involved vehicle. The accident data bases that are useful for hazmat studies are those that contain data on truck accidents, where it can be determined whether or not the truck(s) involved in the accidents were carrying hazmat. Also, it is important to know whether a hazmat release occurred in a particular accident.

Incident data bases contain reports of occurrences where a hazardous material was accidentally released. Incidents of primary interest to communities are releases of hazardous materials during their transportation through the community, releases due to storage, and releases due to transfer or loading from a storage facility to a transporting vehicle or container. Several types of incidents need to be considered. These include releases due to traffic accidents, to valve or container leaks, and to fires or explosions.

Accident and incident data are useful because they indicate the frequency with which particular events occur. However, to make an assessment of accident or incident risk requires corresponding exposure data.

Exposure is a measure of opportunities for accidents or incidents to occur, such as number of hazardous material shipments, tons of hazardous materials shipped, or, best of all, vehicle-miles of hazardous material shipments. Exposure data provides a comparison of accidents or incidents per shipment, or per vehicle-mile, and so forth.

Risk measures, such as accident or incident rates per million vehicle-miles, can be expressed as the ratio of frequency of accidents or incidents to exposure. That is, risk equals number of accidents divided by an equivalent exposure level, or

$$R = \frac{A}{E} \tag{1}$$

where

R represents a measure of risk, such as, accident rate;

A represents a frequency measure, such as number of accidents; and

E represents an exposure measure, such as vehicle-miles of travel.

Thus, equation 1 would calculate a risk in terms of number of accidents per vehicle-mile. Other measures could be used as long as accidents or incidents are known for a corresponding exposure measure.

To be useful in establishing hazardous material transportation policies, risk measures need to be made specific. An accident rate for a particular type of truck traveling on a particular type of road can be obtained if both the accident and exposure populations are categorized accordingly. These rates can then be compared to estimate the safest route, based on the lowest accident rate.

One major weakness in past analyses of truck accidents that is critical in the evaluation of hazardous material transportation risks is that exposure data that correspond well to the available accident data are seldom available. It is often necessary to utilize data from different sources, such as the Bureau of Motor Carrier Safety (BMCS), Motor Carrier Accident Reports, and the Census Bureau's Truck Inventory and Use Survey, to determine truck accident rates. This task is best left to experts. It has many pitfalls, even for experts, and requires a number of assumptions.

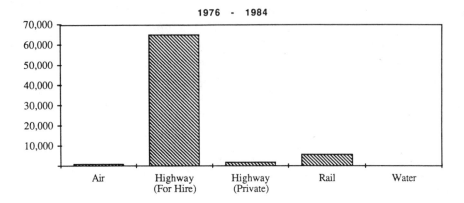

Fig. 9.1. Frequency of hazmat incidents by transportation mode, 1976–1984 (Abkowitz and List 1986)

Frequency of Accidents and Incidents Involving Hazardous Materials

Figure 9.1 illustrates the frequency of hazardous materials incidents by transportation mode for the period 1976–84, as determined by OTA (Abkowitz and List 1986), from the Research and Special Programs Administration (RSPA), Hazardous Materials Incident Reporting System (HMIR). This data base, which is administered by the Office of Hazardous Materials Transportation in the U.S.DOT, includes incidents in which a hazmat was unintentionally released while being transported. The figure shows that the vast majority of reported hazmat incidents involve highway transportation, as opposed to the air, rail, and water modes. The highway incidents include both releases due to traffic accidents and releases due to other causes such as valve or container leaks. The RSPA data make a distinction between highway incidents involving for-hire trucks (those classified as common carriers), where the shipper and the carrier are separate entities, and incidents involving private carriers, where the truck is owned by the shipper of the cargo. For-hire trucks travel substantially more miles per year than private trucks and carry a wider variety of cargos. Figures 9.2 and 9.3 show the trends over time in the frequencies of highway incidents involving a hazmat release in the for-hire and private categories, respectively

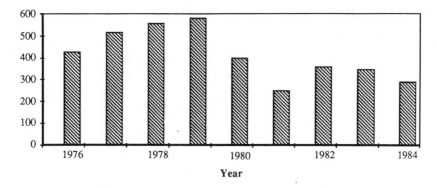

Fig. 9.2. Frequency of hazmat incidents in highway (for-hire) mode by year[5] (Abkowitz and List 1986)

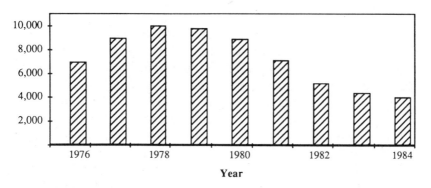

Fig. 9.3. Frequency of hazmat incidents in highway (private) mode by year (Abkowitz and List 1986)

(Abkowitz and List 1986). These data include both incidents that occur on the highway and incidents that occur in truck terminal or yard areas.

Consequences of Accidents and Incidents Involving Hazardous Materials

The consequences of hazmat releases in highway transportation are available from the Hazardous Materials Incident Reporting System. Table 9.2 presents a distribution of the result of highway-related

Table 9.2 Distribution of hazmat incidents in highway transportation by result of release

| | Industry Segment | | | |
Result	For-Hire Trucking	Private Trucking	Total	(%)
None	1,017	18	1,035	(1.7)
Fire	130	26	156	(0.03)
Explosion	21	2	23	(0.04)
Fire and Explosion	48	15	63	(0.01)
Spillage	55,368	3,406	58,774	(97.1)
Spillage and Fire	239	153	392	(0.6)
Spillage and Explosion	22	4	26	(0.04)
Spill, Fire, and Explosion	31	11	42	(0.07)
Total	56,876	3,635	60,511	

Source: Office of Technology Assessment contractor report.

hazmat incidents (Abkowitz and List 1986). Spillage of a hazmat was the result of 97.8 percent of incidents and was the only reported result of 97.1 percent of incidents. Fires resulted from 0.8 percent of highway-related incidents and explosions from 0.25 percent. The nature of the 1.7 percent of incidents that did not involve either a spill, a fire, or an explosion is unknown but could include gaseous or radiation releases.

The consequences of these spills, fires, and explosions are summarized by the HMIR data base in terms of injuries, deaths, and property damage that are the direct result of a hazardous material's release. According to this source, only 0.2 percent of recorded incidents involved one or more deaths. Slightly more than 2 percent of recorded incidents resulted in injury. Property damage occurring from 68,450 incidents totaled nearly $105 million.

There is no single data base that contains records of all vehicular accidents and incidents involving hazmat. One has to go to two or more data bases, all of which have different reporting requirements and are all known to be incomplete to some degree.

Highway Type and Accident Rates

The type of highway on which vehicles operate is known to have a strong effect on accident rates for all vehicle types including trucks. Three factors related to the geometric design of the highway and its

Table 9.3 Fatal accident involvement rates of combination trucks by highway type (nationwide data, 1980–82)

Highway Type	Number of Fatal Accident Involvements	Travel by Combination Trucks (10^6 veh-mi)	Fatal Accident Involvement Rate (per 10^6 veh-mi)
Urban interstate	917	25,551	0.036
Urban noninterstate	1,979	27,164	0.073
Rural interstate	1,750	60,554	0.029
Rural noninterstate	276	—	
All	10,600	179,347	0.059

surrounding environment are generally used to define highway type. They include type of development (urban/rural), access control (freeway/nonfreeway), number of lanes, and presence or absence of median (divided/undivided). The effect of highway type on truck accident rates is a critical factor in comparing the risk of hazmat releases due to traffic accidents between alternative routes.

A recent California Department of Transportation (Caltrans) study by Graf and Archuleta (1985) examined truck accident involvement rates by highway type and truck configuration. The study results indicate that accident rates, both for trucks and for other types of vehicles, are generally lower on freeways than on nonfreeways and are generally higher on urban highways than on rural highways.

A 1987 study by Carsten (1987) determined fatal accident involvement rates by highway type for combination trucks using nationwide accident data from a University of Michigan data base compiled from Fatal Accident Reporting System (FARS) and Bureau of Motor Carrier Safety (BMCS) data and nationwide exposure data compiled by FHWA. The results of this study, presented in Table 9.3, are quite consistent with the results of Graf and Archuleta for fatal accidents.

Previous investigators performing hazmat transportation risk assessments have been frustrated by the lack of reliable data on truck accident rates by highway type. Most investigators have recommended the use of actual accident data for the highway routes in question whenever possible (Urbanck and Baker 1980; Barber and Hilderbrand 1980; Materials Transportation Bureau 1981). This recommendation appears sound, although it increases the effort required for a hazmat routing study and requires careful study design to ensure that the sample sizes

Table 9.4 Estimated truck accident rates (selected sites in California, Texas, and New Jersey)

Highway Type	Truck Accident Rate (accidents per 10^6 veh-mi)
Interstate (freeway)	0.65
U.S. and state highways (rural nonfreeways)	2.26
Interrupted flow due to intersections (urban arterials)	3.65

Source: Abkowitz et al. 1984a; 1984b.

of accidents used are sufficient to provide an accurate measure of the traffic safety differences between the routing alternatives in question. If sufficient local accident data are available, their use is always preferable to national or regional averages.

Due to the lack of truck accident data for hazmat risk assessments, Abkowitz et al. (1984a; 1984b) in a study for the EPA, developed average truck accident involvement rates for three highway types: freeways, rural nonfreeways, and urban arterials. These rates, illustrated in Table 9.4, were based on data for 194 five-mile highway segments in California, Texas, and New Jersey. Abkowitz did not attempt to control for the effects of truck configuration, cargo area configuration, or any of the other factors known to affect truck safety. However, the results in Table 9.4 do provide a reasonable illustration of the differences in truck safety between highway types.

The available findings concerning the effect of highway type on truck safety have important implications for hazmat transportation. First, freeways should be generally preferred to nonfreeways as hazmat transportation routes. Not only do freeways have lower accident rates than nonfreeways, but they are usually (but not always) located farther from residential and other development than nonfreeways and provide a more manageable location to contain and clean up any spills that do occur. Possible exceptions may be elevated freeways, depressed freeways, bridges, and tunnels, which have to be considered on an individual basis. Second, urban highways typically have higher truck accident rates than rural highways, with urban arterial streets having the highest truck accident travel rates of any highway type. However, it must be recognized that if additional distance is required to use freeway routes or avoid urban areas, the exposure to accidents (vehicle-miles of travel) is increased. Thus, there is a tradeoff between accident rate and distance traveled that needs to be considered formally to select a minimum risk route whenever the route with the lowest accident rate is not the shortest route.

Summary of Hazardous Material Accident-Incident Data

This section summarizes the most important findings of a recent analysis of the hazmat incident, accident, and exposure data bases (Harwood 1987).

Hazmat Incidents

Approximately 40 percent of hazmat incidents reported to RSPA occur off the highway in terminal or yard areas. These types of incidents have no direct bearing on the safe operation of the highway system. Of hazmat incidents that occur on the highway, traffic accidents account for only about 8 percent. These incidents are of particular concern because they are likely to involve substantially more deaths, injuries, and property damage than other types of hazmat incidents. The most common causes of hazmat incidents that occur on the highway involve valve or fitting failures (30 percent of incidents), cargo shifting (29 percent), and body or tank failures (21 percent). The majority of these types of incidents are caused by human error, with package or container failure as the second most frequent cause.

The vast majority of hazmat incidents on the highway involve the release of flammable or combustible liquids and corrosive materials. Fires and explosions result from less than 2 percent of hazmat incidents that occur on the highway. However, fires and explosions occur in nearly 9 percent of hazmat incidents that result from traffic accidents.

Traffic Accidents

Approximately 13 to 15 percent of traffic accidents involving hazmat-carrying trucks result in a hazmat release. This estimate is consistent in both the BMCS and Missouri data that were studied and is slightly less than the 20 percent estimate developed indirectly in a previous study by Abkowitz (1984a; 1984b). In such an accident, solids in bulk are most likely to be released, liquids in bulk are less likely to be released (though still above average), and gases in bulk and hazmat in general freight are least likely to be released.

The types of truck accidents most likely to result in a hazmat release are: truck-train collisions at railroad-highway crossings; overturning by single-unit trucks and single-trailer combination trucks and running off the road by single-trailer combination trucks, particularly at freeway ramps; and separation of units in double-trailer combination trucks. Tank trucks are slightly more likely than vans or flatbeds to release their cargo if an accident occurs, and hazmat releases are least likely in multiple vehicle collisions. It is unclear whether or not fixed object collisions are likely to result in a hazmat release, because the BMCS and Missouri data bases do not agree on this point.

Accidents that occur in rural areas are more likely than accidents that occur in urban areas to result in a hazmat release because single-vehicle accidents are more likely than multiple-vehicle accidents in rural accidents and because higher speeds are also likely to be involved in rural accidents.

Hazmat releases are more likely in severe accidents that involve fatalities and injuries than in property-damage-only accidents, since severe accidents typically generate high accident forces that make fatalities, injuries, and hazmat releases more likely. Nighttime accidents are more likely than daytime accidents to result in a hazmat release. Nighttime travel by hazmat-carrying trucks is more likely to be in rural than in urban areas and, even in urban areas, nighttime accidents are more likely than daytime accidents to involve only a single vehicle. Hazmat releases are more likely in accidents that occur on horizontal curves than on tangent highway sections and in accidents that occur on grades or at hillcrests than in accidents that occur on level highway sections.

In general, the BMCS accident data and the state accident data from Missouri produce findings that are in agreement. The primary value of state accident data bases appears to be that they may include accident factors that are not available in the BMCS data.

Exposure

A majority of the trucks that carry hazardous materials at least some of the time are single-unit trucks, and most of these are vans. However, single-trailer combination trucks account for nearly 70 percent of the vehicle-miles of travel by hazmat-carrying trucks. Liquid or gas tankers account for 26 percent of the travel by hazmat-carrying single-trailer combination trucks and 6 percent of the travel by hazmat-carrying double-trailer combination trucks.

The majority of hazmat-carrying trucks carry hazardous materials less than 25 percent of the time. Only 17 percent of hazmat-carrying trucks carry hazardous materials more than 75 percent of the time.

Emergency Planning and Community Right-to-Know*

On 17 October 1986, the Superfund Amendments and Reauthorization Act of 1986 (SARA) was enacted into law. One part of the new SARA provisions is Title III: The Emergency Planning and Community Right-to-Know Act of 1986.

This legislation builds upon the Environmental Protection Agency's (EPA) Chemical Emergency Preparedness Program (CEPP 1985). The community right-to-know provisions of Title III will help to increase the public's knowledge and access to information on the presence of hazardous chemicals in their communities and releases of these chemicals into the environment.

The sections of the law are: emergency planning (301–303), emergency notification (304), community right-to-know reporting requirements (311, 312), and toxic chemical release reporting—emissions inventory (313).

Emergency Planning (301–303)

Title III required that the governor of each state designate a state emergency response commission by 17 April 1987. While an existing state organization can be designated as the state emergency response commission, the commission can have broad-based representation. Public agencies and departments concerned with issues relating to the environment, natural resources, emergency services, public health, occupational safety, and transportation all have important roles in Title III

*From U.S. Environmental Protection Agency (EPA) *Title III Fact Sheet, Emergency Planning and Community Right to Know.*

activities. Various public and private sector groups and associations with interest and expertise in Title III issues also can be included in the state commission.

The state commission must designate local emergency planning districts. The deadline for this step was 17 July 1987. Local emergency planning committees must be established within one month after a district is designated. The state commission is responsible for supervising and coordinating the activities of the local emergency planning committees, for establishing procedures for receiving and processing public requests for information collected under other sections of Title III, and for reviewing local emergency plans.

The local emergency planning committee must include elected state and local officials, public health professionals, environmental, hospital, and transportation officials as well as representatives of facilities subject to the emergency planning requirements, community groups, and the media. The local committee must establish rules, give public notice of its activities, and establish procedures for handling public requests for information.

The local committee's primary responsibility will be to develop an emergency response plan by 17 October 1988. The plan must include: identification of facilities and extremely hazardous substances transportation routes; emergency response procedures, on-site and off-site; designation of a community coordinator and facility coordinator(s) to implement the plan; emergency notification procedures; methods for determining the occurrence of a release and the probable affected area and population; description of community and industry emergency equipment and facilities and the identity of persons responsible for them; evacuation plans; description and schedules of a training program for emergency response personnel; and methods and schedules for exercising emergency response plans.

In order to assist the local committees in preparing and reviewing plans, Congress required the National Response Team (NRT), composed of fourteen federal agencies with emergency response responsibilities, to publish guidance on emergency response planning. This guidance, the *Hazardous Materials Emergency Planning Guide* (1987), will be published by the NRT and incorporates emergency planning aspects of the CEPP Interim Guidance. It also replaces the Federal Emergency Management Agency's Planning Guide for Checklist for Hazardous Materials Contingency Plans (1981, popularly known as FEMA-10).

The emergency response plan must be reviewed by the state commission as well as annually by the local committee. The Regional Response Teams, composed of the Federal Regional officials and state representatives, may review the plans and provide assistance to the local committees upon request.

Those planning activities of the local committees and facilities should be focused on, but not limited to, the 402 extremely hazardous substances published in the 17 November 1986 Federal Register (later increased to 406). The list included the threshold planning quantities for each substance. EPA can revise the list and threshold planning quantities for each substance based on the toxicity, reactivity, volatility, dispersability, combustibility, or flammability of a substance.

Any facility that produces, uses, or stores any of the listed chemicals in a quantity greater than its threshold planning quantity is subject to the emergency planning requirements. Covered facilities must notify the state commission that they are subject to these requirements. If a facility begins to produce, use, or store any of the extremely hazardous substances in threshold quantity amounts, it must notify the state commission within sixty days.

Each state commission must notify EPA of all facilities subject to the emergency planning requirements.

Emergency Notification (304)

Facilities must immediately notify the local emergency planning committee and the state emergency response commission if there is a release of a listed hazardous substance that exceeds the reportable quantity for that substance. Substances subject to this requirement are substances on the list of 402 extremely hazardous substances as published in Federal Register on 17 November 1986 plus the additions and substances subject to the emergency notification requirements under Comprehensive Environmental Response Compensation, and Liability Act of 1980 (CERCLA) Section 103(a).

The initial notification can be by telephone, radio, or in person. Emergency notification requirements involving transportation incidents can be satisfied by dialing 911, or, in the absence of a 911 emergency number, calling the operator.

This emergency notification needs to include: the chemical name; an indication of whether the substance is extremely hazardous; an estimate of the quantity released into the environment; the time and duration of the release; the medium into which the release occurred; any known or anticipated acute or chronic health risks associated with the emergency, and where appropriate, advice regarding medical attention necessary for exposed individuals; proper precautions, such as evacuation; and name and telephone number of contact person.

Section 304 also requires a follow-up written emergency notice after the release. The follow-up written notice or notices must update information included in the initial notice and provide information on actual response actions taken, any known or anticipated data or chronic health risks associated with the release, and advice regarding medical attention necessary for exposed individuals.

Community Right-to-Know Reporting Requirements (311–312)

There are two "community right-to-know" reporting requirements that apply primarily to manufacturers and importers. Section 311 requires that facilities which must prepare or have available Material Safety Data Sheets (MSDS) under the Occupational Safety and Health Administration (OSHA) regulations to submit either copies of its MSDS or a list of MSDS chemicals to the local emergency planning committee, the state emergency response commission, and the local fire department.

If the facility owner or operator chooses to submit a list of MSDS chemicals, the list must include the chemical name or common name of each substance and any hazardous component as provided on the MSDS.

If a list is submitted, the facility must submit the MSDS for any chemical on the list upon the request of the local planning committee. EPA may establish threshold quantities for hazardous chemicals below which no facility must report.

The reporting requirement of Section 312 involves submission of an emergency and hazardous chemical inventory form to the local emergency planning committee, the State emergency response commission, and the local fire department.

The inventory form incorporates a two-tier approach. Under Tier 1, facilities must submit the following aggregate information for each applicable OSHA category of health and physical hazard: an estimate (in ranges) of the maximum amount of chemicals for each category present at the facility at any time during the preceding calendar year, an estimate (in ranges) of the average daily amount of chemicals in each category, and the general location of hazardous chemicals in each category.

Upon request of a local committee, state commission, or local fire department, the facility must provide the following Tier II information for each substance subject to the request: the chemical name of the common name as indicated on the MSDS, an estimate (in ranges) of the maximum amount of the chemical present at any time during the preceding calendar year, a brief description of the manner of storage of the chemical, the location of the chemical at the facility, and an indication of whether the owner elects from the state commission and the local committee.

The public may also request Tier II information from the state commission and the local committee.

Toxic Chemical Release Reporting (313)

Section 313 of Title III requires EPA to establish an inventory of toxic chemical emissions from certain facilities. Facilities subject to this reporting requirement are required to complete a toxic chemical release form for specified chemicals. The form must be submitted to the EPA and those state officials designated by the governor, initially on or before 1 July 1988 and annually thereafter by 1 July, reflecting releases during each proceeding calendar year.

The reporting requirement applies to owners and operators of facilities that have ten or more full-time employees that are in Standard Industries Classification (SIC) codes 20 through 39 (i.e., manufacturing facilities) that manufactured, processed, or otherwise used a listed toxic chemical in excess of specified threshold quantities.

The list of toxic chemicals subject to reporting consists initially of chemicals listed for similar reporting purposes by the states of New Jersey and Maryland. There are over three hundred chemicals and categories on these lists. The EPA can modify this combined list considering the following factors: Is the substance known to cause cancer or serious reproductive or neurological disorders, genetic mutations, or other chronic health effects? Can the substance cause significant adverse acute health effects outside the facility as a result of continuous or frequently recurring releases? Can the substance cause an adverse effect on the environment because of its toxicity, persistence, or tendency to bioaccumulate?

The EPA was required to publish a format for the Toxic Chemical Release form by 1 June 1987. The following information was to have been included: the name, location, and type of business; whether the chemical is manufactured, processed, or otherwise used, and the general categories of use of the chemical; an estimate (in ranges) of the maximum amounts of the toxic chemical present at the facility at any time during the preceding year; waste treatment/disposal methods and efficiency of methods for each wastestream; quantity of the chemical entering each environmental medium annually; and a certification by a senior official that the report is complete and accurate.

The EPA must establish and maintain a national toxic chemical inventory based on the data submitted. This information must be computer accessible on a national database.

Other Title III Provisions

Section 322 of Title III addresses trade secrets and applies to emergency planning, community right-to-know, and toxic chemical release reporting. Any person may withhold the specific chemical identity of a hazardous chemical for specific reasons. However, if the chemical identity is withheld, the generic class or category of the chemical must be provided. The withholder must show each of the following: the information has not been disclosed to any other person other than a member of the local planning committee, a government official, an employee of such person or someone bound by a confidentiality agreement, that measures have been taken to protect the confidentiality, and that the withholder intends to continue to take such measures. The information is not required to be disclosed to the public under any other federal or state law. The information is likely to cause substantial harm to the competitive position of the person. The chemical identity is not readily discoverable through reverse engineering.

Section 323 provides for disclosure under certain circumstances to health professionals who need the information for diagnostic purposes or from local health officials who need the information for assessment activities.

Information claimed as a trade secret, and substantiation for that claim, must be submitted to the EPA. People may challenge trade secret claims by petitioning the EPA, which must then review the claim and rule on its validity.

Section 305 of Title III authorizes the Federal Emergency Management Agency to provide $5 million for each of fiscal years 1987, 1988, 1989, and 1990 for training grants to support state and local governments. These training grants are designed to improve emergency planning, preparedness, mitigation, responses, and recovery capabilities. Such programs must provide special emphasis to hazardous chemical emergencies.

Under Section 305, the EPA is required to review emergency systems for monitoring, detecting, and preventing releases of extremely hazardous substances at representative facilities that produce, use, or store these substances. The EPA will issue a final report of findings and recommendations to Congress by 17 April 1988.

The report must include the EPA's findings regarding each of the following: It must report on the current technological capabilities to monitor, detect, and prevent significant releases of extremely hazardous substances; to determine the magnitude and direction of the hazard posed by each release; to identity specific substances; to provide data on specific chemical composition of such releases; and to determine relative concentration of the constituent substances. It must determine the status of public emergency alert devices or systems for effective public warning of accidental releases of extremely hazardous substances into any media. Finally, it must establish the technical and economic feasibility of establishing, maintaining, and operating alert systems for detecting releases.

The report must also include the EPA's recommendations for initiatives to support development of new or improved technologies or systems that would assist the timely monitoring, detection, and prevention of releases of extremely hazardous substances and improving devices or systems for effectively alerting the public in the event of an accidental release.

Conclusion

Title III, The Community Right-to-Know Act of 1986, will have great impact on such things as community risk analysis, vulnerability analysis, hazardous material emergency planning, and so forth. It is too early to analyze the local impact of this act in practice. It should enable the appropriate local committees to acquire information needed for rational planning. Such data were heretofore difficult to obtain.

Except for incidents where a spill has occurred, Transportation Companies are exempt from the law. This omission may be a weakness in the law as it applies to local planning, because data for transportation risk assessment, routing, and so forth, are also difficult to obtain. Title III will not directly change this policy; however, it may indirectly lead to better hazmat transportation data.

References

Abkowitz, M., and G. F. List. 1986. "Hazardous Materials Transportation: Commodity Flow and Incident/Accident Information Systems." Office of Technology Assessment contractor report.

Abkowitz, M., et al. 1984a. "Assessing the Releases and Costs Associated with Truck Transport of Hazardous Wastes." Draft Final Report, EPA Contract No. 68–02–6621, January 1984.

Abkowitz, M., et al. 1984b. "Estimating the Release Rates and Costs of Transporting Hazardous Waste." *Transportation Research Record* 977.

Barber, E. J., and L. K. Hilderbrand. 1980. "Guidelines for Applying Criteria to Designate Routes for Transporting Hazardous Materials." Report No. FHWA–IP–80–15, Federal Highway Administration.

Carsten, O. 1987. "Safety Implications of Truck Configuration." Presented at Transportation Research Board Annual Meeting (unpublished).

Chemical Emergency Preparedness Program. 1985. Interim Guidance, U.S. Environmental Protection Agency.

Code of Federal Regulations. 1984. Title 49: Transportation, Ports 100 to 177.

Code of Federal Regulations. 1984. Title 49: Transportation, Ports 178 to 199.

Graf, V. D., and K. Archuleta. 1985. "Truck Accidents by Classification." Report No. FHWA/CA/TE–85, California Department of Transportation.

Harwood, Douglas W. 1987. "Present Practices of Highway Transportation of Hazardous Materials." Interim Report, *Analysis of Existing Data Bases*, Midwest Research Institute Project No. 8669–S (unpublished).

Hazardous Materials Emergency Planning Guide. 1987. National Response Team, Washington, D.C.

Materials Transportation Bureau. 1981. "Guidelines for Selecting Preferred Highway Routes for Large Quantity Shipments of Radioactive Materials." Report No. RSPA/MTB–81/5. DOT Research and Special Programs Administration.

National Transportation Safety Board. 1981. "Safety Effectiveness Evaluation— Federal and State Enforcement Efforts in Hazardous Materials Transportation by Truck." Report No. NTSE–SEE–81–2.

Office of Technology Assessment. 1986. "Transportation of Hazardous Materials."
    Report No. OTA–SET–304.
Planning Guide and Checklist for Hazardous Materials Contingency Plans. 1981.
    Federal Emergency Management Agency, FEMA–10.
Transportation Research Board. 1983. "Transportation of Hazardous Materials:
    Toward a National Strategy." *TRB Special Report 197.*
Urbanek, G. L., and E. J. Barker. 1980. "Development of Criteria to Designate
    Routes for Transporting Hazardous Materials." Report No. FHWA/RD–
    80/105, Federal Highway Administration.

Part V

Rural Transportation Educational and Technical Assistance

10

Planning Rural Transportation Systems: Applications of a Statewide Network Model

Dean Linsenmeyer
Azzeddine Azzam
Duane Olsen

The nation's rural transportation system of light density rail lines and rural roads currently faces a critical juncture in its evolutionary history. Beginning with the ordinance of 1785, it was the explicit goal of government to identify private lands through a one-mile rectangular survey grid. Nebraska was no exception. Nebraska's rural road network includes 9,981 state highway miles and 79,137 miles of rural roads (Stauss 1978). Over 75 percent of the rural roads are graveled, nearly 18 percent are earth, and the remainder are hard surfaced.

Present rural road designs and bridge capacities reflect the small-size, low-volume transportation technologies of four or more decades ago. Baumel and Schornhorst estimate that nearly 70 percent of today's rural bridges were built before 1935. As technological and economic changes have impacted rural firms, the average vehicle width and axle weight has increased. Consequently, 81 percent, or 9,439, of the off-federal-aid system bridges in Nebraska are classified as being either structurally deficient or functionally obsolete (Baumel and Schornhorst 1983).

The demand for rural transportation services continues to increase. Agriculture dominates the economy of many midwestern states including Nebraska, where it employs nearly a third of the state's labor force (Johnson 1986). With the rapid development of commercial agriculture, increased tonnage of petroleum fuels and fertilizers must ultimately be transported to nearly every acre of agricultural land. Increased proportions of larger harvests are transported off-farm to commercial markets around the world. Currently, approximately 16.5 million metric tons of grains and oilseeds, 3.2 million metric tons of livestock and dairy products, and 1.8 million metric tons of fertilizer are shipped annually over Nebraska's rural roads serving its 65,000 farms and ranches (U.S. Dept. of Commerce 1980).

In addition to increased volumes of rural freight, changing patterns of commodity flows have also impacted the demands on the rural transportation system. In the last decade, the advent of the unit-train rate and the passage of the Staggers Act have greatly differentiated transportation costs between competitive buyers and sellers of rural commodities. This in turn has resulted in greater price dispersion between rural markets and increased economic incentives to rural producers to transport commodities farther and in larger-sized vehicles in accessing more distant markets. Analysis revealed that the annual ton-miles of rural truck transportation of grains nearly doubled in Nebraska over the 1975–80 period (Linsenmeyer 1983).

Responsibility for the maintenance and upgrading of nearly 90 percent of this rural mileage falls on local county or township authorities. In sixty-six of Nebraska's ninety-three counties, county commissioners are responsible for all rural roads. In the remaining twenty-seven counties, township officials hold most of that responsibility (Stauss 1984). County governments annually receive about $40 million from state and federal highway funds. Reflecting the recession in its dominant industry, agriculture, Nebraska's state revenue dropped by 2.7 percent for 1984–85, while the national average increased by more than 9 percent (Lawson 1986). To augment state and federal sources, Nebraska counties and townships raise approximately $65 million annually for roads primarily from property taxes. Although assessment procedures tend to reduce fluctuations in property tax revenues, substantial declines in Nebraska farmland values will ultimately have an impact on local governments. Limited by these financial constraints, the level of maintenance and investment expenditures necessary to upgrade the entire rural network to meet current and future transportation demands is prohibitive. Selective investment or disinvestment in the rural transportation infrastructure is interrelated with the economic, institutional, and technological developments of both the private user and the public agency. Previous attempts to assist participants have consisted of generalized findings from isolated cross-sectional studies of a single or small range of commodities with little or no regard for intermodal interactions.

The Nebraska Experiment Station and the Cooperative Extension Service in conjunction with the Nebraska Department of Roads set out to assemble, present, and encourage the discussion of information to help local officials meet this challenge. Specific objectives include developing a flexible, intuitively appealing, and updatable rural transportation model (RTM) capable of inventorying transportation conditions and simulating rural flows of major agricultural commodities over alternative transportation networks, and improving public awareness of the issues involved in rural investment/divestment decisions and their impact on the future of the local economy.

The Rural Transportation Model

The procedure to accomplish these objectives involved constructing a multicommodity network model. The rural products considered are corn, sorghum, wheat, soybeans, hogs, fat cattle, and feeder cattle, while fertilizer and bulk petroleum are included as rural inputs. The output from the model includes private user costs and public costs incurred from accommodating the total flow of the above commodities over a specified geographical area. The costs may be calculated under current or simulated road and rail configurations. Tonnage by mile segment is calculated so that planners can identify the exact traffic routings given the transportation network.

Conceptual Formulation

To formulate the problem, denote the state area by A, and the area of its N counties by a_i, for $i = 1, 2, \ldots N$. Subdivide the a_i's further into j components, say square miles j, such that $A = \sum_i \sum_j a_{ij}$, and let P_{ij} be the total production in the square mile a_{ij}.

For a given county i, consider each a_j as a source. Associated with each source is a net non-negative quantity P_j to be shipped to potential sinks (e.g., elevators). If the objective of the shipper is to maximize revenue received at a_j associated with the flow of P_j to potential sinks S_k, for $k = 1, 2, \ldots K$, then there exists a least cost path L^*_j linking the source a_j and a sink S^*_k. The minimum total transportation cost per unit C^* for goods P_j can be written as

$$C^* = C \sum_{r=1}^{S} t_r \tag{1}$$

where t_r denotes the distance in miles of each branch, r, and S indicates the number of branches on the least cost path L^*_j, and C is a constant unit cost per volume/mile, assuming a given vehicle type and a given quality factor for all S branches. If the branches are of unequal quality, as is usually the case, then associated with each branch t_r of a specific quality and vehicle type v is a unique cost, c_{vr}, and C^* becomes

$$C^* = \sum_{r=1}^{S} C_{vr} t_r I_{[0, 0]} \text{ for } v = 1, 2, \ldots V \tag{2}$$

where C^* is the private shipper cost of moving one unit of farm produce from a source to a sink, assuming a specific vehicle type, v. $I_{[0, 0]}$ is a binary indicator of road quality on a specific road segment when two road qualities are differentiated.

For M shippers, the total private costs (TPV) are simply

$$TPV = \sum_{v=1}^{V} \sum_{j=1}^{M} \sum_{r=1}^{S} C_{vr} t_r P_j \tag{3}$$

This formula is illustrated in Figure 10.1. The diagram represents a hypothetical road network indicated by the bold lines in a hypothetical county. Consider the large square as a county in the state and the numbered nodes in the center of each dashed square as sources of the flows P_j from the square with area a_j. Assume all roads connecting the squares are unpaved rural roads. S^* is the sink associated with a least-cost path serving sources 1, 2, 3, 4, 5, and 6. For example, by moving west from source 2, then south on AS^*, L^*_1 can be written as

$$L^*_1 = \{2, 1, 3, 5\}$$

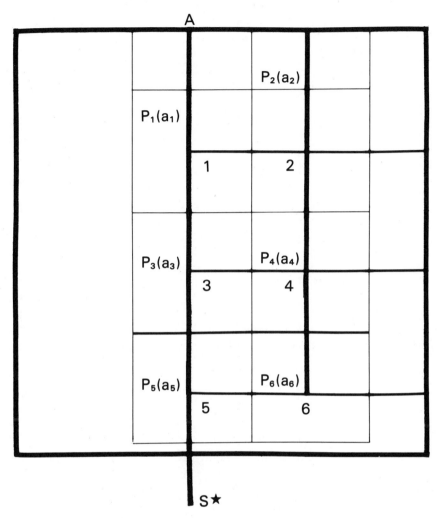

Fig. 10.1 Hypothetical county with six sources and one sink

with $j = 4$ links. The associated cost is

$$C^*_{v1} = C_{v1}{}^2 + C_{v2}{}^1 + C_{v3}{}^3 + C_{v4}{}^5$$

where the superscripts denote the location of a particular segment on $L^*{}_1$, and the subscripts denote the number of the sequential segments on the diagram followed by vehicle type v.

Denote the capacity of truck v by Q_v. Then the proportion of P_j hauled by truck type v is written as

$$H_{vj} = \frac{R_{vj} Q_v}{\sum\limits_{v=1}^{v} R_{vj} Q_v} \qquad (4)$$

where R_{vj} is the probability of truck type v hauling P_j to market.
    The actual volume hauled by truck type v is

$$T_{vj} = P_j{}^* H_{vj} \qquad (5)$$

and the number of trips by truck type v to haul T_{vj} to market is

$$N_{vj} = \frac{T_{vj}}{Q_v} \qquad (6)$$

with appropriate conversion of T_{vj} to 18-kip[1] equivalents (KIP_{vj}), the total number of 18-kips applied to each road segment r on the least-cost path L^*_j is

$$F_{jr} = \sum\limits_{v=1}^{v} (N_{vjr}) (KIP_{vjr}) \quad \text{for } r = 1, 2, \ldots s \qquad (7)$$

Since a particular road segment r may also be part of other least-cost paths L^*_j for $j = 2, \ldots M$, the aggregate number of 18-kips from the M sources is

$$F_r = \sum\limits_{j=1}^{M} \sum\limits_{v=1}^{V} (N_{vjr}) (KIP_{vjr}) \quad \text{for } r = 1, 2, \ldots S. \qquad (8)$$

If the public cost per road segment PC_r are functionally related to F_r, then the total public cost for the region is simply to the total of PC_r over the existing r's which constitute all possible least-cost paths from the M sources.
    The link between traffic dynamics on rural roads and rail lines is formulated as follows. Consider Figure 10.2 where a grid system is imposed on

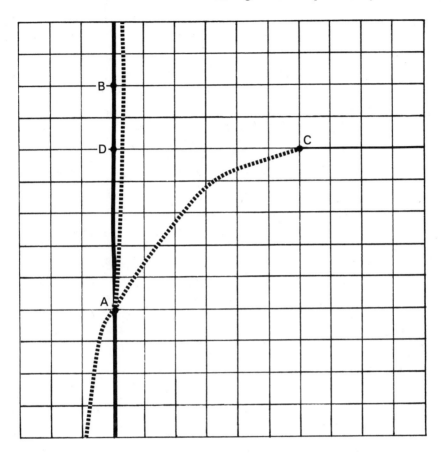

Fig. 10.2 Subterminal-country linkage

a hypothetical county. The squares represent the sources (P_j) of the flow, and the darker lines represent rural roads. Superimposed rural road grids are a state highway in bold print, a north-south main rail line in dashed print, and a branch line, AC, also in dashed print. Assume C is a country elevator, and A is a subterminal elevator. C may ship grain to A or to an external market. The flow from the sources surrounding the two elevators may go to either elevator. The size of each elevator's trade territory hinges on its relative bid price and road accessibility. C has the option of shipping to A either through the rail link, AC, or along the road link, CDA, depending on the relative transport costs.

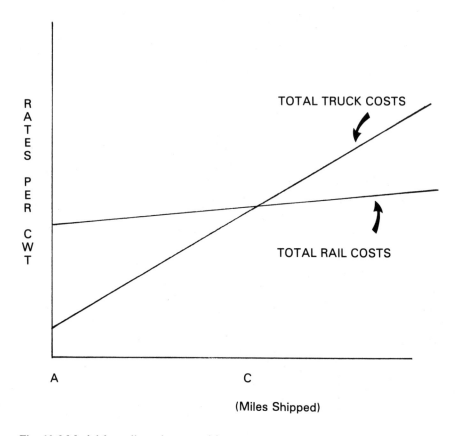

Fig. 10.3 Model for rail-truck competition

Suppose the load out capacity constraint at C and the quality of branch line AC are such that the rail company owning AC and the main line railroad decides to close the branch line. The impact on roads hinges on the interaction of many variables.

First, using the traditional model of rail/truck competition (Fig. 10.3), if the intersection of the rate schedules of the two modes happens to coincide with or exceeds the distance from A to C, then for distances less than AC trucking rates per hundredweight are consistently lower than for rail rates. Therefore, in Figure 10.2, the only effect of rail abandonment on roads would be the flow diverted to the rural road moving west on CD and south on the state highway, DA. Hence, rail abandonment will have no effect on trade territory boundaries and subsequently on the traffic over rural roads.

If the distance to A from C is less than the point where the two rates coincide, then rail abandonment has several repercussions. First, if by branch line abandonment, C loses some of its outlets, its bid price is affected not only by increased transport cost, but also by a shift in its derived demand for grain from producers. Furthermore, because elevators' trade territories are affected by bid prices, one would expect a shift in market share, rerouting of flows, and perhaps greater traffic burdens on certain rural roads.

Empirical Specification

Each square mile in the state has been designated as a commodity producing unit (CPU). Shipment volumes (P_j) include corn, sorghum, wheat, soybeans, fat, and feeder cattle. The volume of grain assigned to each square mile was based on area-specific soil and yield conditions.[2] Fat-cattle volume was based on the number and size of feedlots whose location is public knowledge. Feeder cattle volume was assigned according to rangeland area. The volume of hogs per square mile was distributed according to feed grain availability. All shipments of grain from the sources to the sinks was net of grain fed to local livestock.

Commodity receiving units (CRU), referred to earlier as sinks (S_k), include elevators, livestock, and hog-sale barns. Input distributing units (IDU) include fertilizer, feed, and petroleum dealers. The spatial locations of the CRUs, and IDUs, were obtained from their respective association's directories. Each location was assigned a unique "xy" coordinate. Prices of input and output at each location were also determined.

All rural roads and highways were identified by type and quality. State and federal highway configurations were obtained from the official state map and were arranged in separate arcs connecting various nodes (towns). Each node was assigned an "xy" coordinate. Rural roads, on the other hand, were entered as an empty grid system. This way the county engineer can alter the configuration and quality of the roads under his jurisdiction.

The state rail network was also arranged as arcs linking various nodes (connection points, such as towns). Each node was assigned an "xy" coordinate. Each arc was assigned its actual distance in miles. The distribution of trucks by type was determined, and the probability of using a particular truck type to haul grain and livestock was estimated using multivariate logit analysis of farm survey data (Azzam and Linsenmeyer 1987). The principal covariates used in the logit model are distance to market and grain or livestock shipment size. The trucks considered are single axle, tandem axle, and semis.

The cost per volume mile for all outputs and inputs hauled by truck were estimated for each truck type according to road type and quality. Allowance was also made for turn penalties.[3] The freight rates for rail were obtained from railroad companies operating in the state.

Input receiving units (IRU) are the same as the CPUs. The actual bid prices for corn, wheat, and soybeans at each of the sixty-two subterminal elevators are used.[4] Each subterminal elevator was asked to report its bid price for the last Thursday of each month in the crop year. Those subterminals retailing fertilizers were also asked to report their prices per ton for dry bag fertilizer, liquid fertilizers, and anhydrous ammonia during their peak sales season. Omaha was used as the central livestock market assumed to be the dominant price setter for livestock throughout Nebraska. Preliminary investigation of petroleum prices provided by the American Automobile Association (AAA) Service indicated no apparent geographical pattern. Consequently, the model utilizes a single price for the state. Once all of the variables are inputted, a least-cost-path algorithm (discussed below) is used in a three-step optimization process. The first step transmits prices from the subterminal (wholesale) centers to the country (retail) markets by discounting central market prices by the estimated transportation costs along the least-cost routing. This determines the prices quoted by the local grain elevator, fertilizer, or bulk petroleum retailer, or livestock collection station. Step two utilizes that price to estimate the trade area and affiliated volume of business for each local collector (retailer). In doing so, the least-cost-path algorithm estimates the routing used to transport rural production from the farm (source) to the collection centers (sinks). This step also calculates producer's hauling costs by truck type using the logit functions and determines road impacts caused by the freight flow.[5] Step three then attributes the estimated volume transacted by each rural collector (retailer) to the least-cost routing connecting it with its respective terminal (wholesale) center identified in the first step. By eliminating or adding links to the road and rail network, costs and benefits of subsequent optimal routings are calculated and compared to alternative network configurations.

Specifically, the model defines subterminals as those facilities located on rail lines with at least a fifty-car unit train loading capacity. Those elevators not located on the rail or with less than fifty-car unit train loading capacity comprise the country collectors. The procedure for transmitting grain prices from subterminal centers to country collectors is described below.

Let elevators A and B in Figure 10.2 consist of fifty-car capacity subterminals whose prices were discussed earlier. Let elevator C be a country elevator with a rail load-out capacity less than fifty cars. The bid price at C is determined by comparing the market options that would yield the largest sales revenue per bushel net of transportation costs. In this illustration four separate calculations would be compared: the price at A minus the rail costs over the AC rail routing, the price at A minus the trucking costs over the ADC highway routing, and the price at B minus the trucking costs over the BDC highway routing. The rail rate is differentiated by the rail shipping capacity at the shipping point. The truck rate is differentiated by the quality of the road network for both on-rail and off-rail country elevators. If the second option yields a higher net sales revenue at C than either of the other options, then the bid price at C is set as the net sales revenue per bushel from trucking grain to subterminal A. After the rural trade territory is established, the tonnage of grain acquired at C is then added to the estimated freight flow over the ADC road segment with its associated impact on road quality.

In transmitting fertilizer prices, the procedure is the mirror image of that for determining grain prices at country elevators. The same locations, A and B, in Figure 10.2 are assumed to be the dominant local pricing sources at which fertilizer ingredients are received from distant manufacturers/processors. Fertilizer prices at these subterminal locations are compounded by the rail or truck charges for transporting fertilizers from the source to the country outlets. Once again a least-cost algorithm is used, starting at the subterminal locations and sequentially adding the transportation costs for each segment of the optimal path road linkages in ADC and BDC as well as the rail linkage AC. The source, A or B, that can deliver the fertilizer ingredients to C at the least total delivered cost per ton is the sole supplier of C and, in effect, determines the retail price at C.

In the case of cattle (fat and feeder cattle) and hogs, prices at each auction barn or collection point are determined from the average livestock prices received by farmers at the central market in Omaha. The total delivery cost is computed by multiplying the transportation charge per hundredweight per mile by the distance between Omaha and each respective auction barn/livestock collection point. This delivery cost per hundredweight is subtracted from the Omaha livestock price to establish local prices. Once prices at the local collector/distributor points are calculated, they become an essential input in determining the outcome of the economic interplay between merchandisers and rural producers.

As the country grain merchandiser attempts to obtain the largest sales revenue net of transportation costs, the rural producer aspires to do the same. The merchandiser discounts the grain bids from numerous subterminals, processors, and so forth, by the transportation cost incurred in accessing each market and then compares their equivalent "alongside" prices. In like manner, the producer discounts commodity bids from country collectors by his cost of delivery to each in determining at their respective "farm-gate" prices. The same parallelism applies to producers' economic behavior in the purchase of inputs, except that alternative retail prices are compounded by transportation costs while attempting to minimize total delivered costs.

In attempting to minimize the transportation cost, the producer will try to choose that road system that has the least distance, has the greatest proportion of better quality roads, and has the least constraint on load capacity and safety. Other factors, such as past social-cultural ties to a particular market or the presence of related business firms located at a particular center, will also be important in determining the specific market.

Algorithm of Country Market-Producer Linkage

A least-cost algorithm was built to approximate the interplay described above. A rectangular grid of roads intersecting at one-mile intervals, representing the rural road system, was assumed. This assumption can be relaxed by deleting roads or by specifying diagonal roads. Each potential intersection of two-mile roads was identified as a vertex or node. Data stored describing each of these interconnecting links must be site specific. Two matrices of identifications were used to locate a specific segment being considered: one matrix identifying the east-west roads and one the north-south. Both matrices use the intersection of the fortieth parallel and the sixth principal meridian as the origin from which all mile segments are identified. Diagonal roads were approximated by rectangular movements toward the intersection closest to the diagonal road. The rectangular approximation of any diagonal section overestimates the actual distance. In the rectangular approximation, the links are adjusted proportionally so that their sum equals the distance of the diagonal road itself. Turn penalties, normally assigned to the rectangular corners, are eliminated when it represents a diagonal road. To reflect the shift of traffic off the diagonal, a turn penalty is imposed for traffic going straight when the approximated diagonal turns. The disadvantage of this method is that the road quality, transportation costs, and so forth of the diagonal superimposed on its rectangular road substitute, and the actual conditions of the original rectangular road are lost.

The least-cost-path algorithm is run for each truck type and each commodity type since the cost per mile of a specific road type is unique to the truck type and the commodity being transported. Each mile road segment carries the tonnage produced or required by the quarter section (160 acres) bordering on each side of the road. In addition, any segment may also carry the cumulative tonnage of other roads that feed onto it enroute to market.

When areas larger than one square mile are treated as an aggregate, imaginary roads with an artificially high cost of transport are introduced to drain the interior of the area to the boundary road. The high transportation cost of these imaginary roads prohibits traffic from other roads being routed over them in the least-cost-path algorithm. However, their costs are not included in computing private or public costs as they are essentially incurred in the field.

The least-cost algorithm builds what is technically called a depth-first tree traversal. Figure 10.4 provides an illustration of the operations of the model. Assume two elevators, A and B, with producer corn bids of $2.57 and $2.58, respectively. Tandem-axle costs for trucking corn over each road segment are stored in the data base as illustrated. The algorithm begins building the tree of road linkages one branch at a time connecting a road segment and its associated land area with a market center. It starts with the segment that would deliver the highest net farm gate price (NFGP) to its producing acres. In frame i, the first two segments are 1 and 2 since they originate from elevator B, which has the highest bid price combined with their lowest transportation cost of one cent per bushel per mile. This yields the highest possible NFGP of $2.57

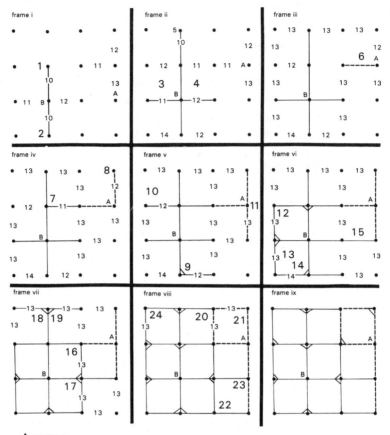

Assumes:
Price @B = $2.58/bu Price @A = $2.57/bu   Turn Penalty = $.0005/bu

Link #	Farm Gate Price	Farm Gate Price	Link #	Farm Gate Price	Farm Gate Price
1	$ 2.57	$	13	$ 2.5555	$
2	2.57		14	2.5555	
3	2.569		15	2.5550	
4	2.568		16	2.5545	
5	2.56		17	2.5545	
6		2.559	18	2.5465	
7	2.5585		19	2.5465	
8		2.558	20		2.5455
9	2.5575		21		2.5455
10	2.5575		22	2.5445	
11		2.557	23		2.5440
12	2.5555		24	2.5425	

Note: Small sized numbers represent cents/10 bushel/mile trucking cost for each respective segment. Large sized numbers represent order in which segment is added to least-cost routing.

Fig. 10.4 Hypothetical ordering of least-cost algorithm for routing corn in a tandem-axle truck

per bushel for the four quarter sections bordering segments 1 and 2. All other segments from either A or B would produce lower NFGPs.

In frame ii, the model now considers all possible linkages radiating from the nodes currently included. After comparing the costs for all of these linkages, the model selects sequentially those segments which result in NFGPs of descending magnitude: Linkage 3, $2.569; Linkage 4, $2.568; and Linkage 5, $2.56. This technique simulates the producer's evaluation of elevator bids and transportation costs that in combination will give him his highest net sales revenue. This is also equivalent to identifying the least-cost routing from each producing area to its respective market center.

The same procedure is repeated in frame iii. When a comparison is made of all remaining linkages spreading out from the included nodes, elevator A now commands the highest net farm-gate price of $2.559 on segment 6. It appears initially that both segment 6 and segment 7 in frame iv produce the same NFGP. However, a turn penalty of $.0005, reflecting the cost of deceleration and acceleration results in a NFGP for segment 7 of $2.5585. Turn penalties are indicated by diagonal lines traversing the relevant corners. The node between segments 6 and 7 begins to identify the trade area boundary between A and B. Segment 8 is added next in the series.

Segments 9, 10, and 11 are added in frame v. Both segments 9 and 10 have turn penalties, and both result in exactly the same NFGP of $2.5575. In the program they would then be added simultaneously. This also applies to links 12, 13, and 14, which share a common NFGP of $2.5555 in frame vi. The program proceeds through frame vii and is completed in frame viii. The completed tree spanning the entire region is presented in frame ix. The least-cost path and the resulting trade area in frame ix is unique to the specific truck type and commodity type considered; therefore, the algorithm is repeated for each. It is evident that any change in bid price or road condition would also alter the flow and the final trade area configuration. The NFGPs at a given point in the boundary of the trade territory are approximately equal with respect to either elevator. However, the NFGPs differ when comparing different points on the boundary.

Now that the least-cost routing is established, the model begins to accumulate tonnage. The algorithm traverses the tree, to the end of a branch first. It then carries that tonnage to the first junction, deposits it, goes to the end of the alternate branch, returns to the same junction,

```
                              1E

        0     1     2     3     4     5     6     7

48   . .04 . .05 . .04 . .08 . .04 . .04 . .14 .
       0     1     0     1     0     0     2     0
       3     2     3     5     4     3     2     4
47   . .06 . .03 . .06 . .25 . .09 . .03 . .07 .
       0     2     0     0     4     0     3     0
       3     5     3     3     1     3     2     3
46   . .03 . .03 . .03 . .09 . .06 . .03 . .04 .
       0     3     0     0     6     0     4     1
8N
       6     5     6     5     0     7     0     4
45   . .39 . .95 . 1.2 . 2.1 . 5.9 . 5.8 . 5.2 .
       2     1     1     7     6     0     2     3
       9     6     6     9     8     8     0     3
44   . .03 . .03 . .03 . .03 . .06 . .03 . .03 .
       2     1           7     5     0     1     1
       6     2     9     3     6     5     6     9
43   . .03 . .03 . .03 . .06 . .14 . .06 . .03 .
       2     0     0     7     3     0     1     1
       3     6     3     0     2     7     2     2
42    .03   .06   .12   .03   .06   .03   .03
```

Fig. 10.5 1984 flows over road system in Saline County assuming (a) a zero-mile-parameter zone and (b) trucks do not cross underweight bridges. *Base Run.* (1,000 18-kips)

and proceeds until the tonnage from all branches are gathered at the main junction before moving to the next major limb. The freight tonnage for each road segment is summed across all truck sizes and all commodities to reveal the total tonnage moving on a given road. The model converts this total tonnage into 18-kips which are used in later sections to estimate the road wear and changes in annual maintenance costs.

The reverse procedure is used for fertilizer and petroleum. Instead of starting with the highest bid price, the algorithm begins with the lowest sales price at the retail centers and adds the trucking costs in an attempt to deliver the input at the minimum net farm-gate cost, resulting in input routings being the minimal cost to all land areas and trade territories drawn accordingly.

Policy Example

Saline County, Nebraska, was selected for a pilot test of the impact of reclassification of low-volume public dirt roads to permit private access only. In an attempt to reduce public maintenance costs without incurring significant increases in private transportation costs, this policy may be considered by county road officials.

The base run of RTM with the public dirt roads in their current condition is illustrated in Figure 10.5. This flow of commodities over the rural road network resulted in an estimated private trucking cost of approximately $225,287 annually to transport all fertilizer, bulk petroleum, feedgrains, wheat, soybeans, feeder cattle, fat cattle, and slaughter hogs. In order to provide these transportation services while maintaining the current road qualities, the public sector paid approximately $6,230 in annual maintenance costs. Figure 10.5 estimates the 1,000 18-kips of freight over each road segment in Saline County in 1984 given the base run conditions.

In the alternative run, all public dirt roads in Saline County were reclassified as restricted access so that they were essentially private access only. All other conditions of the base run, such as truckers not crossing underweight bridges and not considering freight needs in the perimeter outside the county, were held constant. Figure 10.6 provides the user with the estimated 1,000 18-kips of commodity flow over each road segment in Saline County in 1984 under the alternative scenario.

The impact of reclassification of public dirt roads as private access roads was to decrease public expenditures for road maintenance by $254 annually or approximately 4 percent. While one might expect the public savings to be greater, one must consider that the same tonnage must still be transported over other public roads, the closing to public access has forced some redirection of flows possibly increasing the ton-miles hauled, and the dirt roads chosen for reclassification were already very light-density roads.

While the public sector experienced a net savings by the policy, the private sector saw transportation costs rise by $3,706. This change would need to be taken into consideration in evaluating the net gains to the local economy as a whole of reducing the public revenue expenditure.

IE

	0	1	2	3	4	5	6	7
48	.	.04 .	.11 .	.06 .	.04 .	.06 .	.04 .	.05 .
	0	1	0	0	1	0	0	1
	3	9	3	3	2	3	5	2
47	.	.03 .	.10 .	.03 .	.06 .	.18 .	.12 .	.04 .
	0	3	0	0	3	0	0	2
	6	4	3	3	9	3	3	0
46	.	.03 .	.03 .	.03 .	.03 .	.10 .	.07 .	.04 .
8N	0	4	0	1	5	0	0	3
	9	4	6	0	6	7	4	0
45	.	.48 .	1.2 .	1.5 .	1.7 .	6.0 .	5.7 .	5.3 .
	3	2	2	1	9	2	3	0
	6	1	1	0	4	5	9	7
44	.	.03 .	.03 .	.03 .	.03 .	.06 .	.03 .	.04 .
	3	1	1	0	8	2	3	0
	2	5	5	4	2	2	0	3
43	.	.03 .	.03 .	.03 .	.12 .	.03 .	.03 .	.12 .
	2	0	0	0	6	1	1	0
	9	9	8	6	4	6	4	9
42		.03	.03	.03	.06	.06	.03	.03

Fig 10.6 1984 flows over road system in Saline County assuming (a) a zero-mile-parameter zone, (b) trucks do not cross underweight bridges, and (c) all dirt roads are private access only. *Simulation Run.*

Model Summary

The RTM model assists county and state planners in approximating the private and public costs of rural traffic. The model can be updated and is interactive. By displaying the network on the computer screen, the model allows county engineers to graphically witness optimal routings and flows and to maintain a graphical road inventory in which configuration and quality can be altered at the engineer's discretion. Alternative scenarios that the engineer may consider as relevant to the local situation may also be analyzed.

Extension Implementation

While public interest and awareness will be required to reach acceptable solutions, elected county commissioners and supervisors are the primary individuals responsible for investment/disinvestment decisions. However, the potential users of the RTM must also include local road engineers or supervisors who serve as a primary source of information and advice for these elected officials.

Initial extension efforts have centered on the introduction of the RTM. These were primarily targeted toward county engineers and road supervisors. The various software packages of the RTM were presented and demonstrated at their annual summer conference. Subsequently, a day-long workshop was conducted for county roads staff which offered participants hands-on experience as well as copies of the RTM software packages and instructional manuals. Difficulty was experienced in addressing the extreme diversity of hardware available in county offices. Additional workshops are being planned for county road supervisors and engineers utilizing the staff of current pilot counties as resource personnel. Meanwhile, a grant has been obtained to provide these resources to all county road engineers or supervisors who request them.

Pilot programs will be proposed to combine this capacity with planning procedures used in the development of the Pennsylvania "Agri-Access" road network (TenEyck and Lebo 1984). Local leaders should expect to improve their ability to cope with substantive structural adjustments in the local economy and design a road network appropriate for their development plans.

A Nontechnical Summary

The software package contains four disks. The respective contents and purpose of the disks are listed according to the content and order in which the computer software is used by the county engineer:

> *Disk 1*
> Label: Edit. Road
> Purpose: Displays entire state map with state highway network. This helps the user locate a county in which he would like to enter county roads and bridges and actually alter the rural road and bridge conditions on either disks 2 or 3 below.

Disk 2
Label: Eastern. Nebraska
Purpose: Contains data on the grid system of the entire eastern half of the state; i.e., east of a north-south line located 120 miles west of the sixth Principal Meridian. Each mile on grid is initialized to be a "gravel road." The user can reinitialize the grid system to any other road type with accompanying serviceability index and bridge situation using "Edit. Road" above.

Disk 3
Label: Western. Nebraska
Purpose: Contains data on the grid system of the entire western half of the state. Each mile on the grid is initialized to be a "no road." The user can reinitialize the grid system to any other road type using its accompanying serviceability index and bridge situation using "Edit. Road" above.

Disk 4
Label: Flows
Purpose: To be used with disk 2 or 3; to generate commodity flows over a specific grid system and calculate private and public transportation costs.

Disks 1, 2, and 3 serve an accounting function. The county engineer can keep a visual inventory of bridges, the road network, and their inventory. In the event of an unanticipated or anticipated road closure, say due to a snowstorm or repairs, the engineer can "close" the road in the computer screen and simulate the resulting rerouting of the flows.

Disk 4, on the other hand, contains all the basic geographical information on the location of firms. It also contains a matrix of trucking costs by road type and quality and rail rates by main or branchline. In the event of changing fuel costs, rail rates, and so forth, the information can be altered to reflect the new cost conditions. More importantly, as firms enter or leave the area, the engineer can easily eliminate them from the data base. In addition, as rail branchlines are added or deleted from the state map, the engineer can do the same through correcting the data base. Disk 4 also contains the minimum-cost algorithm described in the previous section.

Notes

1. The engineering term 18-kip is used to describe the road surface pressure equivalent to eighteen thousand pounds per axle.

2. The soil types or soil association names (SAN) per square mile obtained from the Agricultural Stabilization and Conservation Service (ASCS) maps. Associated with each SAN are four qualitative categories: farmland suitability, irrigation suitability, slope, and water erosion potential. Each qualitative category is in turn broken down into five categories: high, good, fair, low, and very low. The method for using the above information to assign production per square mile is too lengthy to discuss. Interested readers should contact the authors.

3. Turn penalties are costs of vehicle acceleration and deceleration to turn right or left at a road intersection.

4. Initial data for prices and quantities reflected 1984 conditions. The model is updated for use in subsequent years.

5. In calculating the road impacts, the distribution and total kip equivalents by truck type and by commodity were considered. The weight was distributed over the front axle, tractor drive, and tractor back wheels.

References

Azzam, A. M., and D. Linsenmeyer. 1987. "The Impact of Volume of Marketing and Distance to Market on the Choice of Truck Size." *North Central Journal of Agricultural Economics* 8 (1): 135–44.

Baumel, C. Phillip, and Eldo Schornhorst. 1983. "Local Rural Roads and Bridges: Current and Future Problems and Alternatives." *Transportation Research Record* 898: 374–78.

Johnson, Bruce B. 1986. "The Changing Structure of Agriculture in Nebraska." *Nebraska Policy Choices*. Ed. by Jeffery S. Luke & Vincent J. Webb, Center for Applied Urban Research, University of Nebraska, Omaha, Nebraska.

Lawson, Michael. 1986. "The Impact of the Farm Recession of Local Governments." *Intergovernmental Perspective* 12 (3): 17–24.

Linsenmeyer, Dean. 1982. "Effect of Unit-Train Shipments on Rural Nebraska Roads." *Transportation Research Record* 875: 60–64.

Stauss, Connie. 1988. "Nebraska Can Work." Part I, Policy Prescriptions for Solving the Infrastructure in Nebraska, Research Division, Ne. Department of Economic Development, Lincoln, Nebraska, 21–26.

TenEyck, Thomas E., and Dennis E. Lebo. 1984. "Benefits of Pennsylvania's Agricultural Access Study," Bureau for Strategic Planning, Pennsylvania Dept. of Transportation.

U.S. Department of Commerce, Bureau of Census. 1980. *Nebraska Census of Agriculture*.

11

Adjusting to a Changing Transportation Regulatory Environment—The Case of Trucking-Exempt Commodities

Wesley W. Wilson
Gene C. Griffin
Kenneth L. Casavant
Daniel L. Zink

Grain production accounts for a significant portion of farm income in the northern plains region of the United States, particularly for North Dakota where food grains, feed grains, and oilseeds amounted to 55 percent of total farm income in 1984, exclusive of government payments. Since much of the production must be exported out of the state and the region, an efficient, competitive transportation system is critical to both the state and the agricultural economy.

More than 550 million bushels of field crops were shipped from North Dakota origins in the 1983–84 crop year. All shipments made were provided by either truck or rail, which are the only two modes of transportation available to North Dakota shippers. (Some grain moves by truck-barge and rail-barge combinations after the grain leaves the state.) The two modes, while different, are very good substitutes in originating grain. Two railroad firms (Burlington Northern and Soo Line) dominate grain shipments from North Dakota, hauling 74 percent of all grains and oilseeds in 1985–86. By contrast, between 600 and

1,000 trucking firms capture the remaining 26 percent of the grain traffic. Thus, truckers provide the only competition to an otherwise oligopolistic transport industry in the Upper Midwest. Shippers of agricultural commodities in the region rely heavily on the trucker to maintain a reasonably competitive transportation market by limiting the market power of the railroads.

During the late 1970s and early 1980s a variety of legislation was passed that affected the transportation industries. Legislated changes, coupled with rising costs and a depressed economy, represented a wide variety of net circumstances facing the grain distribution system, particularly the grain truckers' role in that system. A program was therefore initiated to educate truckers, shippers, and others about this changing economic and regulatory environment. In addition, the program addressed the long run implications of these dynamic forces and the truckers' changing role in the distribution system.

The program consisted of management topics presented by economists and attorneys. Specific topics discussed included truck costs, pricing, competitive factors, policy changes, the impact of truck and rail deregulation, the importance of the industry to agriculture, and growth in the industry (see the appendix).

The program was conducted at one-day seminars at two different North Dakota locations in August of 1981. Since 1981 portions of the program have been given several times at related workshops and seminars. In this chapter a brief summary of the program is provided in conjunction with the rationale for including each component. In the final section a discussion of the problems encountered and suggestions for organizing similar programs are provided.

North Dakota's "Exempt" Truckers

The first presentation, entitled "Exempt Trucking: The Case in North Dakota," was intended to summarize an ongoing research effort investigating the nature, role, and economic viability of exempt agricultural truck transportation. The rationale for this presentation was based on the proposition that as independent truckers, the firms might be unable to track industry trends and performance and were in need of somewhat simplistic formulas and mechanisms upon which to base pricing decisions. With these purposes in mind, the presentation covered broad industry trends and descriptions of the industry, followed by a discussion of pricing decisions with particular emphasis on the role of costs and differing revenue sources (i.e., the availability of backhaul loads.)

Exempt truckers serving North Dakota are composed of a variety of different types of operations. These truckers range from farmers hauling their own agricultural products to relatively large trucking firms serving large market areas. This sector of the industry is exempt from regulation when carrying bulk, unprocessed agricultural products. It is therefore difficult to estimate the number of firms—estimates range from 600 to 1,000 (Cosgriff 1978). Of the firms identified, 77 percent were located in North Dakota, while the remainder were located in the bordering states of Minnesota, Montana, and South Dakota. The distribution of firms is heavily weighted to the eastern part of North Dakota, reflecting both greater production and truckers' comparative advantage in shorter hauls as the major markets for the region's agricultural products are in Minnesota.

Truck and rail market share data suggested that transportation by truck, relative to rail, grew in every year between 1974 to 1979. Truck competition was strongest in the northeastern and southwestern part of North Dakota. While the number of truckers was quite large in the northeastern part of the state, the number of firms in the southwest was considerably smaller. Therefore, the larger market share of trucks in southwestern North Dakota may be due to lack of reliable rail service or low density of production, rather than truckers' inherent economic advantages in the southwest.

This opening session of the workshop gave a general overview of trucking in North Dakota including number of firms, geographical dispersion of firms, and intermodal competitive relationships. The next part of the discussion provided average industry characteristics and data that firm managers may use to evaluate their own performance. This discussion centered around a sample of firms operating in 1979. In general, the truckers in the state are of relatively small size (two to four tractors). A high degree of industry concentration was noted in the sample; the largest eight firms accounted for 56.8 percent of the loaded miles in the survey. In explaining this level of concentration, it is noted that the largest firms traveled greater distances (635 miles versus about 450 miles per one-way trip) and a greater proportion of their return legs of round trips were loaded (59 percent versus about 25 percent). Larger firms had been in business about 13.5 years, while medium-sized firms and owner-operator had been in business only about eight years. This may be reflective of some inherent efficiencies or market strength associated with larger carriers.

The final segment of the initial presentation covered cost concepts and an integration of cost and backhaul availability into fronthaul pricing decisions. Statistical analysis was used to generate average cost estimates per mile based on firm size, utilization (miles per year per truck), average length of haul, and equipment age. Greater efficiencies were associated with larger firms; these firms had about a 4.5 cent per-mile cost advantage over single truck firms. These results were discussed with the audience and provided as a standard from which firms could evaluate their own performance. After reviewing cost concepts and results of the cost estimates, a costing worksheet was provided to the firm managers. The format of the worksheet was based on cost accounting principles and was relatively easy to use. It corresponded closely to the statistical formulae used to calculate costs discussed above, and therefore could be used by truckers to compare their costs with those from the statistical analysis.

Based on the discussion of costs, pricing and the seasonality of rates were then presented. With regard to pricing decisions, it was pointed out that backhaul traffic has a minimal impact on costs, but a profound impact on revenues. The firms were encouraged to incorporate expected revenues associated with backhaul traffic in evaluating the fronthaul price they need. It was noted that the critical decision the trucker makes is whether or not to provide the service at the price offered, given that the truckers' role in establishing the fronthaul rate is minimal (Cosgriff 1978). The role, nature, and level of costs and backhaul traffic was emphasized in that decision. Means of attracting backhaul traffic were then discussed.

A Changing Regulatory Environment

The conference was conducted in 1981, one year after passage of two major transportation bills, The Motor Carrier Act of 1980 and The Staggers Rail Act of 1980. The second and third presentations were based on the assumption that an extension effort was needed to educate all parties in the state concerning not only the specific changes in law, but also the long-run implications of each act. Each of these presentations are summarized below and were conducted by attorneys actively specializing in transportation law.

The Motor Carrier Act of 1980 and its Effects

The first presentation, dealing with the Motor Carrier Act of 1980, consisted of several components. No overview of recent legislation is complete without a description of the source of the change. The first component of this presentation was therefore a cursory overview of the history of motor carrier regulation. Second, the recent pressures for deregulation were discussed. Deregulation or partial deregulation of transport has occurred in virtually all freight transport sectors. Since much can be learned from experiences in other sectors, a brief discussion of the adjustment of airlines to deregulation was presented. Finally, the recent changes emanating from the Motor Carrier Act of 1980 were detailed and implications for both exempt and regulated truckers were discussed.

History of Motor Carrier Regulations

Federal regulation of interstate motor carrier transportation was nonexistent prior to 1925. However, interstate motor carriage was regulated in most regions of the United States by state regulatory authorities. Some forty states at this time required truck operators to obtain operating authority, regardless of whether they operated intrastate or interstate. In 1925, the Buck versus Kuykendall decision by the United State's Supreme Court effectively eliminated state controls on entry into interstate routes by motor carriers. As a result, there was pressure and perhaps need for legislation at the federal level.

The Motor Carrier Act of 1935 was passed in response to a variety of pressures not only from state regulatory bodies, but also from railroads, shippers, and large established motor carriers. This act provided for regulation of interstate motor carriage under the umbrella of the Interstate Commerce Commission. The act grandfathered operating authority to those carriers already providing the service, and thereafter required new entrants to obtain operating authority. Not all traffic, however, was subject to the jurisdiction of the ICC. Most notably, private motor carriage and the interstate transportation of unprocessed agricultural commodities were exempted from ICC jurisdiction.

Pressures for Deregulation

Several events lead up to the eventual passage of the Motor Carrier Act of 1980. Some of these events included: experiences with other deregulated transportation sectors; problems with the then-current regulatory system; the fuel shortage of the 1970s; and finally, a growing consensus of the public in favor of less government intervention in the marketplace. In 1978, total economic deregulation of the airways was initiated, culminating with the recent sunsetting of the Civil Aeronautics Board. While in the initial years there were some adverse price and service effects, the general attitude toward air deregulation has been favorable due to benefits accruing from innovative fare structures by new entrants.

A number of problems identified with current motor carrier regulation also promoted moves toward less regulation. The problems were primarily associated with the bureaucratic morass associated with the fragmented jurisdiction of the ICC, as well as restrictions on routes and backhauls. Exempt and nonexempt classification of commodities raised serious concern for the workability of regulation. For example, as Representative Millicent Fenwick testified:

> The ICC has 36 categories of exempt and nonexempt products listed under the heading of "Milk and Cream." Buttermilk is exempt, but butterfat and buttermilk with condensed cream are regulated. Concentrated skim milk, and powdered, are exempt, but condensed and evaporated are not.
>
> And believe it or not, Mr. Chairman, manure in its natural state is an exempt commodity but mature, fermented with additives such as yeast and molds, producing a rich liquor which in water solution is used for soil enrichment, is not. (Depsey 1980)

In addition, restrictions on routes and backhauls seemed an anomaly at a time when fuel shortages abounded and Americans were being told to save gasoline. An example provided by Snow (1977) is demonstrative of an inefficiency introduced by regulation.

> A company ships two loads per week from North Carolina to New England and the trucks return empty. A subsidiary firm ships a like number of truckloads from New England to Georgia. These also return empty. Total annual mileage is 330,000, almost

half of which is needlessly empty because of ICC restrictions on intercorporate hauling by private carriers. If these artificial restrictions were eliminated, either of the present fleets could pick up the other's cargo on its return haul. Total annual mileage would be 170,000, of which 5,000 miles would be empty. Fleet capacity would be reduced by half, mileage savings would be 160,000 per year, and fuel savings would be 40,000 gallons per year. There would be no impact on regulated traffic. (Snow 1977)

In short, public attitudes, inefficiencies, and positive experiences with other transportation deregulation were all contributory factors in the drive for passage of the Motor Carrier Act of 1980.

Specific Changes in the Regulatory Environment

The primary audience for the conference was the "exempt" trucker; that is, they haul commodities exempt from interstate or intrastate economic regulation. The data suggest these firms regularly serve the same elevator for most of their trips. Hence, they return back to the same North Dakota origins. As discussed earlier, they often travel empty on the return trips, a situation not unlike the private carrier example given earlier. There are many possible reasons for traveling empty on these return trips, not the least of which is that North Dakota is a region exporting agricultural commodities and importing regulated commodities. Unless these carriers of exempt commodities have some form of operating authority, they are restricted from serving the regulated transport market directly.

The changes in the regulatory system afforded by the Motor Carrier Act of 1980 went far in relaxing these entry barriers. First and foremost, entry restrictions into transport markets of regulated commodities were greatly reduced. To gain entry under the old law, carriers had to prove they were "fit, willing, and able" and show that the proposed service was required for the public convenience and necessity. Under the new legislation, these criteria were continued but greatly changed. Now the applicant need only show that the proposed service will serve a useful public purpose and be responsive to public demand. The burden is now on the protestants to show that the service is inconsistent with the public convenience and necessity. In addition, there are now cases wherein applicants need only show they are fit, willing, and able. These include service to communities that are not regularly served by another motor carrier, service to locations where rail service has been abandoned, movements of U.S. government property (with some exceptions), small shipments (under 100 pounds), and movement of foodstuffs and fertilizer by an owner-operator (provided the owner-operator remains with the truck at all times). Many of the truck firms are based in small, rural communities which may qualify under the fitness only application criteria. In addition, many communities in North Dakota faced the rail line abandonment issue. Finally, many carriers in the state were of relatively small size, and the owner typically is a driver, hence, an owner-operator.

The legislation also expanded the list of exempt commodities. Fish and shellfish by-products, livestock and poultry feed, agricultural seeds, and plants transported to a farm or to a business selling to farmers are now exempt. Some of these commodities are inputs to the agricultural economy and therefore represent new potential backhaul traffic to the exempt trucker.

Finally, cursory overview of some of the remaining changes of the legislation was provided. These included new rules for contract carriage, private carriage, pricing, and so forth. Specific attention was paid to how these new changes created problems or opportunities for the trucking firm.

The Staggers Rail Act—Bane or Boon?

The two modes of transportation serving North Dakota's agricultural community are truck and rail. The partial, yet substantial, deregulation of the railroads occurred in 1980. The success or failure of the Staggers Act is a subjective topic, and specific interests certainly have differing viewpoints depending on the individual's perspective.

Much of the new transportation legislation reflected a movement toward greater reliance on the market to determine prices which was accomplished by removing regulatory lags in price adjustment and enhancing profitability of the railroads by enabling unprofitable dimensions of the business to be divested. Each of these factors and the implications for trucking were addressed in the third presentation.

Rail Price Adjustment

A cost index was introduced into rail rate making by the Staggers Act to expedite recovery of inflationary cost increases. Under the new legislation, rail rates can be adjusted quarterly using an inflationary index. It was pointed out that when rail rates increase under this provision, more traffic could accrue to truckers. However, it was also noted that in attracting the added traffic it was important to have a knowledge of costs and not to "cut each others throats."

Price Determination and Market Dominance

The concept of market dominance was introduced to regulatory policy under the 4-R Act but was changed somewhat by the Staggers Rail Act. In essence, if the railroad is not found to have market dominance, the jurisdiction of the ICC with respect to maximum rate controls is removed and the price is determined by the marketplace. The traffic had to demonstrate a revenue to variable cost ratio of at least 160 percent before the ICC had authority to determine the existence of market dominance (the 160 percent threshold increasing over time). If the rate in question was more than 160 percent of variable cost, the ICC then considered a variety of other standards before rendering a decision on market dominance. If the traffic was found market dominant, only then could the question of whether or not the rate was reasonable be addressed. It was pointed out that most grain traffic in the region yielded a revenue to variable cost ratio greater than 160 percent, and that in five out of nine grain reporting districts in North Dakota the railroad had a market share over 70 percent. Given the current regulatory policy, the proposition was that very little of the traffic would be found market dominant. Hence, rates were expected to be the result of market processes. The important role of the exempt truck as the only competitor of the railroad was stressed, again as it affected transport rate determination.

Surcharges on traffic (economically, a means to abandonment) was a second provision of the Staggers Rail Act having serious implications on grain transportation in the state. Under the new legislation, carriers can place surcharges on a variety of traffic, including any joint line rate that does not yield 110 percent of variable cost, rates applying to carriers with inadequate revenues on lines carrying less than three million gross ton miles per year, and rates applying to carriers with adequate revenues on lines carrying less than one million ton miles per year.

Most, if not all, North Dakota branch lines fall within the second category. Thus, railroads have the potential to effectively abandon unprofitable or marginal branch lines by applying rate surcharges. Truckers serving those areas could then anticipate added potential loads if appropriate pricing and service decisions were made.

The new legislation also greatly facilitates the direct abandonment of unprofitable or marginal branch lines. Each rail line abandoned represents added potential traffic for motor carriers. Those authorized for abandonment were identified for the audience. In addition, just prior to the conference, representatives of one of the two railroads serving the state identified rail lines either up for, pending, or under consideration for abandonment. These lines were identified for planning purposes of motor carriers, shippers, and other affected parties.

This presentation was concluded with a warning. While much of the regulatory change suggests a boon to truckers, the long-term implications of the railroad industry painted a different picture; that is, much of the above discussion dealt with marginal or low-volume branch lines. The long-term strategy identified with the railroads in the region is to publish multiple-car rates and provide the incentive for a "subterminal" system of transportation in the state. The implication over the long-term for the trucker is they would be displaced from long haul traffic and placed into short haul traffic feeding the subterminal distribution system.

Agricultural Trucking Growth in North Dakota

The previous presentations were structured by conference planners to outline the existing transportation infrastructure and shifts in regulatory policy. The next presentation provided an overview of trends in trucking, railroad pricing responses to growth in trucking, and expected future behavior of railroads and truckers.

During the 1970s trucking in North Dakota grew at a consistent rate. In 1974 the truck share of agricultural products was only about 19 percent, increasing to about 40 percent in the late 1970s. The increase was not only in terms of relative market shares but in absolute volumes as well. The growth in trucking was attributed to rail car shortages occurring in the time period, rail pricing policies (higher prices, perhaps to obtain rents associated with the car shortage), and a rapidly growing agricultural economy. Most of the growth occurred in the eastern third of the state, where sunflower and wheat production growth was largest and where firms were located closer to the major markets in Minnesota. While both Minneapolis and Duluth truck markets experienced growth, the growth was highest in the Duluth markets (where backhauls are generally not available), emphasizing the fronthaul rate available to truckers.

Railroad reactions had consisted of meeting truck competition by decreasing the single car rail rate. However, this policy was changed somewhat in the late 1970s and early 1980s as a reaction to a growing truck share of shipments from western North Dakota to the Pacific Northwest. In 1981 the truckers' share of that market had increased to over 45 percent. Much of this growth was attributed to the growing availability of backhauls from the West Coast. Truckers were able to compete over this longer haul if loaded in both directions. In addition to continued price competition with decreases in single-car rates, for the first time railroads also responded with greater product differentiation. The railroad introduced multiple-car rail rates as a strategy to meet truck and truck-barge competition in the west. The result was that continued backhaul traffic from the West Coast was essential in order for truckers to compete with the railroad for the long haul agricultural traffic from North Dakota to the West Coast.

The railroad was expected to continue to base competitive pricing decisions on long-run truck costs. Also, product differentiation by multicar merchandising was expected to be the principal competitive tool used by the railroads in meeting truck competition. Finally, it was pointed out that in short-run pricing decisions the railroad could well abandon the above strategies and increase prices to gain profits associated with rail car shortages. Under the new legislation railroads could be expected to react much faster to such shortages and other changes in the market, again providing short-run opportunities for the aggressive trucking firm.

An Overview of Agricultural Trucking in North Dakota and the Nation

The last presentation was a review and synthesis of the four presentations summarized above and provided, an overview of other issues facing these and other trucking firms throughout the nation. Included in the presentation was transportation as a derived demand; that is, transportation is only useful in terms of the time and place utility it creates. As such, there is a need for truckers not only to drive, but also to identify what needs to be moved, where it needs to be moved, and the value of the service.

While earlier presentations pointed to advantages of the large firm over the small firm, the conclusion was not that small truckers cannot compete; rather, the results suggest that progressive and successful truckers have more opportunities. The cost information provided a mechanical means to calculate costs as well as industry averages to evaluate performance. Carriers were again encouraged to use the cost information in conjunction with backhaul prospects to form a basis for their pricing decisions.

By integrating these concepts with a changing regulatory environment, the Motor Carrier Act of 1980 was considered as having opened many opportunities for the trucker. These opportunities, when used, could make a trucking firm a more efficient and profitable business. The Staggers Rail Act of 1980 was considered as positive in the short run. The role of the trucker may change in the long run from providing service in long haul markets to being a critical factor in short haul markets, serving as a feeder to the grain subterminal system.

Trends in trucking, regulation, and competition suggest that for truckers to compete over long hauls they simply must look to backhaul traffic—a theme throughout the conference. Unit and multiple car rail rates will cause extreme competition for truckers, and the only way they will be able to compete is to enhance revenues on a total trip basis.

Finally, a variety of national trends and issues will continue to affect the trucker. These include not only a deregulated transportation industry, but also continued debate about size and weight restrictions. Recent analyses had shown that truckers were not paying for the cost of the damage they did to the road system. Thus, increases in user fees were identified as a coming possibility. In addition, there appears no end in sight to the continuing problem of different weight and length restrictions across states. The final parting point given to all attending the conference was that a number of changes were taking place in transportation and that truckers could no longer afford to just drive; they must make both management and merchandising decisions.

Lessons of Organization

As a concluding note to this chapter, the lessons learned from both organizing and conducting the conference are summarized. First, the conference was held in mid-August to correspond with the beginning of the harvest of commodities. While an alternative time period could not have been chosen for the initial effort, later attempts have been coordinated with off-peak time periods.

Second, three different mechanisms were used in publicizing the conference. These included direct mailing to the known truckers, contact with the local news media, and contact with the national trade magazines. All had some benefit; attendance was about forty to fifty people at each location. The locations chosen were in the northeast and lower central parts of North Dakota, based on the geographical dispersion of truckers. Future attempts at this type of a program may well be advised to also contact the customers of these carriers as well as truck stops located throughout the region. Finally, contact with the local news media was essential. Notice was given to the public, and television coverage of the event in each of the two cities was obtained.

Third, the content of the conference was well received by most of the public attending, with some exception. The content was broad and integrated; however, one possible omission was that of the process of locating and negotiating for backhaul loads. As demonstrated in the initial presentation and throughout the remaining conference, backhaul loads have a profound impact on the economic viability of the trucker. Mechanisms to enhance the likelihood of obtaining backhauls could have been better developed.

The inclusion of two specific items in the conference program may have been warranted. First, the mechanics of obtaining fitness applications and other operating authority may have been a fruitful area of discussion. Second, little is known of the mechanics of obtaining a backhaul load in a given market. The inclusion of a broker from one of the major markets may have been very useful.

References

Casavant, Ken. 1981. "An Overview of Agricultural Trucking in North Dakota and the Nation." Papers and Proceedings of the Trucking in North Dakota Management Conferences, Upper Great Plains Transportation Institute, North Dakota State University, Fargo, North Dakota.

Cosgriff, John G. 1978. "The Cost and Operations of Exempt Motor Carriers in North Dakota." Upper Great Plains Transportation Institute Report No. 33, North Dakota State University, Fargo, North Dakota.

Dempsey, Paul Stephen. 1980. "The Expanse of Deregulation: Erosion of the Common Carrier System." Transportation Law Institute, 1.

Finsness, John. 1981. "The Staggers Rail Act—Bane or Boon?" Papers and Proceedings of the Trucking in North Dakota Management Conferences, Upper Great Plains Transportation Institute, North Dakota State University, Fargo, North Dakota.

Griffin, Gene C. 1981. "Agricultural Trucking Growth in North Dakota." Papers and Proceedings of the Trucking in North Dakota Management Conferences, Upper Great Plains Transportation Institute, North Dakota State University, Fargo, North Dakota.

Snow, John W. 1977. "The Problem of Motor Carrier Regulation and the Ford Administration's Proposal for Reform." Ed. by Paul W. MacAvoy and John W. Snow, Washington, D.C.: American Enterprise for Public Policy Research.

Thoms, William E. 1981. "Rollin' On . . . To Deregulation—the Motor Carrier Act of 1980 and its Effects." Papers and Proceedings of the Trucking in North Dakota Management Conferences, Upper Great Plains Transportation Institute, North Dakota State University, Fargo, North Dakota.

Wilson, Wesley W. 1981. "Exempt Trucking—The Case in North Dakota." Papers and Proceedings of the Trucking in North Dakota Management Conferences, Upper Great Plains Transportation Institute, North Dakota State University, Fargo, North Dakota.

Appendix Trucking in North Dakota / A Management Seminar

Program for 12 and 13 August 1981

12 August 1981
   Location: Ramada Inn, Coronado Room
   Grand Forks, ND at 1:00 P.M.

13 August 1981
   Location: Holiday Inn, Hall of Ports
   Bismarck, ND at 1:00 P.M.

A Management Seminar Discussing:

- Costs
- Competition
- Growth
- Pricing
- Deregulation
- An Overview of the Industry

Agenda

1:00   Introduction and Coffee
1:30   "Trucking: The Case in North Dakota" by Wesley W. Wilson, Research
        Assistant, Upper Great Plains Transportation Institute, NDSU, Fargo,
        ND
2:00   "Truck Deregulation: What Now?" by Dr. William E. Thoms, Professor of
        Law, University of North Dakota School of Law, Grand Forks, ND
2:30   "Railroad Deregulation: Its Effects on Motor Carriers" by John I. Finsness,
        Director of Traffic, North Dakota Public Service Commission, Bis-
        marck, ND
3:00   "Agricultural Trucking: Growth" by Gene C. Griffin, Director Upper Great
        Plains Transportation Institute, NDSU, Fargo, ND
3:30   "Trucking in North Dakota: An Overview" by Dr. Kenneth L. Casavant,
        Professor of Agricultural Economics, Washington State University, Pull-
        man, WA

Sponsored by: Upper Great Plains Transportation Institute

Transportation Institute Advisory Council:
    Greater North Dakota Association
    North Dakota Public Service Commission
    North Dakota Farm Bureau
    North Dakota Farmers Union
    North Dakota Stockmans Association
    North Dakota Wheat Commission
    Economic Development Association
    North Dakota Grain Dealers Association
    North Dakota Railway Lines
    North Dakota Motor Carriers Association
    North Dakota Aeronautics Commission

For more information call or write:
    The Upper Great Plains Transportation Institute
    Ceres—Room 202
    North Dakota State University
    Fargo, ND (701) 237-7767

12

A Short-Line Solution to Rail Branch Line Abandonment: A Comparative Case Study

Henry M. Bahn

Prior to the late 1970s and early 1980s, when new legislation increased the flexibility of railroads to abandon unprofitable lines as a method of reducing costs and enhancing revenue, the Interstate Commerce Commission (ICC) had used a policy of cross-subsidization to maintain service on marginally profitable or unprofitable lines. The railroads' problems were magnified by their difficulty in adjusting rates on individual lines to reflect costs. As a consequence, rail services were sometimes provided at below-cost rates, sometimes attracting additional traffic, but often maintaining traffic at essentially subsidized rates.

In addition to these difficulties, new technology and publicly funded projects for highway and waterway development eroded the competitive advantage of railroads. Relative to other modes, the quality of rail service deteriorated, resulting in loss of market share, reduced profitability to the rail industry as a whole, and, in some cases, bankruptcy.

The relatively large number of rail lines identified as candidates for abandonment represents many lines that would have been abandoned years ago had the regulatory climate allowed such action, and "the quick about-face policy has unleashed pent-up desires to abandon low traffic lines only recently, creating an atmosphere of crisis rather than measured evolution" (Johnson 1982).

The abandonment process is normally streamlined, allowing abandonment if the railroad can show that maintaining service results in a financial loss based on a simple formula:

$$\pi = R - C - .167NLV$$

where

π = Profitability;

R = Revenue;

C = Avoidable Costs;

NLV = Net Liquidation Value.

The railroad estimates revenue based on a reasonable approximation of projected traffic and rates over time. Avoidable costs include direct costs associated with operating the lines, such as wages, maintenance, fuel, and so forth, and indirect costs, such as administration needed in moving traffic over the line. Net liquidation costs are estimated for both land and equipment salvage value (track, ties, etc). The ICC has determined that railroads should be allowed to earn a 16.7 percent pre-tax return on rail lines (Ming and Zink 1982).

The rail abandonment process can proceed rapidly, with ICC approval within seventy-five days of application if no protests are received. In the event of protest or appeal, a final decision can be made within one year of application.

Community Considerations in Dealing with Abandonment

When abandonment is proposed for a rail line, two groups of people are affected. Shippers and receivers located on the line are faced with a direct change in the operation of their firms, and the community as a whole may be impacted by the loss of or change in service.

Directly affected firms respond by making changes based on profitability considerations, that is, by minimizing procurement or marketing costs by seeking other transportation alternatives, such as truck, truck/rail transfer, or truck/barge transfer. Such adjustments may be costly,[1] particularly for those who enjoyed below-cost rail rates prior to abandonment.

Community responses may be harder to quantify and may include emotional or psychological as well as economic components. In some rural areas the abandonment may be the culmination of a long-term economic decline and may become a symbol of the overall deterioration of the community. Saving the branch line may therefore include non-transportation considerations.

Transportation changes affect the community in a variety of ways. Loss or stagnation of industry causes employment losses and thus reductions in tax revenues and increased social service costs. The reduced potential for new industrial development can result in diminished economic growth rates. Reduced transportation service can cause personal hardship and can result in accelerated deterioration of highways and bridges and generally increased transportation costs to businesses, farmers, and families. In addition there may be environmental effects, changes in demand for public services, highway or rail safety impacts, and others. These adjustment are essentially offsetting (e.g., railroad-generated noise replaced with highway noise) and are not significant (Dickerson et al. 1981).

Responses to Rail Abandonment

When faced with the abandonment of rail service, firms and communities have three alternatives: to allow abandonment to proceed unchallenged and seek alternative transportation sources; to prevent abandonment by protest, litigation, or subsidization of the line; or to take over the line as a public or private entity.

Private-market solutions include accepting abandonment, subsidization through shipper-paid surcharges, and private takeover of the line. Private solutions are undertaken by shippers who determine that private subsidization or renovation will be a profitable investment or that paying surcharges or utilizing alternative transportation modes are least-cost solutions.

Public solutions may be preferable when potentially abandoned lines are very long, when private takeover is difficult, or when non-transportation objectives exist. Public solutions imply subsidies to directly affected parties (Johnson 1982).

The Case Study

Response to rail abandonment often centers on continuation of service by public takeover. While acceptance of abandonment or private-market solutions should be considered, public solutions are often attractive or are justified on grounds of a greater public good. Shipping firms would generally agree, since a public solution can be expected to reduce the direct cost to individual shippers, while a private solution may not.

Advocates of public solutions should cautiously evaluate the takeover proposal based on the condition of facilities, existing and potential traffic, transportation competition, operating costs, and the overall cost of the public solution (ICC).

The comparative case study presented below represents two analyses of a hypothetical short-line solution to a proposed rail abandonment. The data are similar to those that might be presented in the executive summary of a feasibility study by a consultant or public agency to justify public takeover as a nonprofit or state or municipally operated short-line railroad.

The comparative analysis is designed to provide the reader with a vivid contrast of the often conflicting methodologies and interpretations of private consultants, groups with a specific interest, or advocates of publicly funded projects. This approach has been successfully applied as an inservice training method for Cooperative Extension professionals and community/economic development practitioners.

Although hypothetical, the analyses presented here are drawn largely from actual short-line development projects in the Midwest and western United States. Example A, GRIPE, represents a highly optimistic approach, while Example B, CANT, is more conservative.

Case Study Assumptions

A 30.6-mile light-duty branch line is proposed for abandonment by BigLine Railroad Company. The line provides service, predominantly outbound grain shipments, for agricultural communities in a rural area with a population of approximately twenty thousand. The branch connects with the only major railroad for east-west service to major domestic and export markets. An inventory of the line and its accompaniments is presented in Table 12.1.

BigLine proposes abandonment because existing traffic cannot sup-

Table 12.1 Line and equipment summary, BigLine branch line abandonment proposal

Length—30.6 miles
FRA Safety Standard—Class I (10 mph)
Rail—75 lb., fair to good condition
Ties—treated hardwood, poor condition
Plates/Anchors—single, inadequate
Ballast—poor condition
Bridges—37, good condition; 1 (1600′ × 70′ high) poor condition, needs major repair or replacement within 2 years
Crossings—30, good condition
Road bed/ditching—unstable, poor condition
Tunnels—1, fair but serviceable condition
Rehabilitation cost (excluding bridges)—$9,398,300
Net liquidation value—$1,750,000

port the continuing cost of operation and maintenance. Revenues are grossly insufficient and the line ties up assets that could be used more productively elsewhere. Operating losses are estimated at $426,505[2] based on 600 cars annually.

Other Considerations

Recent rail use was 600 cars, but the potential for 1,200 cars exists, assuming 4.2 million bushels of grain are transported by rail annually. Five grain elevators merchandise approximately 3.5 million bushels annually. Another 2.5 million bushels are trucked directly to other elevators outside the area. Little or no potential exists for rail shipments (inbound or outbound) of other commodities. Shippers say they are willing to use a short line if service and rates are "reasonable." Commercial and farm truck costs are approximately $.07 to $.09/bushel to the nearest mainline rail loading facilities. Two-lane highway service connects the local area with major east-west interstate highways and mainline rail connections.

Community support for maintaining the branch line exists but is not unanimous, as some local residents are concerned about potential tax increases. Two other important factors are that the unemployment rate is 8.5 percent, about 2 percent higher than the state average, and that BigLine Railroad Company owes $2.5 million in back property taxes and is protesting its tax assessments through the courts.

Table 12.2 Summary data—short-line solution, GRIPE and CANT analysis

	GRIPE (Example A)	CANT (Example B)
Operating Revenue/Yr	$ 554,400	$ 344,400
Avoidable (Operations) Costs/Yr	$ 455,595	$ 445,595
Acquisition Costs	N/A	$ 1,750,800
Rehabilitation Costs	$9,398,300	$12,428,300
Lost Jobs Avoided	87	6
Income Loss Avoided/Yr	$1,554,000	$ 75,600
Tax Revenue Loss Avoided/Yr	$ 465,310	$ 208,783
Population Loss Avoided	168	12
Highway Impact Avoided/Yr	$4,071,244	$ 198,872
Trucking Costs Avoided/Yr	$ 504,907	$ 327,600
Benefit/Cost Ratio	3.45	.51

Situation

The Group for Rail and Industrial Preservation and Expansion (GRIPE) has retained a consultant to study the feasibility of a public takeover of the line with the intent of leasing it to a cooperative or non-profit operator at one dollar per year. GRIPE has protested the abandonment application, and the ICC will consider its counter proposal. BigLine is willing to sell the property at the net liquidation value ($1.75 million) or will continue to provide service if its losses are reimbursed with a subsidy or surcharge sufficient to offset rehabilitation costs and operating expenses. Another group, Citizens Against New Taxes (CANT), retained its own consultant, who was instructed to assess the benefits and costs of a public takeover of the BigLine branch line.

Findings of the two consultants, from the executive summaries of their final reports, are presented in Table 12.2.

The summaries were presented to lay groups, local business and political leaders, and to state legislators and agency leaders for their recommendation.

GRIPE recommends immediately proceeding with the public project, noting that operating revenue exceeds annual avoidable costs, total rehabilitation costs are offset by only a few years' highway deterioration cost saving, abandonment will result in a substantial increase in unemployment, and the cost benefit ratio is positive.

CANT argues that the cost of rehabilitation will never be recovered, net operating losses will be sustained, and that individual shippers should absorb additional transportation costs just as they do other business expenses.

Revenue Calculations

Average truck rates in the area are approximately $.0025 per bushel per mile for farm trucks and $.004 per bushel per mile for custom haul. This effectively limits the average rail tariff to approximately $.0035 per bushel per mile.[3] Both analyses assume that a potential for 1,200 cars annually exists. At approximately 3,500 bushels per car, this figure accounts for 4.2 million bushels of grain, or about 70 percent of the grain normally exported from the region. Both analyses also agree that an average tariff no larger than $.0035 per bushel-mile will be required to capture a 70 percent market share.

The GRIPE analysis includes a surcharge or subsidy of $175 per car (or $.05 per bushel) to be paid from state lottery revenue or as a direct contribution by the state grain growers association or the grain merchants association.[4] Gross revenue estimates are summarized in Table 12.3.

Table 12.3 Annual gross revenue, GRIPE and CANT analysis

	GRIPE	CANT
Average Tariff Revenue	$344,400	$344,400
Surcharge or subsidy @ $175 × 1,200 cars	$210,000	N/A
TOTAL REVENUE	$544,400	$344,400

Avoidable Costs

Both consultants agree on operating expense figures provided by BigLine Railroad Company and the State Department of Transportation (State DOT). When BigLine calculated its profitability, it did not use annual right of way maintenance costs since it is currently not maintaining the line. Both consultants included maintenance for equipment and right of way as an annual operating expense since these costs would be incurred if the line were reactivated. BigLine provided the following avoidable costs: maintenance of right of way $195,339; maintenance of equipment $138,146; and operations $122,109; total avoidable (operations) costs $455,595.

Both GRIPE and CANT summarized the expected annual revenue

Table 12.4 Annual return over avoidable costs, GRIPE and CANT analysis

	GRIPE	CANT
Revenue	$544,400	$344,400
Avoidable Costs	$455,595	$455,595
RETURN OVER AVOIDABLE COSTS	$98,805	−$111,195

and avoidable costs. However, their projected returns over avoidable costs, presented in Table 12.4, differed significantly.

Rehabilitation Costs

Rehabilitation costs provided by BigLine and State DOT were the same for both analyses, with a notable exception. The GRIPE proposal did not consider replacing or repairing the large bridge that BigLine indicated needs major renovation within two years. GRIPE's consultant felt the deterioration was overstated and that normal right of way maintenance would suffice. Total rehabilitation costs estimated by GRIPE were $9,398,300.

CANT estimated a bridge renovation cost of $3.03 million (immediate renovation would increase expected life by ten years) and a net replacement cost, including engineering, of $6 million, citing State DOT reconstruction figures. The renovation cost was included in CANT's analysis for a total of $12,428,300.

Acquisition Costs

GRIPE noted that BigLine is delinquent in property tax payments and suggests that a settlement can be reached by forgiving the $2.5 million in taxes in return for a donation of the line. BigLine has not responded to the proposal, nor has it withdrawn its protest against its tax assessment.

CANT budgeted $1.75 million, the net liquidation value that BigLine has indicated is an acceptable selling price.

Community Impacts—Employment and Income

The two studies differ greatly in community impacts. While both used some similar State Commerce Department data, the interpretation appears to be significantly different.

GRIPE surveyed grain elevators, farmers, farm implement dealers, agricultural suppliers, and other businesses, and asked them if grain farmers lost rail service, would they go out of business. GRIPE also asked how many employees were associated with each firm surveyed. It was determined that thirty-seven jobs would be lost if all firms responding negatively would actually cease operation.

The State Commerce Department provided an employment multiplier[5] of 1.35 for rural communities, an aggregate figure for the state that includes mining, lumber, and other extractive industries, as well as agriculture.

GRIPE adjusted the direct employment estimate by the multiplier and interpreted the product as indirect jobs that were then added to the direct job loss:

37 direct jobs $\times$ 1.35 multiplier = 50 indirect jobs;

37 + 50 = 87 total jobs lost.

CANT noted that agriculture is the primary activity in the area and that similar rail abandonments have not resulted in a substantial loss of agricultural production jobs or employment in agricultural support businesses. Abandonment would result in the loss of four freight agents' positions that, when adjusted by the multiplier, result in the loss of approximately six jobs in the area.

GRIPE's income effect was estimated from a study of small business in the area. CANT used the average income for rail freight agents, which it obtained from BigLine.

Both consultants agreed on 1.93 family members per job, an unverified figure received from a State Commerce Department clerk, and estimated total population loss based on that figure.

Community Impacts—Highway Deterioration

GRIPE's highway impact cost was based on the estimated reduced effective life of existing highways resulting from increased truck traffic due to loss of rail service. Approximately seventy-five miles of main highway routes were expected to be subjected to an additional fifty-five truck trips per business day (including backhaul) according to State DOT. Accelerated deterioration, based on 18-kip equivalent factors[6] and a twenty-year effective lifespan, requires renovation or replacement at an earlier date (Mason 1984). Average accelerated deterioration was estimated at $67,161 per mile by State DOT. GRIPE reported this figure as an annual deterioration cost.

CANT estimated the marginal damage impact for the same traffic level by determining the additional highway overlay thickness, corresponding to the increased axle loads, that would be required to maintain present highway surface condition (Fortenberry 1984). The marginal cost was estimated to be $2,841 per mile on an annual basis.

Community Impacts—Taxes

Both groups concurred with State Department of Revenue estimates of $189,781 annually in lost tax revenue from the abandoned rail line. GRIPE and CANT estimated tax revenue losses from lost population using the average tax burden per family, a figure obtained from the county tax assessor based on average property values, the existing mill levy and sales, and state income tax estimates. GRIPE computed an annual tax loss of $275,529, based on an average tax revenue of $3,167 for eighty-seven households. CANT used the same revenue figure and six households for an annual tax loss of $19,002.

Impacts on Grain Shippers

Both consultants also estimated additional transportation costs to affected shippers. GRIPE noted that "at projected traffic levels the additional cost of trucking grain to transloading facilities on the mainline would be at least $504,907 annually," but the estimation method was not disclosed.

CANT estimated the average additional trucking distance from farms to transloading facilities at 25.5 miles, and a weighted average annual cost of transporting in both farm and custom hire trucks at $.003 per bushel mile for an annual cost of $321,600 (4.2 million bushels $\times$ 25.5 miles $\times$ $.003 = $321,600).

Benefit/Cost Analysis

Both groups computed a benefit/cost ratio associated with the proposed short-line solution. The present value of annual costs or receipts was computed as follows:

$$PV = AF \frac{1 - (1+i)^n}{i} \tag{1}$$

where

PV = Present Value;

AF = Annual Receipt or Cost Flow;

i = Interest Rate;

n = Number of Years.

The present value of rehabilitation salvage value (excluding land) was computed as follows:

$$PV = SV(1 + i)^{-n} \tag{2}$$

where

SV = Salvage Value.

Both present value analyses used an effective life of ten years (n = 10). GRIPE used the current interest rate of 12.5 percent, (i = .125), while CANT used a "real" interest rate, adjusted for inflation, of 4 percent (i = .04). Both analyses assumed that all rehabilitation costs were allocated at the beginning of the project period. The benefit/cost analyses of GRIPE and CANT are summarized in Tables 12.5 and 12.6, respectively.

Conclusions

It is important to identify both private and public goals when dealing with rail abandonment. Public goals may include nontransportation or noneconomic aspects that have broadly defined benefits. While the total cost of any project must be thoroughly analyzed, costs and benefits should be considered from a marginal perspective; that is, considering the additional benefit relative to the additional cost.

Costs and benefits and their justifications can vary substantially de-

Table 12.5 Summary of present value of costs and benefits—GRIPE

	ANNUAL COST OR RECEIPT, ORIGINAL COST, OR SALVAGE VALUE	PRESENT VALUE*
Annual Avoidable (Operations) Costs	$ 455,595	$ 2,522,370
Rehabilitation Costs	$9,398,300	$ 9,398,300
TOTAL COSTS		$11,920,670
Annual Operating Revenue	$ 554,500	$ 3,069,397
Annual Income Loss Avoided	$1,554,000	$ 8,603,613
Annual Tax Loss Avoided	$ 465,310	$ 2,576,157
Annual Highway Impact Avoided	$4,701,244	$26,028,112
Net Salvage Value Rehab.	$2,829,546	$ 871,348
TOTAL BENEFITS		$41,148,627
Net Present Value (Benefits minus Costs)		$29,227,957
Benefit/Cost Ratio ($41,148,627 ÷ $11,920,670)		3.45

*i = .125
n = 10

Table 12.6 Summary of present value of costs and benefits—CANT

	ANNUAL COST OR RECEIPT, ORIGINAL COST, OR SALVAGE VALUE	PRESENT VALUE*
Annual Avoidable (Operations) Costs	$ 455,595	$ 3,695,284
Rehabilitation Costs	$12,428,300	$12,428,300
Acquisition Costs	$ 1,750,000	$ 1,750,000
TOTAL COSTS		$17,873,584
Annual Operating Revenue	$ 344,400	$ 2,793,393
Annual Income Loss Avoided	$ 75,600	$ 613,184
Annual Tax Loss Avoided	$ 208,783	$ 1,693,417
Annual Highway Impact Avoided	$ 198,872	$ 1,613,030
Net Salvage Value Rehab.		$ 2,527,818
TOTAL BENEFITS	$ 3,741,788	$ 9,240,842
Net Present Value (Benefits minus Costs)		–$ 8,632,742
Benefit/Cost Ratio ($9,240,842 ÷ $17,873,584)		.51

*i = .04
n = 10

pending upon the methodology and assumptions of the analyst. Erroneous calculations or misinterpretation can distort real costs and benefits and can be used (intentionally or otherwise) to justify a marginal or uneconomic project. "Pork barrel" projects are sometimes justified using questionable methods.

Although most decisions have non-economic components, economic considerations should not be distorted in order to justify them. A correct economic analysis can help decision makers to understand the real cost associated with noneconomic components of any proposal. Comprehensive analysis may be difficult to achieve however, and conflicts between affected parties (e.g., independent truckers and farmers) may arise.

Professional planners, consultants, and others responsible for developing and presenting proposals should strive to use correct methods and should critically examine other studies and supporting evidence. Concerned citizens, legislators, and agency decision makers should critically examine proposals and should require substantial justification and documentation of methodologies and assumptions.

Notes

1. The author is aware of no verified bankruptcies or relocations of firms solely in response to loss of rail service.

2. $\pi = R - C - .167\,NLV$

where:

π = Profitability $(-\$426,505)$

R = Revenue $(\$126,000)$

C = Avoidable Costs $(\$260,255)$

NLV = .167 Net Liquidation Value $(\$1,750,000)$

3. Both analyses were based on a State Department of Agriculture report that grain would be loaded at three assembly points on the line. Approximately 1 million bushels would originate at the termination point (30.6 miles), 1.2 million bushels at the midpoint (24.0 miles), and 2 million bushels at a second mid-point (19.5 miles). All three origins have adequate existing elevator and loading facilities:

$\$.0035 \times 1.0$ million bu $\times 30.6$ Mi. = $\$107,100$
$\$.0033 \times 1.2$ million bu $\times 24.0$ Mi. = $\$100,800$
$\$.0035 \times 2.0$ million bu $\times 19.5$ Mi. = $\$136,500$

4. GRIPE is unwilling to attempt to raise a surcharge sufficient to maintain BigLine service on the branch line on the ground that the total surcharge would be excessive and that it would not eliminate the risk that BigLine would proceed with abandonment at a later time.

5. A multiplier provides an estimate of the total impact of a change; i.e., if employment in the base economy changed by one job, a total change of 1.35 jobs would be expected. Stated differently, losing one job in the base industry would result in an additional 0.35 job loss, for a total loss of 1.35 jobs.

6. 18,000-pound load equivalent single axle; this approximates a farm truck loaded with 300 bushels or a commercial dual-axle tractor-trailer combination loaded with 1,000 bushels.

References

Dickinson, Glen, et al. 1981. *An Analysis of the Impacts of Railroad Abandonment and the Costs and Benefits of Reinstituting Service Along Certain Rock Island Lines in Southwestern Iowa*. Technical Report 137, Institute of Urban and Regional Research, University of Iowa, Iowa City.

Fortenberry, T. Randall. 1984. "The Effects of Branch Line Abandonment on Local Highways: A Site Specific Study." Master's thesis, Department of Agricultural Economics and Economics, Montana State University, Bozeman.

Johnson, Mark A. 1982. *Policy Choices Regarding Railroad Branch Lines*. Economic Special Report No. 70, Department of Economics and Business, North Carolina State University, Raleigh.

Mason, John M., Jr. 1983. "Effects of Oil Field Development on Low Volume Roadways: An Overlook Energy Related Cost." *ITE Journal*.

Ming, Dennis R., and Daniel L. Zink. 1982. "Rail Line Abandonment." Paper presented at Great Plains Extension Transportation Workshop, 16–17 December, Denver, Colorado.

Rail Services Planning Office. Interstate Commerce Commission. 1982. *Guidelines for Evaluating the Feasibility of Short Line Operations*. Washington.

13

Highway Salt Management

Donald J. White

Keeping highways and roads clear in the winter in New York State is vital to local and regional businesses and to the traveling public. At the present time, the most effective and economical method of clearing roads is through the use of deicing materials in connection with plowing. Sodium chloride (NaCl), ordinary salt, is most commonly used. In some situations the sodium chloride is mixed with calcium chloride or sand.

There are both benefits and costs of salt-enhanced deicing on highways and roads. The work of Murray and Ernst indicates that annual benefits of road salting include: lives saved in reduced traffic accidents and shortened response time to medical emergencies; fuel energy saved; reduced wage loss due to lateness to work and absenteeism; and reduced production losses and losses in goods shipments.

The costs of salt-enhanced deicing are reflected in a number of factors, as indicated in Table 13.1.

Governments at all levels can to varying degrees implement programs and practices that will begin to reduce both the direct costs—purchasing, storage, and application—and the indirect costs—impact on vegetation and water supplies. Municipal governments (county, town, and village) at the local level often find their highway operating budgets increasing, with a sizable portion being used to keep the roads clear of ice and snow.

Compounding the cost factor has been the increase in salt loss from

Table 13.1 Annual cost of salt use
(in millions of dollars)

Purchasing and Application	400
Vehicle Damage	4,000
Highway Structures	1,000
Vegetation	100
Water Supplies	300
Utilities	20
Total	5,820

Source: EPA Report 600/2–76–105; updated to 1985 prices.

outside storage piles, contamination of private well-water supplies, and
law suits resulting from water contamination and damage or destruction
of vegetation from salt.

Development of an Educational Program

Cornell Cooperative Extension, through its local government program,
in conjunction with the Cornell Local Roads program, identified a
number of important concerns that local officials had regarding the
costs of salt storage and application. Based on situational documentation with local government officials in a number of municipalities, an
educational program was developed.

The cooperatively developed educational program had several objectives. First, to create an awareness on the part of local government
officials, highway superintendents, and highway maintenance employees regarding the most cost-effective ways of storing and applying salt.
Second, to create an awareness of potential damage to groundwater
supplies and vegetation as a result of poor storage and application
methods. Third, to create a better understanding of potential liability
and develop ways to cope with liability issues.

Program Audience

The program was designed for all city, county, town, and village personnel involved with the management of streets and highways. Supervisors, mayors, and other government officials were encouraged to
attend.

Program Approach

Based on the success of a pilot educational program, held in one county in August of 1984, a statewide program was designed to reach a broader, more encompassing audience. This program was based on a delivery system that had the potential for workshops across the state. It was based on one seminar in each of the New York State Department of Transportation's ten regions. The workshops involved county Co-operative Extension agents in hosting some of the programs in their extension headquarters and local/county highway superintendents in hosting the others. This method was successful in involving local resource people and facilities.

Program Components

First, two types of teaching materials were developed. One was a series of slides encompassing three components: the effects of salt on roadside vegetation, types of salt-storage facilities, and construction aspects of pole buildings for salt storage. The other was overhead transparencies related to the potential effects of open storage piles of salt on both public and private groundwater supplies and to deicing materials, costs, and effectiveness.

Second, a participants' reference manual entitled "Highway Salt Management Handbook for Local Government Officials" was created. It contained information on ground water and surface water, vegetation, location and site selection for new storage facilities, storage area considerations, storage design, types of storage buildings, storage design considerations, blending materials, general precautions in the handling of deicing chemicals, and legal aspects. It also had appendices covering steps to be taken when water contamination is suspected, testing for salt, the salt required per season, a storage area check list, and a reference list. A set of salt storage building plans is available as a complementary reference to the manual.

Third, case examples regarding legal aspects of highway salt application were gathered. These examples were useful for discussions of handling municipal liability.

Finally, publicity materials were developed. They were disseminated through the direct mailing of a flyer to key elected and appointed officials, through a listing of the seminars in the Local Roads newsletter

Nuggets and Nibbles, through contacts with the New York State Department of Transportation officials, and through contacts with county Cooperative Extension agents.

Program Implementation

The program was implemented in ten different locations across the state during the summer and fall of 1985. Several additional seminars were held at various locations during the spring, summer, and fall of 1986.

The agenda for each seminar included the following topics: environmental impacts, deicing considerations, salt-storage methods and structures, and legal considerations (see appendix).

Supporting Case Examples

Two case examples may be helpful in identifying situations faced by town and village governments in New York State. These factual case examples illustrate the situation and steps being taken to do a better job of management. The action results are definitely attributable to participation in the educational program.

Town Case Example

For twenty years the town of Peaceville had piled its highway salt-sand mixture outside, unprotected, behind the Town Barn. Two years ago the house adjacent to the Town Barn was sold. Several days after a heavy spring rain, the new family, the Browns, noticed that their well water had changed from a fresh taste to one of a salty taste. Even after the rain had stopped, the family still had a salt taste to the water for several weeks. Then it seemed to clear up. Another soaking rain several weeks later again brought the same salty taste to the water.

The Browns began to do some checking around with neighbors, but none of them had the problem. One of the neighbors suggested that perhaps the town salt-sand pile might be at fault. That seemed to be logical. The Browns proceeded to examine the salt-sand pile, which was on a piece of ground slightly higher than the location of their well. Drainage could indeed come from the pile toward their drilled well. There even seemed to be a pathlike area, with a whitish coloring to it, fanning out from the salt-sand pile toward the well area and the lawn. The family contacted the well driller, who had put in the 145-foot drilled well. He checked to see if there was any possible leakage at the surface around the casing. None seemed to be apparent. However, the well was cased down about 60 feet, and there could be some infiltration of surface water into the aquifer and hence into the well.

The town highway superintendent was contacted and he allowed that his salt-sand pile could be contaminating the Browns' well. But he decided to talk to the town board and get their ideas.

After several meetings with the family, it seemed that the best decision was to help the family obtain a new and deeper well. (Some water testing had been done and there was a positive test for sodium chloride in the well water, but it was extremely difficult to tell where the NaCl was coming from.) The offer of a new well seemed to be the best solution for both parties.

A new well was located and drilled at a different location on the property, to a depth of 225 feet with the casing to a depth of 85 feet. To date, there have been no problems with the new water supply. But then again, salt has a funny way of traveling and moving around in the soil and the water-bearing area. Both the family and the town board hope that the cost of $4,800 (mostly covered by the town) has solved the problem.

The town board and the town highway superintendent of the town of Peaceville, in their infinite wisdom and futuristic vision, have undertaken a project to place the salt-sand pile under cover. An enclosed structure is being built to house the 2200 cubic yards of salt-sand. It is hoped that this effort will reduce any future well contamination in the surrounding area.

Several events occurred in this hypothetical case. Let me comment briefly on each of these. First, the Browns recognized a problem that they did not want to live with. They did the best they could in locating the potential source of contamination. They decided to try and work with the local officials rather than bring about a law suit or an Article 78 proceeding. They also checked with the neighbors to see if they had the problem. Fortunately for both the neighbors and the town board, the problem was limited. Had it not been, the town board could have become even more financially involved.

Second, the town board and the town highway superintendent were willing to listen, help with an analysis of the situation, and help to correct the situation without costly court action. Further, the town highway superintendent and the town board were very willing to work together to cope with the problem. They recognized the interdependence each had with the other.

Various sections of the Highway Law, starting with Section 140 as well as Section 32 of the Town Law, outline the powers and duties of the highway superintendent and the relations with the town board. Not all the relations are clear cut, but it seems both groups need each other in order to serve the residents of the community.

Third, the town highway superintendent, with the cooperation and support of the town board took action to move the salt-sand pile into a protected storage building. While this initially costs money, in the long run, it hopefully will pay off in reduced salt losses, reducing possible water contamination, and making for a better work situation during the times when the salt-sand mixture is handled for ice and snow control.

Village Case Example

The village of Valley View, located in a rural area, has in recent years been accommodating an increase in population from an urban area fifteen miles to the northeast. An increased population of approximately 700 residents during the past three years has resulted in higher traffic volume during rush hours for both commuters and school bus transportation. Traditionally, the village has stored its salt and sand mixture outdoors, but usually covered with a tarp for weather protection. The storage pile, located on a vacant lot several miles from the equipment buildings, provides a challenge for motorbikers and ATV riders. The challenge of riding up one side and down the other has led parents in the neighborhood to be concerned about safety; and it has meant a potential liability for the village trustees. Additionally, there has been some leaching of salt from the pile when exposed for a period of time. The increased travel on village roads has meant more frequent plowing and salting to keep the roads clear.

With increased operating costs for keeping the roads clear, the village trustees have begun to consolidate operations. They have purchased additional land, adjacent to the current village equipment maintenance buildings, and using salt storage plans developed by the Agricultural Engineering Department at Cornell, will construct an adequate storage facility. The building will house salt-sand mixes and liquid calcium chloride. The use of the calcium chloride will, under certain conditions, reduce the applications of sodium chloride and in the long run be more cost effective.

The background information needed by the village trustees and highway superintendent to make the changes in the operating procedures was provided through the Cornell Highway Salt Management Program.

Program Benefits

More than 300 city, county, town, and village personnel involved with the management of streets and highways participated in the seminars. In addition, there have been over 250 requests for the participants' reference manual by highway superintendents and other local government officials not able to attend the seminars.

Seminar Evaluation

An evaluation (Appraisal Questionnaire) was given to each participant at the end of each seminar. Some of the key components of the evaluation were as follows. Topics covered in the seminar that were most useful, in order of priority, were legalities and liability, salt storage, and application rates and mixtures. Of those topics covered, the following two should have been covered in more detail: legalities and liability; application rates and mixtures. Ninety-eight percent of the seminar participants felt the workshop had improved their knowledge significantly. The estimated cost to the participants' municipality for their time and travel to attend the seminar averaged $113. Eighty-eight percent of the participants indicated the cost to the municipality for time and travel was under $200, with approximately half of these indicating the cost was under $100. Ninety-eight percent also indicated that their time at the seminar was well spent. Estimated savings the next year to the municipality by having participated in the seminar ranged from under $1,000 to over $5,000 with an average savings of $3,217. The best time of the year for future workshops is in the fall, followed by spring, with summer next, and winter last.

Further Use of Materials

Within New York State, other state agencies, as well as private businesses and consultants, have requested copies of the seminar materials. These materials will help them in working with local governments in an advisory capacity.

The program has been presented in two New England states and materials have been sent to several midwestern state extension offices. Our experience with the Highway Salt Management Program indicates that a similar program could be conducted by other land-grant universities in an educational format for local governments. Those states faced with problems of winter highway maintenance might well find the program of benefit.

Conclusion

Based on a two-year educational effort, the Cornell Cooperative Extension "Highway Salt Management Program" has met an important need in protecting community and individual natural resources, while reducing municipal operating costs and potential liability.

Reference

Murray, D. M., and Ernst, U. F. W. 1976. *An Economic Analysis of the Environmental Impact of Highway Deicing*, Report No. EPA 600/2–76–105 (May). U.S. Environmental Protection Agency.

Appendix

Sample Agenda for Highway Salt Management Workshops

AGENDA

8:30 A.M.   Registration
9:00 A.M.   Welcome, Program Overview
9:15 A.M.   Environmental Impacts: Ground and Surface Water; Vegetation
10:15 A.M. Break
10:30 A.M. Deicing Materials, Abrasives, Mixing, Applications, and Costs
Noon   Lunch (catered, cost included in registration fee*)
1:00 P.M.   Salt Storage Methods and Structures
2:00 P.M.   Legal Considerations
3:00 P.M.   Adjourn

*Participant Registration Fee: $10, included cost of the reference manual, coffee break, and lunch.

14

How Technology Transfer and Cooperative Extension Depasture Highways and Maintain Rural Roads

Kate Skelton
Lynne H. Irwin

Meeting major transportation needs in this century and developing a clear vision for highway agencies have been described as "getting and keeping the nation out of the mud." At the beginning of this century, rural highway agencies throughout the country did, indeed, struggle to keep the nation's travelers "out of the mud." At that time, the nation was a growing and vast network of regions linked together by narrow, and most commonly, unpaved roads.

Rural communities faced a number of other transportation problems as well. But highway engineers and public works officials in the 1980s face problems that are not only different, but proportionately greater in magnitude, cost, and economic significance to the country.

The 1906 edition of the *State of New York Road Red Book for the Improvement, Repair, and Maintenance of Public Highways* noted that it was lawful to drive cattle in the highway, but the Code of Civil Procedure "now prohibits cattle, horses, colts, asses, mules, swine, sheep or goats from running at large or being herded or pastured in the highways" (211). This change in statute noted in the 1906 *Red Book* reflected the beginning of major changes in the use of our public road networks. Increased traffic volumes were to bring challenges not only in terms of constructing new roads, but also in terms of maintaining and reconstructing existing roads whose geometry was safe for the new vehicular patterns of motorists and commercial and farm transport.

Cooperative Extension services based in the state's land-grant colleges have been providing training and information to our rural communities for a century. More recently, in 1951, Cornell University's College of Agriculture and Life Sciences initiated one of the first formal extension programs designed specifically for rural public works and highway officials, known today as the Cornell Local Roads Program.

The services and manner in which training and technology assistance have been provided by the Local Roads Program have evolved as our rural communities and road systems have undergone social and economic change. The program and the constituency it has served have a familiarity that, as the following history relates, has made it possible for a successful venture in innovative and effective training to take place.

In the fall of 1986, a highway superintendent contacted the engineer who directs the Cornell Local Roads Program, seeking advice on how to maintain a low volume road whose surface was being torn up by the shoes on the hooves of carriage horses. His community had seen a recent increase in the number of Amish settlers whose horse-drawn carriages traveled on the village roads. The 1906 Road Book would be expected to provide clues to the technical solution for this superintendent's problem. In fact, the design, structure, materials, and management of rural low-volume roads have changed so drastically over succeeding generations that the solutions today are quite different. (The solution, by the way, was determined by "technology transfer" from a neighboring state, Pennsylvania. There, they use rubber shoes on the horses.)

A review of these changes and the evolution of the Cornell Local Roads Program follows. In many important respects, New York State is not unique in terms of its road system. However, the success of the Cornell Local Roads Program and the manner in which it has developed its training and technical assistance programs have been, if not unique, at least in the vanguard of educational extension services.

Our Nation's Roads

Low-volume roads, those carrying no more than 1,000 vehicles per day, play a vital role in our transportation system. In the United States, more than 2.9 million miles of roads are considered low-volume, and more than 70 percent of the roads constructed since the turn of the century are low-volume (FHWA, A World of Technology for Sharing 1986, 37).

"Rural two-lane highways comprise 97 percent of the total rural highway mileage in the United States. Travel on this two-lane system amounts to 66 percent of all U.S. Highway Travel" (Brinkman and Smith 1984). In a nation whose public attention appears to be dominated by concerns about Interstate, multi-lane highway systems, these statistics are worth considering. It places the current concerns about infrastructure rebuilding in perspective. As the deterioration of the nation's infrastructure captures the attention of government officials at all levels, the vital significance of the low-volume road system for the nation's health becomes evident.

It is estimated that "40 percent of the secondary system of rural arterials is in need of capital improvements now, and . . . there are over two million miles of local roads and streets in even worse condition. Seventy-five percent of the nation's bridges are on local roads and half of these—some 213,000 bridges—are currently deficient and need improvement. Local roads are in the poorest condition and have the greatest unaddressed needs of the entire transportation system" (Local Road Position Statement 1986, 7).

When our road systems deteriorate, as they have, and fail in their function of facilitating the movement of people, goods, and services, the "life of our communities" can be drastically altered.

In New York State, for example, the neglect of highways in rural communities has had a serious impact on the economy of many upstate municipalities. Agriculture is a major industry in the state. A 1983 survey of rural road deficiencies documented the negative impact of the neglect of roads and bridges on the cost of doing business and providing services and access to markets for rural communities. The New York State Commissioner of Agriculture and Markets reported that the survey identified 494 roads and 195 bridges across the state that hindered the movement of goods and supplies to and from farms (New York State Department of Agriculture and Markets 1985).

> Agriculture is a major industry generating more than $2.6 billion in cash farm receipts in 1983. An efficient transportation system is important to agriculture's continued economic vitality. A criti-

cal link in the State's agricultural transportation system is the local rural road and bridge network. . . . The larger feed, fertilizer and petroleum delivery trucks as well as the bulk milk trucks used in today's agriculture require roads and bridges designed to accommodate heavy equipment. . . . The deterioration of roads and bridges in rural New York is causing increasingly serious problems resulting in higher costs of doing business and in some cases, loss of service or markets. (New York State Department of Agriculture and Markets 1985, 1)

This story is not unusual. Three-quarters of the rural roads in the state were constructed more than fifty years ago. Over this half century, traffic patterns, vehicle loads, and volume have introduced demands on road networks that many rural communities cannot accommodate because of tight budgets and lack of trained personnel.

Changes in industry, in all sectors, have impacted on the road system and on community tax bases to support public works services. Our rural communities have not been suburbanized as much as they have been impoverished in the last fifty years. The loss of public revenues in our smaller communities has had a dramatic impact on the ability to provide and maintain transportation networks adequate to meet the demands of our changing nation. "Without more resources, road maintenance costs will have to be contained or reduced. . . . Local rural government officials and their constituents will have to find more cost-effective methods and organizational structures to meet service demands" (Walzer et al. 1987, 20).

As the economic and social health of rural communities worsens and pressure to find those cost-effective methods to meet service demands increases, Cooperative Extension programs have a unique responsibility and role to play. Extension services traditionally have focused on providing training and information for the farming industry, but New York State expanded its programs to include assistance to public works and highway personnel in rural communities informally as early as the 1920s. The goal has been to train local superintendents, whether elected or appointed, in the new engineering and design standards, changing technologies, and in the management skills needed to maintain the vital transportation system on which rural and suburban life depends.

Extension Services and Public Works: The 1930s

There are more than 1600 units of local government in New York State that have a responsibility for roads, including 930 towns, 57 counties, 555 villages, and 61 cities. Turnover of personnel among town highway departments is quite high, with as many as 300 or more new superintendents coming into office in elections that are held every other year. Many of the town and village highway officials have very little formal training in the field of highway engineering before they take office. In general, their training is gained by experience "up through the ranks."

In 1951, to provide formal training and assistance to local rural road agencies in New York State, Cornell University's Cooperative Extension brought together the efforts of the Departments of Agricultural Engineering, Agricultural Economics, and the School of Civil and Environmental Engineering.

During the early years, activities were devoted to a great extent to providing extension services such as technical bulletins, training schools, and seminars. Responsibility for instruction of an undergraduate course in low-cost roads was added in 1958 and even later, graduate training and research activities were added. The services remained university-based.

In 1938 a School of Highway Superintendents, co-sponsored with the Town and County Officer's Training School (New York State Association of Towns), was first conducted on campus. At that time it was hosted by the Department of Agricultural Economics. In 1951 this responsibility was transferred to the Local Road Program in the Department of Agricultural Engineering and a full-time extension faculty member was hired. In 1960 a Public Works School was begun by the Local Roads Program, in co-sponsorship with the Municipal Training Institute (New York State Conference of Mayors and Municipal Officials). The Highway School primarily serves the counties and towns, while the Public Works School, now conducted independently, primarily served the cities and villages.

Research and Technical Assistance: The 1950s

By the late 1950s, demographic changes in the nation had accelerated the stress on rural roads that had been witnessed earlier. The need for training rural highway officials now required a more sophisticated approach to the problems facing our communities. There was a need to develop new technologies, provide new road design and safety standards, and to assist rural agencies with low-cost solutions to road construction and maintenance.

In anticipation of these changing demands, the Local Roads Program added laboratory facilities and a technician in the early 1950s, and research became an integral activity. The intensity of the research effort has gradually increased, and by the mid-1960s projects for the study of improved road materials were formally established. Under the direction of a professional engineer and an experienced laboratory technician, the program developed a highway materials testing laboratory, and in the 1970s research efforts were expanded considerably.

In addition to providing technical assistance to individual highway agencies or personnel in the field, the program also offered and continues to offer periodic training programs in materials and technology at its laboratory and classroom facilities on campus. Augmenting the training program provided through the annual Highway School, which just completed its forty-second conference, short courses for public works and highway superintendents have been offered on topics such as pavement recycling and mix design methods for asphalt. These programs, like the extension services developed in the 1930s, have been campus-based training activities.

The laboratory has been more than a training ground, however. The Local Roads Program's research efforts have been diverse, devoted to hydrology and highway drainage design, land use planning along watershed boundaries, evaluation of a laboratory kneading compactor, mixing and compaction influences on strength of cement-stabilized soils, resilient behavior of base and subgrade materials, and nondestructive testing of highway pavements.

Applied research has been an integral part of the program. In 1986, for example, a joint research venture was undertaken with the USDA Forest Service to develop a Road Dust Monitor capable of quantitatively measuring levels of road dustiness. Road dust is a significant safety problem for motorists and a costly maintenance problem. A good dust control program would greatly reduce the money now spent annually on aggregate replacement on the more than two million miles of aggregate and earth-surfaced roads in the continental United States.

The instrumentation developed in the laboratory and field tests proved capable of providing a repeatable and reliable method of measurement that could form the basis for good dust control management (Irwin, Taylor, and Aneshansley 1986). Utilizing and implementing the research results is an important next step in the process of technology transfer.

Technology Transfer and the 1980s

As an adjunct to its research efforts, the program added a full-time computer specialist to its staff in the 1980s. Since that time, in addition to providing support services for laboratory research, a number of practical user's guides have been developed to assist researchers and engineers in the field.

One example is the mainframe computer program, NELAPAV, developed in 1980 (Irwin and Fellers 1980) and followed by a microcomputer version in 1984 and 1985 (Irwin and Speck 1986). NELAPAV stands for the Nonlinear Elastic Layer Analysis for PAVements. It allows the user to compute stresses, strains, and displacements at any point in an n-layered pavement system. "The primary feature which sets this program apart from its linear elastic predecessors is its ability to accommodate layers having moduli of elasticity which vary with the level of stress or strain in the layer. Most unbound granular pavement materials, to some degree, exhibit this behavior" (Irwin and Speck 1986, 1).

The application of this research tool to the day-to-day concerns of highway engineers is significant. Transferring this technology to the world of the highway superintendent who has no engineering training requires skill and sensitivity. Computation of stress in a pavement system is the domain of the researcher and the design engineer. Utilizing information about the rates of deterioration of pavements is the domain of the highway superintendent. Learning to translate both the knowledge and the technology from the laboratory to the local highway superintendent is the challenge facing extension services today. The ability to analyze pavement stress might even hold the answer to restoring roads impacted by Amish horses!

Pavement stress is only one application of computer modeling. Financial management, personnel management, traffic operations, road surface management, sign inventories, bridge inspection, rural public transportation, purchasing, safety improvement scheduling, solid waste management—nearly every function of a public works department is amenable to computerization. Efficiency and the need to cut costs, to manage maintenance and personnel scheduled, to develop maintenance programs, and to respond to public need quickly have prompted a growing interest in computer use among rural highway agencies and transportation officials. In response to this need, the Cornell Local Roads Program computer specialist has developed an on-site training course in computer applications for highway personnel and is available to highway officials who need individualized assistance regarding computerization of their own agency functions.

Extension Services and Technology Transfer: A Model for the 1990s

Microcomputer technology in transportation agencies, while it portends a real change in the look and function of our rural highway and public works departments, eclipses a much more fundamental set of needs. How can training and technical assistance be provided effectively to a constituency plagued with undersized budgets, high rates of personnel turnover, deficiencies in engineering training, and undeveloped management skills?

Part of the answer relies on a philosophical change on the part of educators and trainers. Moving training programs out into the community and away from a wholly university-based educational system requires a parallel shift away from a teacher-led training program to a user-based training. Technology transfer, a buzzword of the 1980s, in fact, reflects a major shift in the way in which knowledge is transmitted.

A 1984 study of the process of technology transfer in highway maintenance identified four basic principles for successful dissemination of information and innovation. First, it was concluded that research use will increase with greater user involvement in problem definition and other phases of the research. Second, for effective research use to occur, it is essential that the results of the research be put into the language of the user. Third, research use will increase when researcher and user are close to each other. Finally, the study concluded that researchers must recognize what users can change and what they cannot change, in order to perform relevant research (Schmitt et al. 1984, 10).

The urgency of finding relevant solutions to our transportation crises has prompted this new way of thinking about the process of bringing innovative change to the local user in an effective manner.

In 1982 the United States Congress appropriated $5 million to provide technical assistance to local highway agencies through the Rural Technical Assistance Program (RTAP). The principal delivery system for the program was a network of Technology Transfer Centers. Putting research results into practice quickly and effectively is a critical need in the transportation sector. Under the Federal Highway Administration RTAP program, the Technology Transfer Centers were designed to provide training and other technology transfer products to local users. One of the primary objectives of the program was "to serve as a communications link among the various sources of new technology and the state and local agencies which can apply the technology in daily operations" (FHWA's Technology Transfer Program).

In 1983 ten Technology Transfer Centers were named. Today, there are more than forty such Centers around the country. Most of the Centers created under this program were new. The designation of the Cornell Local Roads Program as the Technology Transfer Center in New York State did not represent the creation of a new program as much as it represented a natural evolution of a training program. The Technology Transfer Center status brought the program into full maturity.

Organization of the Cornell Technology Transfer Center

At the local level, closest to the user, what does this program look like? The program is tailored to the user's perspective so that the trainer and trainee see the same problem and visualize the same solution. An identification of and with the local needs and resources has been a central component of the technology transfer process. An audience that is receptive to innovation is an audience whose own needs and capabilities are acknowledged and incorporated directly into the communication process.

For the Cornell Local Roads Program, this has taken the form of "institutionalizing" local input. For example, in the early 1980s the Cornell Local Roads Program conducted two surveys to assess the critical job issues of its constituency. Priority issues were materials and pavements, public relations, manpower, management, safety, liability, traffic, highway maintenance, and equipment maintenance. Many of these critical issues remain today. A 1986 assessment conducted by the program showed that these issues are still critical, although the order of priority has changed. Liability and risk management, for example, has far greater impact on the operations of a highway department today than was the case a few years ago.

With this user input, and with the direction provided by a Steering Committee representing all levels of government, the Cornell Local Roads Program has developed a user-based, integrated program of services for disseminating information. Under the Rural Technical Assistance Program mandate, this program includes providing local training programs throughout the state, an information and publication service, technical assistance provided by a professional engineer, computer specialist, and laboratory technician, a quarterly newsletter, regional seminars and conferences, and publication of a directory of highway officials designed to facilitate communication among local roads and public works personnel.

On-site Training Programs

In its first two years as a formally designated Technology Transfer Center, the program conducted 95 workshops on ten topics. More than 1,500 highway officials participated in these training programs. In order to maximize accessibility to the training programs, workshops are conducted throughout the state so that driving time is no greater than one hour from the place of work. All workshops are offered "at cost," with registration fees typically being set at ten dollars. This is possible because of the cooperation of local highway agencies that serve as hosts for the workshops. Accessibility to low cost, quality training has become a hallmark of the program.

The workshop topics are largely "user" defined. They have included workshops on the rehabilitation of existing bridges, computer applications for local road agencies, maintenance and welding workshops, communications workshop, highway salt management seminars, local road design for safety, road surface management workshops, the basics of a good road, power and duties of local highway and public works officials, and pavement maintenance and pavement management. In response to numerous requests for information and seminars on tort liability, a workshop currently is being developed on liability and the related issue of risk management.

To date, the program has published six workbooks to accompany training programs. Each manual is written by the technical trainer who conducts the workshop and is field-tested and revised to accommodate the users' input. While designed for use in the workshop, each manual also stands on its own as a reference guide and is distributed, free of charge, to highway officials who request copies.

Information Service

Technology Transfer Centers are required to provide an information service for the constituencies they serve. The Cornell Local Roads Program provides copies of research reports and bulletins, state Department of Transportation and Federal Highway Administration publications, and its own training publications free of charge. In addition, technical information is available on a request basis from the Director and other technical personnel on staff. In the first two years of operation, the program responded to more than 900 requests for information, the majority of them coming from local highway officials.

Quarterly Newsletter

Predating the Technology Transfer Center as part of the program services, a quarterly newsletter entitled *Nuggets and Nibbles* has been published. Translating nuggets of technical information into nibble-sized bites, the newsletter now has a current circulation of more than 3,000 readers. Typically, *Nuggets and Nibbles* includes a section on publication abstracts of research reports relevant to low volume road engineering, a calendar of events, special feature articles usually prepared by the program staff, and information from readers. The program's publication service provides free reprints of those articles and reports abstracted or otherwise featured in the newsletter.

The Personnel Network in the Road Network

Each Technology Transfer Center is required to maintain a mailing list of highway officials. An annual directory of such officials is published at Cornell. The intent of this publication is to enhance the networking or ability of highway officials to communicate with one another and to share information and resources directly. This process is facilitated if the local officials have easy access to each other's names, addresses, and telephone numbers.

Measuring Effectiveness

Evaluation of program efforts and needs assessment have been integral components of the Local Roads Program. All workshops are evaluated by participants. The results then are shared with instructors, the steering committee, the director, and the project coordinator for the purpose of developing future training programs that reflect the needs, criticisms, and suggestions of the constituency. In addition, an annual evaluation and needs assessment is carried out to measure the effectiveness of all the program services.

The cost-effectiveness of a program is an important measure, yet many feel it is difficult to assess with accuracy. The Local Roads Program has incorporated direct questions about potential cost savings into its program evaluation form in an effort to begin to assess the value of its program to the many municipalities it serves. Basically, the evaluation tool attempts to determine whether the program saved the taxpayer money.

Overall, as reported in a 1987 survey conducted by the program, the taxpayers in New York State realized a savings of $1,620,830 in 1986. Of those answering the question, 79 percent provided a specific example of how they had saved money. For example, information in a training course on pavement materials led one superintendent to use cold-mix at $22 a ton against hot-mix paving material at $28 a ton. The municipality saved $15,180—a significant amount when one considers that for about half of the municipalities in the state the highway budget is more than 50 percent of the annual town budget.

Dollars are, of course, only one measure of program effectiveness. As difficult as it is to assess the direct monetary savings of training programs provided to highway agencies, it is even more difficult to assess the larger and long-run impact of technology transfer. One hint of effectiveness comes from the fact that inquiries for technical information and request for training have increased and highway officials, after attending one workshop, attend subsequent training programs offered by the Technology Transfer Center. The ultimate and most meaningful assessment, however, will come from a combination of well-trained public officials and a mobilization of public opinion that supports meeting our transportation needs.

Will technology transfer keep the nation "out of the mud"? It is a question many are asking. "It is generally recognized that bad roads cannot be afforded. . . . Greater emphasis on training programs for highway organizations is urgently needed. Modification of traditional training programs probably will be necessary to prepare for changing demands, using the latest tools, methods, and approaches" (Smith 1986, 136).

Getting out of the mud and raising our sights through better training is a first step. In a recent address at the Technology Center Directors meeting in Colorado, Lowell Jackson, head of the Colorado Department of Highways, reminded his audience of the power of technology when combined with public will.

> Eighteen years ago, Neil Armstrong set foot on the surface of the moon. Yet, today we have been unable to mobilize the needed resources to take care of the most commonplace of needs: the maintenance of our country's infrastructure.
>
> There are no quick fixes for this or any other major challenge facing America. Our only resolve is to think grandly and practically about these commonplace things; this will assure their continuity, and our safety and economic survival.
>
> To have done so in space, but not here on earth will be tragic. (Jackson 1987)

References

Albany State Engineer and Surveyor. 1906. *State of New York Red Book: Improvement, Repair and Maintenance of Public Highways.* Bulletin No. 12.

A World of Technology for Sharing: America's International Highway Program. Federal Highway Administration, 1986.

Brinkman, C. P., and S. A. Smith. 1984. "Two Lane Rural Highway Safety." *Public Roads* 48 (2).

Cornell Local Roads Program Technology Transfer Center. 1987. Final Evaluation Report, Cornell Local Roads Program Report 87–1.

Federal Highway Administration. N.d. "FHWA's Technology Transfer Program."

Irwin, Lynne H., and Daniel P. T. Speck. 1986. NELAPAV User's Guide. Cornell Local Roads Program Report 86–1.

Irwin, Lynne H., Deborah J. Taylor, and Daniel J. Aneshansley. 1986. *Device to Measure Road Dustiness on Aggregate Surfaced Roads*. Cornell Local Roads Program Report 86–5.

Jackson, Lowell. 1987. Address to Technology Center Directors meetings—Colorado. National Symposium on Local Roads. Position Statement for Local Roads, America Runs on Local Roads.

New York State Department of Agriculture and Markets. 1985. *Rural Road and Bridge Survey: Identification of Problems Impeding the Efficient Movement of Agricultural Goods in New York State*. Division of Rural Resources and Development.

Schmitt, Robert P., Edward A. Beimborn, and Mary J. Mulroy. 1984. *Methods of Effective Transfer and Implementation of Highway Maintenance Technology*. Federal Highway Administration Report No. FHWA/RD–84–501.

Smith, Wilbur S. 1986. "Current Highway Transportation Interests." *Transportation Quarterly* 40 (1): 131–41.

Walzer, Norman, David L. Chicoine, and Ruth T. McWilliams. 1987. "Rebuilding Rural Roads and Bridges." *Rural Development Perspectives*, 15–20.